ENCYCLOPEDIA OF

Source Illustrations

VOLUME ONE

ENCYCLOPEDIA OF

Source Illustrations

A PORTABLE PICTURE LIBRARY OF 5000 STEEL ENGRAVINGS.
ILLUSTRATING IN SYSTEMATIC ARRANGEMENT THE FIELDS OF
Mathematics and Astronomy: Physics and Meteorology: Chemistry, Mineralogy and Geology
Botany: Zoology: Anthropology and Surgery: Geography and Planography: History and Ethnology

Comprising all of the 266 plates contained in the above sections of the ICONOGRAPHIC ENCYCLOPAEDIA OF 1851

Edited by Johann Georg Heck.

With a descriptive index to the plates, glossaries and an analytical introduction.
MORGAN & MORGAN, INC., Publishers, Hastings-on-Hudson, N.Y. 10706

Introduction © Copyright 1972
Morgan & Morgan, Inc.

International Standard Book Number 0-87100-026-1
Library of Congress Catalog Card Number 72-78034
First Printing of Facsimile Edition, 1972
Printed in the United States of America

CONTENTS

PREFACE

The *Encyclopedia of Source Illustrations* is a reprinting, in two series, of the five hundred plates containing over 12,000 steel engravings that appear in *The Iconographic Encyclopaedia of Science, Literature and Art*. This was published in Philadelphia in 1851, under the editorship of Spencer Fullerton Baird. This in turn was an "Anglicized" edition of the great *Bilder Atlas* of Brockhaus. The latter was considered one of the greatest encyclopedias of its time and while its text has been superseded, the engravings remain a sharp and clear picture of the subjects as they were and, in most cases, still are. To complement the illustrations we have included the full description of each plate together with glossaries of such German words as appear therein.

The *Iconographic Encyclopaedia* is familiarly known as the "Heck" after its original compiler Johann Georg Heck. As such it has long been an elusive treasure for artists and designers. Copies are difficult to come by and even when found are seldom complete. A perfect copy can now bring several hundred dollars.

Anyone who has recently fumed at the time and cost of making a simple engraved card or letterhead will be awed by the care that went into this work. The men whose names appear on the plates as engravers must have been the most dedicated and meticulous of craftsmen. To do full justice to their work we have found it best to reproduce the plates in halftone. This will permit clear copying in most instances. But should some use arise that would be inhibited by the screen, a special print may be arranged for by writing to the publisher.

INTRODUCTION

MATHEMATICS AND ASTRONOMY

Mathematics is not a subject that cries for illustration in the usual sense of the word but there are in these plates many spots of intrinsic beauty. The diagrams of mathematical and geometric problems could grace a textbook, spark a computer advertisement, or decorate an annual report.

The instruments though superseded in use are particularly charming as designs. In the illustrations for astronomy, the artists begin to come in to their own. All of the planetary systems from Ptolemy on are represented. Graphically shown are latitude and longitude and the changing of the seasons. There are maps of the heavens and a classic early map of the moon.

PHYSICS AND METEOROLOGY

The first part of this section is a brief graphic course in basic physics, covering as it does, Mechanics, Acoustics, Optics, and Magnetism and Electricity. It is so thoroughly illustrated that from it could well come *all* of the illustrations for a history of physics.

Meteorology, as would be expected, is a very photogenic section with its beautiful drawings of frost and dew, diagrams of snow crystals, the sun's rays and such nugets as the Alpine snow line. Clouds get a full treatment as does the wind and its aberrations.

CHEMISTRY, MINERALOGY AND GEOLOGY

Chemistry is mainly illustrated here by its implements and utensils and, while many of these are outmoded, they are pictorially beautiful and historically important. Mineralogy is literally a mine of graphic treasures. Particularly in those plates showing the forms of crystallization. Nature is still a top designer and a daring one. The geology plates begin with fossils and go on to such things as volcanoes (including a volcanic chart of the world) and icebergs.

BOTANY

The classification and geography of plants were followed strictly in the preparation of these plates, but who cares. These plates are simply beautiful. Each one hits you as a picture or design in itself and then you realize that each is made up of many pictures. The range of uses for the pictures that make up these plates is almost unlimited, whether it be a

formal botanical use or the most whimsical decorative use from a postage stamp to wallpaper.

ZOOLOGY

Like Botany, the Zoology section is based on a sound classification and a reading of its contents makes it seem most formidable. But a glance at the plates themselves is like looking into a secret jungle. Insects, fish, reptiles, birds, and mammals. Each user will quickly find his favorite plate or plates. This is truly a portable zoo, aquarium and aviary with as much source material for nature illustration as could be found under one "roof."

ANTHROPOLOGY AND SURGERY

The illustrations in this section are in the main a detailed treatment of human anatomy. And detailed it is indeed. It is both sound and comprehensive. Less authoritative but of use and interest to an artist is a section on the varieties of mankind.

GEOGRAPHY AND PLANOGRAPHY

This section is really a book in itself—an atlas of the world as it was. The maps are works of art and masterpieces of craftsmanship. They are made useful and understandable by a long and detailed glossary. There are the usual physical maps of Europe and the other continents and regions but there are also many special maps. The mountain and river systems of central Europe. Maps of the world according to Herodotus . . . and Ptolemy. The kingdom of Alexander the Great. The list is long and the maps a delight.

HISTORY AND ETHNOLOGY

This is not dry history. Stress is laid upon the national types . . . their culture, costume, customs and way of life. A reading of the contents of these plates is necessary to grasp the full scope of their coverage. Just looking at the 81 plates is not in itself enough. They are not just pictures. They teem with the artifacts of history. They *are* history.

CONTENTS OF THE PLATES

MATHEMATICS AND ASTRONOMY

PLATES 1—3.

Mathematical and Geometrical problems, 1–28.

GLOSSARY.

Milchstrasse, Milky Way.

PLATE 4.

Problems in Geodesy or Surveying, and Projection in vertical and horizontal planes, ... 28–53

PLATE 5.

Mathematical and Surveying Instruments.

Figs. 1, 2. Hair compasses, . . 53
" 3, 4. Proportional compasses, . 54
" 5. Do. with micrometer screw, . 54
" 6, 7. Beam compasses, . . 54
" 8, 8a. Triangular compasses, . 54
" 9, 10. Elliptograph, . . 55
" 11–13. Farey's do., . . 55
" 14. Excentric compasses, . 56
" 15. Pantograph, . . . 56
" 16. Wallace's eidograph, . 57
" 17. Spring compasses, . . 57
" 18, 19. Parallel ruler, . . 57
" 20. Lehman's plane table, . 59
" 21. Mayer's do. . 59
" 22. Mayer's fork and plummet, . 60
" 23, 24. Tubular level, . . 60
" 25. Diopter ruler, . . . 60
" 26. Do. with telescope, . 61
" 27. Measuring chain, . . 58
" 28. Measuring staff, . . 58
" 29. Arrow or picket, . . 59
" 30. Zollman's instrument for measuring angles, ... 62
" 31. Astrolabe, . . . 62
" 32. Hadley's sextant, . . 66
" 33, 34. Compass and telescope, . 63
" 35, 36. Schmalkalder's prismatic compass, . . . 64
" 37. Graphometer, . . . 66
" 38. Theodolite, . . . 64
" 39. Borda's reflecting circle, . 67
" 40, 41. Water level and movable diopter, . . . 68
" 42–44. Keith's mercurial level, . 68
" 45. Level and compass, . . 69
" 46. Levelling telescope, . . 69
" 47. Levelling compass, . . 70

Figs. 48. Levelling circle, . . . 70
" 49, 50. Explanation of the vernier, . 67
" 51, 52. Levelling staves, . . 70
" 53, 54. Target of levelling stave, . 71
" 55. Plate compasses, . . 55
" 56. Mason's level, . . . 68
" 57. Application of plane table, . 61
" 58–60. Lehman's method of topographical drawing, . . 33

GLOSSARY.

a = der Projection des Bergstriches, a = Projection of the mountain tract.
b = der Höhe der horizontalen Schicht, b = Height of the horizontal stratum.
c = wahre Länge des Bergstriches, c = True length of the mountain tract.

PLATE 6.

Figs. 1, 2. The armillary sphere, . 76
" 3. Illustrating the properties of the circle, ... 97
" 4. Ill'g the properties of the ellipse, 97
" 5. Ill'g the parallax, . . 97
" 6. Ill'g the centrifugal force of the earth, ... 124
" 7. Ill'g the rotation of the earth, 123
" 8, 9. Ill'g the proof of the earth's being of spherical shape, . 78
and an elliptical spheroid, . 124
" 10. Ill'g the local variation of gravity, 125
" 11. The parallelogram of forces, . 126
" 12. Illustrating the points, circles, and terms of the terrestrial sphere, . 79
" 13. Ill'g the apparent rotation of the celestial sphere, . . 79
" 14. Ill'g the heliocentric and geocentric place of the planets, . 98
" 15. Ill'g the perihelion distance, . 99
" 16, 17. Ill'g refraction, . . 126
" 18. Ill'g the theory of eclipses of the sun and moon, . . 100
" 19. Ill'g the phases of the moon, . 83
" 20. Ill'g the moon's nodes, . 84
" 21. Ill'g the apparent course of Venus, 80
" 22. Ill'g the theory of twilight, . 127
" 23. Ill'g the theory of ebb and flow, 129
" 24, 25. Ill'g the apparent course of superior and inferior planets, 80
" 26. Ill'g the resistance of the ether, . 130

PLATE 7.

Fig. 1. Planetary system of Ptolemy, . 102

Figs. 2. Planetary system of the Egyptians, 103
" 3. Do. of Tycho de Brahe, 103
" 4, 5. Do. of Copernicus, . 103
" 6. Illustrating the velocity of planets, 104
" 7. Ill'g the inclination of the planetary orbits to that of the earth, . 104

PLATE 8.

Figs. 1. Group of stars in Hercules, . 144
" 2. Do. in Aquarius, . 144
" 3, 4. Do. fan shaped, . 144
" 5. Nebula in Ursa, . . 144
" 6. Do. in Gemini, . . 144
" 7. Do. in Leo Major, . 144
" 8, 9. Nebulæ in Monoceros, . 144
" 10. Nebula in Canes Venatici, . 144
" 11. Do. in Sagittarius, . 144
" 12, 13. Do. in Auriga, . . 144
" 14. Do. in Andromeda, . 144
" 15. Comet of 1819, . . 142
" 16, 17. Do. of 1811, . . 142
" 18. Surface of Mars, . . 140
" 19. Do. of Jupiter, . . 141
" 20. Do. and rings of Saturn, . 141

PLATE 9.

Figs. 1. Illustrating the seasons, . . 109
" 2, 3. Daily and yearly motion of the earth, ... 85
" 4. Illustrating the parallel sphere, . 86
" 5. Ill'g the right sphere, . . 86
" 6. Ill'g the 13 transits of Mercury in the 19th century, . . 111
" 7, 8. Ill'g the phenomena of the transit of Mercury, May 4, 1786, ... 112
" 9–13. The sun's spots, . . . 131

PLATE 10.

Fig. 1. Illustrating the determination of longitude and latitude, . 86
" 2. Ill'g the theory of the elliptical orbit of the earth, . . 107
" 3. Ill'g the duration of a revolution of the moon, . . . 113
" 4. Ill'g the daily revolution of the moon around the earth, 112, 113
" 5. Ill'g the phases of the moon, 83, 113
" 6. Orbits of the moons of Jupiter, . 116
" 7. Do. of the moons of Saturn, . 117
" 8. Do. of the moons of Uranus, . 117

Figs. 9. Orbit of the earth's moon, . . 118
" 10. Serpentine projection of the moon's course on the plane of the earth's orbit, . . 113

GLOSSARY.

Abend, Evening ; — *stern,* Evening star.
Abnehmender Mond, Decreasing moon.
Aphelium, Aphelion.
Apsidenlinie, Line of Apsides.
Aufsteigender Knoten, Ascending node.
Austritt beim Aufgang der Sonne, Emersion at sunrise ; — *beim Untergang der Sonne,* Emersion at sunset.
Axe der Ekliptik, Axis of the Ecliptic.
Bahn des Merkur, Orbit of Mercury ; — *der Venus,* Orbit of Venus.
Colur des Frühlings-Æquinoxiums, Colure of the vernal equinox ; — *des Herbst-Æquinoxiums,* Col. of the Autumnal equinox ; — *der Nachtgleichen,* Col. of the equinoxes ; — *des Sommersolstitiums,* Col. of the Summer solstice ; — *des Wintersolstitiums,* Col. of the Winter solstice.
Comet von 1811 *vor seiner Erscheinung. Projectirt auf die Ekliptik am 25 März* 1811. *Neigung der Bahn* 75° 5', Comet of 1811 before its appearance. Projected on the ecliptic March 25, 1811, Inclination of the orbit 75° 5'. — *von* 1811 *nach seiner Erscheinung b. am 1 März* 1812, Comet of 1811 after its appearance until March 1, 1812.
Dauer der längsten Nächte, Duration of the longest nights ; — *des längsten Tages,* Duration of the longest day.
Dichteres Medium, Denser medium.
Drei Uhr Morgens, 3 o'clock A. M. ; — *Nachmittag,* 3 o'clock P. M.
Dritter Octant, Third octant.
Dünneres Medium, Rarer medium.
Ebene der Pallas, d. Juno, &c., Planes of the orbits of Pallas, Juno, &c.
Eintritt beim Aufgang der Sonne, Entrance at sunrise ; — *beim Untergang d. Sonne,* Entrance at sunset.
Ekliptik, Ecliptic.
Erdaxe, Axis of the earth.
Erdbahn, Orbit of the earth.
Erde, Earth.
Erster Octant, First octant.
Erstes Viertel, First quarter.
Excentricität, Eccentricity.
Frühling, Spring.

*Page numbers to the right of each listing refer to the full descriptive text which will be published at a later date.

Frühlingsnachtgleiche, Vernal equinox.
Gemässigte Zone, Temperate zone.
Grosse Axe, Axis of the heavens.
Halley'scher Comet v. 1759 u. 1835, Neigung seiner Bahn, Halley's Comet of 1759 and 1835, inclination of its orbit.
Heisse Zone, Torrid zone.
Herbst, Autumn.
Herbstnachtgleiche, Autumnal equinox.
Horizont, Horizon.
Kalte Zone, Frigid zone.
Kometenbahn, Orbit of a comet.
Letztes Viertel, Last quarter.
Millionen Meilen, Millions of miles.
Mittag, Noon.
Mittelkraft, Mean force.
Mitternacht, Midnight.
Monate, Months.
Mond, Moon; — -bahn, Orbit of the moon; — -finsterniss, Eclipse of the moon.
Morgen, Morning; — -stern, Morning star.
Neumond, New moon.
Neun Uhr Abends, 9 P.M.; — Morgens, 9 A.M.
Niedersteigender Knoten, Descending node.
Nord, North; — -pol, Northpole.
Nördliche Declination der Sonne, Northern declination of the sun.
Nördlicher Polarkreis, Arctic circle.
Obere Conjunction, Superior conjunction.
Œstliche Digression, East digression.
Ost, East.
Perihelium, Perihelion.
Polarstern, Polar star.
Polhöhe über dem Horizont, Elevation of the pole above the horizon.
Richtung des Schattens um Mittag, Direction of the shadow at noon.
Rotationsaxe, Axis of rotation.
Scheinbarer Himmelsbogen, Apparent arch of the heavens; — Horizont, visible horizon.
Sechs Uhr Abends, 6 P.M.; — Morgens, 6 A.M.
Solstitial oder Wendepunktlinie, Solstitial colure.
Sommer, Summer; — -Sonnenwende, Summer Solstice.
Sonne, Sun; — Sonnen-Æquator, Sun's equator; — -finsterniss, Eclipse of the sun; — -scheibe im Grössenverhältniss zu den Planeten, The sun's disk; its size compared to the diameters of the planets.
Stunden, Hours; — Entfernung, Hours' distance; — -ring, Hour-circle.
Süd, South; — -pol, South pole.
Südliche Declination der Sonne, Southern declination of the sun.
Südlicher Polarkreis, Antarctic circle.
Südwestlicher Sonnenrand, Southwestern edge of the sun.
Trabanten des Jupiter; — des Saturn; — des Uranus, Satellites of Jupiter, Saturn, and Uranus.
Untere Conjunction, inferior conjunction.
Vierter Octant, Fourth octant.
Vollmond, Full moon.
Vom Pol bis zum Zenith, From pole to zenith;
— Zenith bis zum Æquator, From zenith to equator.
Wahrer Horizont, True horizon.
Wendekreis des Krebses, Tropic of Cancer; — des Steinbocks, Tropic of Capricorn.
Westliche Digression, West digression.
Winter-Sonnenwende, Winter solstice.
Zoll, Digit, inch.
Zunehmender Mond, Increasing moon.
Zweites Octant, Second octant.
☞ For names of Constellations of the Zodiac, see p. 90.

PLATE 11.
PAGE

Beer and Mädler's Map of the Moon, 133–137

PLATES 12, 13.

Map of the Northern Heavens (Nördliche Sternkarte), and of the Southern Heavens (Südliche Sternkarte), ... 93
Names of constellations, . . . 90–93

PLATE 14.

Figs. 1–11. Relative sizes of the planets with respect to the sun's diameter, . . . 118
" 12–15. Positions of Saturn and its ring with respect to the earth, . . . 119
" 16–35. Apparent size of the planets in their perigee and apogee, 120
" 36–45. Apparent size of the sun as seen from the planets, 120
" 46–54. Comparison of the diameters of the moon and the planets to the diameter of the earth, 121
" 55. Mode of observing a transit of Venus, . . . 121
" 56. Total eclipse of the sun, . . 122
" 57. Aurora borealis, . . . 145
" 58. Aurora australis. . . . 145
" 59. Mock suns, ... 145

GLOSSARY.

Anfang bei Sonnenaufgang, Beginning at sunrise; — bei Sonnenuntergang, beginning at sunset.
Arabien, Arabia.
Atlantischer Ocean, Atlantic Ocean.
Azorische Inseln, The Azores.
Berberey, Barbary.
Berührung des Sonnen-, und Mondrandes, Contact of the edges of sun and moon.
Canarische Inseln, Canary Islands.
Capverdische Inseln, Cape Verd Islands.
Centrale oder totale Verfinsterung, Central or total eclipse.
Drei Zoll Verfinsterung, Three digits eclipsed.
Ende bei Sonnenaufgang, End at sunrise; — bei Sonnenuntergang, End at sunset.
Grönland, Greenland.
Grossbritanien, Great Britain.
Grosser Ocean, Pacific Ocean.
Indisches Meer, Indian Sea.
Island, Iceland,
Mittel bie Sonnenaufgang, Middle at sunrise; —
bei Sonnenuntergang, Middle at sunset.
Mittelländisches Meer, Mediterranean Sea.
Mongolei, Mongolia.
Neun Zoll Verfinsterung Nine digits eclipsed.
Nordpol, North pole.
Norwegen, Norway.
Nubien, Nubia.
Ost Indien, East Indies.
Russland, Russia.
Sechs Zoll Verfinsterung, Six digits eclipsed.
Sibirien, Siberia.

PLATE 15.

Astronomical Instruments.
PAGE

Figs. 1. Herschel's reflecting telescope, . 158
" 2. Fraunhofer's achromatic refractor at Dorpat, . . . 156
" 3–10. Meridian circle at Pulkowa, . 163
" 11, 12. Meridian circle at Hamburg, 163
" 13. Roemer's transit instrument, . 160
" 14. Dollond's repeating circle, . 162
" 15–17. Repsold's Equatorial at Hamburg, ... 164
" 18. Troughton's quadrant, . 160
" 19. Tycho's mural quadrant, . 159
" 20. Clockwork of Fraunhofer's refractor, ... 157
" 21. Ptolemy's triquetrum, . 167
" 22. Portable transit instrument, . 160
" 23. Reflecting sextant, . . 166
" 24. Reflecting sector, . . 167
" 25–34. Repsold's small transit instrument at St. Petersburg, . 161
" 35–37. Ertel's theodolite, . 165
" 38. Henderson's planetarium, . 171
" 39. Henderson's explanation of the seasons, . . . 172

PHYSICS AND METEOROLOGY

PLATE 16.

Fig. 1. Parallelogram of forces, . . 179
" 2. Triangle of forces, . . 179
" 3. Polygon of forces, . . 180
" 4. Parallelopipedon of forces, . 180
" 5. Centre of gravity of a line, . 181
" 6. Do. do. triangle, . 181
" 7. Do. do. polygon, . 181
" 8. Do. do. parallelogram, 181
" 9. Do. of irregular surfaces, 182
" 10. Do. of a cube, . 181
" 11. Do. do. parallelopipedon, 181
" 12. Do. do. pyramid, . 181
" 13. Do. of two different bodies, . . 181, 182
" 14. Illustrating Varignon's funicular machine, . . . 182
" 15, 16. Ill'g the theory of the pulley, 187
" 17, 18. Atwood's machine for demonstrating the laws of freely falling bodies, . . . 202
Fig. 19. The fixed pulley, . . . 187
" 20. Illustrating the oscillation of the pendulum, . . 206
" 21. The gridiron pendulum, . 208
" 22. The mercurial pendulum, . 208
" 23. Lever of the first class, . 182
" 24. Application of the same in the steelyard, . . . 183
" 25. Lever of the second class, . 182
" 26. Lever of the third class, . 182
" 27, 28. Illustrating the theory of equilibrium, . . . 184
" 29. Lever and pulley, . . 183
" 30. Bent lever, . . . 183
" 31. Compound lever, . . 184
" 32, 33. Wheel and axle, . 186
" 34. Endless screw attached to windlass, . . . 190
" 35. Wheel and axle with pulley, 186
" 36–40. Movable pulleys, . . 187
" 41, 42. White's pulley, . . 188
" 43. Pulley with cords working obliquely, . . . 188
" 44–46. Inclined plane, . . 188
" 47, 48. The wedge, . . . 188
" 49–52. Illustrating theory of strength and stress of materials, . 195

PLATE 17.

Fig. 1–3. Illustrating the theory of the screw, ... 189
" 4. Hunter's differential screw, . 190
" 5–21. Illustrating the theory of strength and stress of materials, ... 191–199.
" 22. Ill'g the theory of uniformly varying motion, . . . 201
" 23. Ill'g the theory of unequably accelerated motion, . . 201
" 24. Ill'g the influence of gravitation on the motion of projectiles, 204
" 25–20. Ill'g the theory of projectiles, 204
" 29. Ill'g the centrifugal force, . 204
" 30. Ill'g the lateral pressure of moving liquids, . . . 221
" 31–33. Ill'g the velocity of efflux, . 220
" 34. Ill'g the forcing pump, . 234
" 35. Prony's swimmer, a contrivance to regulate the velocity of efflux, ... 220
" 36. Ill'g the hydraulic ram, . 222
" 37, 38. Ill'g the ballistic pendulum, . 211
" 39, 40. Valve and parachute of the Hampton balloon, . . 237
" 41. Henson's flying machine, . 238
" 42–48. Illustrating the pneumodrome of Partridge, . . . 238

PLATE 18.

Fig. 1–8. Illustrating the pressure of liquids, ... 212

Fig. 9, 10. Ill'g the law of Archimedes, . 213
" 11. The Cartesian devils, . . 214
" 12–14. Hydrostatic balance, . . 214
" 15. Nicholson's areometer, . . 216
" 16. The scale areometer, . . 216
" 17–19. Illustrating capillary attraction, ... 217
" 20–30. Ill'g phenomena of attraction
of liquids and solids, . 218
" 31. Dutrochet's endosmometer, . 219
" 32. Common barometer, . . 224
" 33–35. Gay Lussac's syphon barometer, . . . 225
" 36–38. Fortin's barometer, . . 225
" 39–41. Arago and Dulong's apparatus
for proving Mariotte's law, 226
" 42. Kopp's differential barometer, . 227
" 43. Kopp's volumeter (Quoted in the
text as fig. 93), . . 228
" 44. Gay Lussac's hand air-pump, . 229
" 45, 46. Larger air-pump, . . 229
" 47. Two-cylindered air-pump, . 230
" 48–50. Babinet's cock for obtaining
the greatest rarefaction, . 230
" 51–53. The condensing pump, . 230
" 54–56. The syphon, . . . 232
" 57, 58. Apparatus involving the
theory of the syphon, . 232
" 59. Cup of Tantalus, . . . 232
" 60. Fountain involving the syphon, . 233
" 61. Hero's ball, . . . 233
" 62. Intermitting spring, . . 233
" 63, 64. Hero's fountain, . . 234
" 65–71. Hydraulic press, . . 235
" 72. Apparatus to measure the pressure
of falling water, . . 221
" 73. Ordinary air balloon, . . 238
" 74. Marey Monge's copper balloon, . 238
" 93 see 43. (The figure is marked 93
by mistake of the engraver.)

PLATE 19.

Fig. 1. Gasometer, . . . 240
" 2, 3. Cylindrical blower, . . 240
" 4. Water regulator, . . . 241
" 5. Wind measurer, . . . 241
" 6. Common bellows, . . . 240
" 7. Mercurial thermometer, . . 259
" 8. Apparatus for measuring the expansion of solids, . . 260
" 9–11. Do. for higher tempera-
tures, . . . 260
" 12. Metal, or quadrant thermometer, 262
" 13. Breguet's thermometer, . . 262
" 14. Air thermometer, . . . 263
" 15. Pneumatic apparatus, . . 264
" 16. Illustrating the relative expansion
of mercury, water, and
alcohol, . . . 263
" 17. Ill'g the laws of vaporization, . 265
" 18. Ill'g the tension of vapor in un-
equally heated places, . 266
" 19, 20. Apparatus for measuring the
elasticity of vapor, . . 266

Fig. 21. App's for ascertaining the density
of watery vapor, . . 267
" 22. App's for mixing vapors with
gases, ... 269
" 23. App's for measuring the tension
of this mixture, . . 269
" 24. App's for boiling water by the
condensation of vapor, . 270
" 25. Papin's digester, . . . 270
" 26. Papin's first steam-engine, . 273
" 27–34. Watt's steam-engine, . 273
" 35. Illustrating the transmission of
heat, ... 278
" 36. Rumford's differential thermometer, ... 278
" 37, a, b. Melloni's thermo-multiplier, 279
" 38–40. Locatelli lamp, &c., . . 279
" 41. Illustrating the refraction of heat
rays, ... 281
" 42. Apparatus for ascertaining the
laws of cooling, . . 281
" 43. Calorimeter of Lavoisier and
Laplace, . . . 276
" 44, 45. Apparatus for determining the
specific heat of bodies, . 276
" 46. App's for determining the specific
heat of gases, . . . 277
" 47. Cooling tube, . . . 271
" 48. Cooling vessel, . . . 272
" 49. Apparatus for measuring latent
heat, ... 272
" 49, a. Illustrating the transmission of
sound, ... 246
" 50. Savart's monochord, . . 253
" 51, 52. Vibration of strings, . . 244
" 53–58. Illustrating the construction
of organs, . . . 250
" 59–61. Cagniard de la Tour's system
of determining the number
of vibrations in a tone, . 251
" 62. Apparatus for causing plates to
vibrate, . . . 244
" 63–90. Figures produced by the vibration of plates, bells, &c., 245, 257
[By mistake of the engraver this
figure is numbered 76. It stands
in the centre of the plate.]
" 91. Apparatus for producing tones
by the combustion of hydro-
gen gas, . . . 250
" 92. Illustrating the manner of com-
municating vibrations to the
air, ... 249
" 93. Ill'g the echo in arched rooms, . 248
" 94. Hearing tube, . . . 258
" 95. Illustrating the metal tongue, . 254
" 96, 97. Tongue work of the organ, . 254
" 98. Illustrating the nature of the
human voice, . . . 257

PLATE 20.

Fig. 1. Attraction of a natural magnet, . 314
" 2. Att'n of an artificial magnet, . 314
" 3. Curves of filings over a magnet, . 314
" 4. Influence of a magnet on an iron
rod, ... 315
" 5. The same without contact, . . 315
" 6. Magnetic needle, . . . 315

Fig. 7. The various poles of a magnet, . 316
" 8. Compass, ... 316
" 9. Variation of the compass, . . 316
" 10. Inclination of the compass, . 316
" 11. Action of the earth upon the
magnetic needle, . . 317
" 12. Intensity compass of Gambey, . 317
" 13, 14. Coulomb's torsion balance, . 318
" 15. Coulomb's determination of the
strength of the magnet at
various distances from its
pole, ... 319
" 16, 17. Duhamel's method of preparing artificial magnets, . 319
" 18. Œpinus's method of doing the
same, ... 319
" 19. Horse-shoe magnet, . . 320
" 20, 21. Armature of natural magnets, 320
" 22. Electrical pendulum, . . 321
" 23. Coulomb's electroscope, . . 321
" 24. Pith ball electroscopes, . . 322
" 25. Electric pistol, . . . 323
" 26. Volta's straw electrometer, . 321
" 27, 28. The electrophorus, . . 325
" 29. Plate electric machine, . . 324
" 30, 30a. Rubbers of the same, . . 324
" 31. Van Marum's electric machine, . 325
" 32. Nairne's electric machine, . . 324
" 33. Franklin plate, . . . 326
" 34. Discharging rod, . . . 326
" 35, 36. Leyden jars, . . . 327
" 37. Electrical battery, . . . 327
" 38. Henley's universal discharger, . 327
" 39. Electrical mortar, . . . 323
" 40. Kinnersley's thermometer, . 323
" 41. Leyden jar with movable coatings, 328
" 42. Lightning plate, . . . 329
" 43. Lightning tube, . . . 329
" 44. Electrical light, . . . 328
" 45. Wheatstone's apparatus for determining the velocity of electricity, ... 329
" 46. Electric wheel, . . . 330
[By mistake of the engraver this
figure is numbered 76. It stands
in the centre of the plate.]
" 47. Influence of Galvanism, . . 330
" 48. Volta's galvanic double plate, . 331
" 49. Voltaic pile, . . . 331
" 50, 51. Fechner's improvement of
Bohnenberger's electrometer, 335
" 52. Trough apparatus, . . . 332
" 53–55. Wollaston's battery, . . 332
" 56. Volta's simple galvanic series, . 332
" 57. Hare's calorimeter, . . 332
" 58. Becquerel's constant battery, . 332
" 59, 60. Daniel's Do. . 333
" 61. Grove's battery, . . . 333
" 62, 63. Bunsen's carbon battery, . 333
" 64, 65. Apparatus for decomposing
water, . . . 335
" 66. App's for decomposing salts, . 336
" 67. Becquerel's galvanoplastic apparatus, . . . 336
" 68. Influence of the galvanic current

on the magnetic needle, . 337
Fig. 69. Schweigger's galvanometer, . 337
" 70. Nobili's improved do. . 338
" 71–74. Tangent compass, . . 338
" 75. Sine compass, . . . 338
" 76. [See 46.]
" 76–78. Magnetic action of the galvanic current, . . . 339
" 79–81. Electro-magnets, . . 339
" 82. Rotation of the magnet under the
influence of the galvanic current, ... 350
" 83–85. Ampère's apparatus for determining the influence of terrestrial magnetism on the
galvanic current, . . 346
" 86. Neutralization of terrestrial magnetism, ... 347
" 87. Rotation of vertical currents, . 350
" 88. De la Rive's apparatus showing
that feeble currents are af-
fected by magnetism, . . 347
" 89, 90. Disconnecting and severing
of magnetic currents, . . 349

PLATE 21.

Fig. 1. Refraction of light in its passage
from water into air, . . 283
" 2, 3. Full shadow and half shadow, . 284
" 4. Inverted image caused by a ray of
light entering a dark room
through a small aperture, . 284
" 5. Angle of reflection of light, . 284
" 6. Apparatus to prove the equality of
the angles of reflection and
of incidence, . . . 285
" 7. Proof of the symmetry of images
reflected by plane mirrors, . 285
" 8. Construction of reflected images, . 285
" 9. Mirrors placed together at an
angle, . . . 285, 286
" 10–12. Wollaston's reflecting goniometer, ... 286
" 13. Gambey's goniometer, . . 287
" 14, 15. Reflecting sextant, . . 287
" 16–18. Concave mirror, . . 288
" 19, 20. Nature of images formed in
concave mirrors, . . 289
" 21. Spherical convex mirror, . . 289
" 22. Image formed on the same, . 289
" 23. Caustic curve, . . . 290
" 24. Angle of refraction, . . 290
" 25. Laws of refraction, . . 290
" 26. Total reflection, . . . 291
" 27. Prism stand, . . . 291
" 28. Solar spectrum, . . . 292
" 29. Prismatic refraction, . . 292
" 30. Hollow prism, . . . 293
" 31. Dulong's apparatus for determining the refractive powers of
gases, ... 293
" 32. The six kinds of lenses, . . 293
" 33. Refraction by lenses, . . 294
" 34. Focus of lenses, . . . 294
" 35. Divergence of rays in concave
lenses, ... 295

Fig. 36. Secondary axis of lenses, . . 295
" 37–39. Images formed in lenses, . 295
" 40. Aperture of the lens necessary to
    unite all rays in one point, . 295
" 41, 42. Fresnel's polyzonal lens, . 295
" 43, 44. Decomposition of light into
    various colored rays, . . 296
" 45. Composition of white light from
    various colored rays, . . 297
" 46. Decomposition of the natural
    colors of bodies by the prism, 297
" 47. Achromatic prism, . . . 297
" 48. Achromatic lens, . . . 298
" 49. Mosaic composite eye, . . 298
" 50. Simple human eye, . . . 299
" 51. Illustrating double sight, . . 300
" 52. Ill'g the possibility of seeing vari-
    ous objects at once, . . 300
" 53, 54. Irradiation, . . . 300
" 55. The phenakistoscope, . . 301
" 56. Wollaston's camera lucida, . 302
" 57, 58. Camera obscura, . . 302
" 59. Solar microscope, . . . 303
" 60, 61. Compound microscope, . 303
" 62. Gregorian telescope, . . 305
" 63. Cassegrainian telescope, . . 305
" 64. Newtonian telescope, . . 305
" 65. Galilean telescope, . . 304
" 66. Astronomical telescope, . . 304
" 67. Determination of the magnifying
    power of telescopes, . . 304
" 68. Fresnel's apparatus for determin-
    ing the interference of
    light, ... 306
" 69. Nörremberg's polariscope, . . 310
" 70. Angle of polarization, . . 311
" 71, 72. Rochon's micrometer, . 312
" 73. Soleil's apparatus for measuring
    the rings of polarization, . 313
" 74–76. Daguerreotype apparatus, . 314
" 77. Reflexion by spherical concave
    mirrors, . . . 288
" 78. Refraction in water, . . 291
" 79. Common prism, . . . 291
" 80. Refraction by prisms, . . 292
" 81. Construction of the hollow prism, 293
" 82. The direction of emerging rays
    shown to be parallel with
    that of entering ones, . 293
" 83. Divergence of rays emerging from
    lenses, . . . 294
" 84. Convergence of rays emerging
    from lenses, . . . 295
" 85. Angle of vision, . . . 300
" 86. Vanishing of small objects on the
    punctum cœcum, . . 300
" 87. Apparatus for exhibiting the dura-
    tion of an impression on the
    retina, . . . 301
" 88. **Apparatus for experiments on the
    interference of light,** . 306
" 89. Undulation of rays, . . 306
" 90. Illustrating the theory of interfer-
    ence, . . . 307

Fig. 91. Illustrative of the explanation of
    reflexion by the undulatory
    theory, . . . 307
" 92. The law of refraction similarly
    illustrated, . . . 307
" 93–99. Fraunhofer's spectra, . . 308
" 100, 101. Polarization of light, 310, 311
" 102, 103. The magic lantern, . . 304
" 104. Camera lucida, . . . 302
" 105, 106. Brewster's kaleidoscope, . 286

PLATE 22.

Fig. 1. Apparatus for observing the action
    of terrestrial magnetism on
    vertical currents, . . 347
" 2, 3. Faraday's apparatus for observ-
    ing the rotative action of
    terrestrial magnetism on
    horizontal currents, . . 349
" 4. Action of parallel currents upon
    each other, . . . 348
" 5, 6. Apparatus to show the action of
    crossing currents upon each
    other, ... 348
" 7. App's for determining the plane of
    the terrestrial currents, . 349
" 8. Declination spiral wire, . . 347
" 9, 10. Ampère's apparatus for ex-
    plaining the rotation of the
    magnet, . . . 350
" 11. Thermo-electric currents, . . 356
" 12. Thermo-electric multiplier, . 356
" 13. Apparatus to show the develop-
    ment of electricity by com-
    bustion, ... 337
" 14. Illustrating induction currents, . 351
" 15–17. Neef and Wagner's induction
    coil, ... 351
" 18. Apparatus to show the production
    of electrical currents by
    magnetism, . . . 352
" 19. Induction coil in connexion with
    magnets, . . . 353
" 20–22. Ettinghausen's magneto-elec-
    tric rotating machine, . . 353
" 23–27. Stöhrer's triple magneto-elec-
    tric machine, . . . 355
" 28. Differential galvanometer, . . 356
" 29. Apparatus for determining the
    conducting powers of me-
    tals, ... 356
" 30. App's for determining the re-
    quisite qualities of conduct-
    ing wires, . . . 357
" 31, 32. App's for obtaining an un-
    alterable thermo-electric
    current, . . . 357
" 33–35. Thermo-electric pile, . . 357
" 36–38. Stöhrer's improvement of
    Daniel's electro-magnetic
    machine, . . . 339
" 39. Ritchie's improved machine, . 341
" 40. Wheatstone's telegraph, . . 342
" 41, 42. Steinheil's telegraph, . . 344

Figs. 43–47. Illustrating Ampère's theory
    of the rotation of magnets, . 348
" 48, 49. Astatic multiplier, . . 338
" 50, 51. Weber's apparatus for demon-
    strating the laws of magnet-
    ism, ... 317
" 52, 53, 53a. Arago's apparatus for
    investigating phenomena in
    rotation magnetism, . . 355
" 54. Illustrating the intensity of electri-
    city in combined elements, . 338
" 55–58. Clarke's magneto-electric ma-
    chine, ... 354
" 59. Henley's quadrant electrometer, . 325
" 60. Apparatus for proving that free
    electricity is confined to the
    surface of bodies, . . 322
" 61. Gold leaf electrometer, . . 321
" 62. Buff's app's for determining the
    kind of electricity in a body, 323
" 63. Apparatus to show the separation
    of the combined electricities
    when an electrified body is
    brought near, . . . 323
" 64. Apparatus to show that the con-
    nexion of two similar electro-
    scopes by an insulated
    conductor will separate
    their electricities, . . 324
" 65. Construction of the electrometer, 321
" 66, 67. Different windings around the
    electro-magnet, . . . 346
" 68. Rotation of the magnet around its
    own axis, . . . 350
" 69. The voltaic pile, . . . 331
" 70. Illustrating the action of electri-
    cal currents, . . . 320
" 71. Production of electric light in a
    vacuum, . . . 329
" 72. Electric dance, . . . 322
" 73–75. Eisenlohr's hydro-electric ma-
    chine, ... 325

PLATE 23.

Fig. 1. Howard's diagram to elucidate the
    action of the sun's rays on
    the earth, . . . 360
" 2. Illustrating the snow line, . 366
" 3. Curvature of the Alpine snow line, 366
" 4–23. Forms of snow crystals, . 395
" 24–35. Forms of hailstones, . 397
" 36–38. Illustrating the amount of dew
    on trees and herbs, . 384
" 39, 40. Ill'g the amount of dew on
    differently inclined surfaces, 384
" 41–43. Ill'g the greatest deposit of
    dew on the highest points of
    an object, . . . 384
" 44–47. Ill'g the increase of dewdrops, 385
" 48. Ill'g that an object rolled up in a
    ball receives less dew than
    if spread out flat, . . 385
" 49–52. Ill'g that gilt paper is bedewed
    only when its unmetallic side
    is in contact with wood, . 385
" 53, ab. Zone of dew deposited in the
    cavity of a watch-glass, . 385
" 54. Regular deposit of dew *around*
    wafers on a glass plate, not
    on them, . . . 385
" 55. Deposit of dew on a window, . 383
" 56, 57. Deposit of dew on spiders'
    webs, ... 385
Fig. 58. Perpendiculars from the widest
    boughs of a tree marking the
    limits of the formation of
    frost, ... 386
" 59. Curious formation of frost on the
    chiselled star of a tombstone, 386
" 60, 61. Curious formation of frost on
    leaves, ... 386
" 62. Illustrating the theory of
    winds, . . . 370
" 63. Ill'g the theory of whirlwinds, . 376
" 64. Rain gauge, ... 391

GLOSSARY.

Februar, February.
Fische, Pisces.
Frühling 90 Tage, Spring 90 days.
Heisseste Temperatur, Hottest temperature.
Herbst 90 Tage, Autumn 90 days.
Januar, January.
Juli, July.
Jungfrau, Virgo.
Juni, June.
Kälteste Temperatur, Coldest temperature.
Krebs, Cancer.
Löwe, Leo.
Mai, May.
März, March.
Mittlere Temperatur, Medium temperature.
Schütze, Sagittarius.
Skorpion, Scorpio.
Sommer 93 Tage, Summer 93 days.
Steinbock, Capricornus.
Stier, Taurus.
Waage, Libra.
Wassermann, Aquarius.
Widder, Aries.
Winter 93 Tage, Winter 93 days.
Zwillinge, Gemini.

PLATE 24.

Fig. 1. Peculiar crystallization on the win-
    dow of a drug store, . 386
" 2. Two trees trained on a wall, only
    in part exposed to frost, . 386
" 3–6. Ice flowers, . . . 386
" 7. Formation of fog over rivers, . 387
" 8. Overtopping of trees by fog, . 387
" 9. Formation of fog over rivers in-
    closed by hills, . . 387
" Ill'g the different appearance of clouds
    to observers at different
    places, . . . 390
" 11. Ill'g the difference of shape of
    clouds according to their
    elevation, . . . 390

Fig. 12. Ill'g the difference of currents of
air at different heights, . 372
" 13–18. Different formations of fog
near the harbor of Plymouth
(England), . . . 387
" 19. Mirage in Lower Egypt, . . 403
" 20, 21. Mirages at sea, . . . 404
" 22. Theory of mirages, . . . 405
" 23. Mirage on the lake of Geneva, . 405

PLATE 25.

Fig. 1–8. Forms of clouds, . . . 389
" 9. Halo around the sun, . . 407
" 10, 11. Haloes around the moon, . 408
" 12. Halo and colored ring, . . 408
" 13–20. Mock suns, ... 409

PLATE 26.

Fig. 1–9. Ill'g phenomena in clouds, . 390
" 10–12. Rainbows, ... 405
" 13. Aurora borealis, . . . 428
" 14. Midnight sun in the polar regions.

PLATE 27.

Fig. 1. Whirlwind and waterspout, . 379
" 2, 3. The sun behind clouds, . . 391
" 4. The drawing of water, . . 402
" 5. Converging in the east, of the
shadow of the setting sun, . 391
" 6. Illus'g that objects on earth can
throw shadows into space, . 391
" 7. Shadows thrown on a bank of fog, 408
" 8, 9. Coloring of clouds by the sun, . 391
" 10, 11. Phenomena of the sun's apparent contact with clouds, 391
" 12. Apparent contact of clouds, . 390
" 13. Zodiacal light, . . . 410
" 14–19. Lightning rod, . . . 422
" 20–26. Magnetic observatory at
Greenwich, . . . 424

PLATE 28.

Fig. 1, ab. Inclination charts, . . 426
" 2, ab. Isodynamic charts, . . 427
" 3 (centre). Chart of magnetic declina-
tions, ... 426
" 4, ab. Barometrical wind rosettes, . 376
" 5, ab. Thermometrical wind rosettes, 376
(For Glossary see after plate 29.)

PLATE 29.

Fig. 1. Map of Humboldt's isothermal lines
showing the distribution of
heat and rain on the earth, . 363
" 2. Diagram of the mean annual temperature at various places, . 363
" 3. The mean decennial temperature
of various places, . . 363
" 4. Comparison of temperature, . 363

GLOSSARY.

Ægypten, Egypt.
Æquator-Grenze des Schneefalls, Equatorial
boundary of the snow region.

Aleuten, Aleutian Islands.
Arabien, Arabia.
Asien, Asia.
Barometer steigt, — fällt, Barometer rises, — falls.
Berberei, Barbary.
Beständiger Regen, Perpetual rain.
C. der guten Hoffnung, Cape of Good Hope.
Canarische Inseln, Canary Islands.
Capverdische Inseln, Cape Verd Islands.
Deutschland, Germany.
Erd-Æquator, Terrestrial equator.
Europa, Europe.
Frankreich, France.
Freundschafts Inseln, Friendly Islands.
Gebiet der Monsun Regen, Region of the Mon-
soons.
Gesellschafts Inseln, Society Islands.
Grönland, Greenland.
Grossbritanien, Great Britain.
Grosser Ocean, Pacific Ocean.
Herbst und Winter Regen, Autumn and winter
rains.
Indisches Meer, Indian Sea.
Italien, Italy.
Kopenhagen, Copenhagen.
Kurve von Leith, Br., Curve of Leith, latitude.
Kurve von Padua, Br., Curve of Padua, latitude.
Linie ohne Inclination, Line without inclination.
Magnetischer Æquator, Magnetic equator.
Manschurei, Mandshoo territory.
Maximum der magnet. Kraft, Maximum of
magnetic power.
Mittlere Tageswärme, Medium daily temperature.
Mongolei, Mongolia.
N. O., N. E.
Neufundland, Newfoundland.
Neu Guinea, New Guinea.
Neu Sealand, New Zealand.
Niedrige Inseln, Low Islands.
Nord Amerika, North America.
Nördlicher Gürtel der beständigen Nieder-
schläge, Northern zone of perpetual deposits.
Nördliche Hemisphäre, Northern Hemisphere.
Nördlicher Polarkreis, Arctic Circle.
Nördliches Eismeer, Arctic Sea.
Nordpol, North pole.
Nord See, North sea.
Norwegen, Norway.
Nubien, Nubia.
Oceanien, Oceania.
Ost Indien, The East Indies.
Ostseite, East side.
Persien, Persia.
Provinz des Herbstregens; — des Sommer-
regens; — des Winterregens, Region of
autumnal, of summer, and of winter rains.
Regenloses Gebiet, Rainless region.
Russland, Russia.
Schwacher Sommerregen, Light summer rain.
Sibirien, Siberia.
S. O., S. E.
S. O. Monsun im Apr.–Oct., N. W. Monsun im
Oct.–Apr., S. E. Monsoon from April to
October, N. W. Monsoon from October to April.

Spanien, Spain.
Süd Amerika, South America.
Südpol, South pole.
Südlicher Continent, Southern continent.
Südlicher Gürtel der beständigen Niederschläge,
Southern zone of perpetual deposits.
Südliche Hemisphäre, Southern Hemisphere.
S. W. Monsun im Apr.–Oct., N. O. Monsun im
Oct.–Apr., S. W. Monsoon from April to
October, N. E. Monsoon from October to April.
Thermometer steigt, — fällt, Thermometer rises,
— falls.
Turkei, Turkey.
Vereinigte Staaten, United States.
Wärme-Æquator, Equator of heat.
Wendekreis des Krebses; — des Steinbocks,
Tropic of Cancer; — of Capricorn.
West Indien, The West Indies.
Westseite, West side.
Winterregen, Winter rains.
Wüste Schamo oder Gobi, Desert of Shamo, or
Gobi.
Zone häufiger, fast beständiger Niederschläge,
stets mit electrischen Explosionen, Zone of
frequent, nearly perpetual deposits, always ac-
companied by electrical explosions.

CHEMISTRY, MINERALOGY AND GEOLOGY

PLATE 30.

Fig. 1. Ground-plan of the chemical laboratory at Giessen, . . 470
" 2. Perspective view of part of the analytical laboratory at Giessen, 470
" 3, 3a. Portable wind furnace, . . 434
" 4, 5. Portable distilling apparatus, . 438
" 6, 7. Fixed furnace, . . . 434
" 8, 9. Sand bath furnace, . . . 437
" 10. Small table for raising or lower-
ing receivers, . . . 438
" 11, 12. Small alembic, . . . 438
" 13. Pharmaceutical steam apparatus, 468
" 14–20. Do. with its utensils, . 469
" 21, 22. Crucible furnace, . . . 435
" 23. Tongs for handling hot crucibles, 435
" 24. Splitting iron, ... 438
" 25, 26. Retorts, ... 437
" 27–29. Globes or matrasses, . . 438
" 30–34. Hessian crucible, . . . 434
" 35, 36. Evaporating dishes, . . 439
" 37–41. Thermometers, . . . 466
" 42. Separating funnel, . . . 466
" 43. Bent tube with bulb, . . 441
" 44, 45. Walter's safety tube, . . 443
" 46. Filtering funnel, . . . 465
" 47. Separating funnel, . . . 466
" 48. Special funnel, ... 466

Fig. 49. Washing bottle, ... 465
" 50. Measure, ... 470
" 51–54. Florentine flasks, . . . 466
" 55. Pneumatic tub, ... 444
" 56, 57. Wolff apparatus, . . . 468
" 58, 59. Gasometer, ... 452
" 60, 61. Davy's apparatus for inves-
tigating earths, . . . 468
" 62. Apparatus for generating prussic
acid, ... 468
" 63. Apparatus for producing small
quantities of illuminating gas
from various substances, . 470
" 64. Argand's oil lamp, . . . 470
" 65–68. Pharmaceutical extract presses, 469
" 69–73. Chemical balance, . . . 466

PLATE 31.

Fig. 1, 2. Oxy-ethereal lamp, . . . 435
" 3. Distilling apparatus, . . 438
" 4, 5. Gasometer, ... 452
" 6, 7. Apparatus for rendering carbonic
acid liquid, . . . 440
" 8. App's for obtaining phosphorus, . 445
" 9. Furnace for obtaining caustic soda, 446
" 10. Furnace for heating matrasses, . 456
" 11. Berzelius lamp, . . . 447
" 12. Triangle of iron wire, . . 457
" 13. Apparatus for obtaining the gase-
ous elements, . . . 442
" 14. App's for obtaining chlorine, . 444
" 15–23. Drying apparatus, . . . 457
" 24. Air pump, ... 459
" 25. Calcium tube, ... 459
" 26. Chloride of calcium tube, . . 460
" 27–29. Combustion tubes, . . . 459
" 30–32. Combustion furnace, . . 459
" 33. Apparatus for elementary analysis
with application of oxygen, 461
" 34–38. App's for determining the
nitrogen in organic sub-
stances, ... 462
" 39. App's for filling the potash apparatus, ... 460
" 40, 41. App's for determining the
specific gravity of vapor, . 461
" 42. Muffle furnace, ... 455
" 43. Cupel, ... 455
" 44. Muffle, ... 455
" 45, 46. Apparatus for generating
carbonic acid gas, . . 454
" 47. Two-branched tube for washing
precipitates, . . . 465
" 48, 49. Washing bottles, . . . 465
" 50–52. Filtering apparatus, . . 460
" 53. Suction tube, ... 465
" 54. Washing bottle, ... 465
" 55. Galley furnace, ... 455
" 56. Gas generator, ... 444
" 57. Crucible, ... 454
" 58. Apparatus for ascertaining the
amount of pure metal in
oxydes, ... 447
" 59. Davy's safety lamp, . . . 467
" 60. Apparatus for procuring oxygen, 443

Fig. 61. Safety tube, . . . 444
" 62, 63. Blowpipe, . . . 435
" 64. Iron pincers for handling heated vessels, . 447
" 65. Apparatus for obtaining nitrogenous substances from organic matter, . . . 464
" 66. Eudiometer, . . . 451

PLATE 32.

Fig. 1. Blowpipe, . . . 474
" 2. Attenuated point of flame caused by the blowpipe, . . 474
" 3. Forceps, . . . 474
" 4. Berzelius blowpipe, . . 474
" 5. Nicholson areometer, . 474
" 6. Magnetic needle, . . 475
" 7, ab. Instrument for detecting electricity in minerals, . 475
" 8. Common goniometer, . 483
" 9. Gambay's do. . 484
" 10. Wollaston's do. . 483

Forms of Crystallization.

Fig. 11, 12. Regular octahedron, . 477
" 13. Octahedron abbreviated to a six sided plate, . . 477
" 14. Cube, . . . 278
" 15. Relation of the cube and octahedron, . . . 478
" 16, 17. Cubic octahedron, . 478
" 18. Rhombic dodecahedron, . 478
" 19. Relation of the rhombic dodecahedron and cube, . 478
" 20. Pyramidal cube, . . 478
" 21, 24. Cube with dodecahedral faces replacing its edges, . 478
" 22. Octahedron with dodecahedral faces, . . . 478
" 23. Octahedron passing into a dodecahedron, . . . 478
" 24. See 21, . . . 478
" 25. Combination of cube faces and those of the pyramidal cube, . . . 478
" 26. Tetrahedron, . . 478
" 27. Octahedron passing into a tetrahedron, . . . 478
" 28. Cube with its edges replaced by three faces, . . 478
" 29. Pentagonal dodecahedron, . 478
" 30. Trapezohedron, . . 478
" 31. Octahedron passing into a trapezohedron, . . 478
" 32. Obtuse square octahedron, . 479
" 33. Acute do. do. . 479
" 34. Square octahedron with two corners truncated, . . 479
" 35. Right square prism, . . 479
" 36. Regular eight sided prism, . 479
" 37. Right square prism with its corners truncated, . . 479
" 38. Square octahedron with truncated basal edges, . 479
" 39. Do. with truncated lateral edges, 479

Fig. 40. Eight sided pyramid, . . 479
" 41. Twelve sided prism, . . 479
" 42. Six sided prism with bevelled edges, . . 481
" 43. Right square prism, with basal edges truncated, . 479
" 44. Rectangular octahedron, . 480
" 45. Do. truncated, . 480
" 46. Square octahedron with bevelled lateral edges, . 479
" 47, a. Obtuse rhombic octahedron, . 480
" b. Acute rhombic octahedron, . 480
" c. Rectangular octahedron, . 480
" 48. Rhombic octahedron with two corners bevelled, . 480
" 49. Octahedron with the corners of the vertical axis replaced by four plane faces, . 479
" 50. Right rhombic prism, . 480
" 51. Do. with obtuse edges truncated, 480
" 52. Irregular eight sided prism, . 480
" 53-55. Combination of prisms belonging to the trimetric system, 480
" 56. Rectangular prism, . . 480
" 57, 58. Modified octahedrons, . 480
" 59, 60. Oblique six sided prism, . 481
" 61. Octahedron with half the edges truncated, . . 481
" 62. Prism with half the basal edges truncated, . . 481
" 63-65. Oblique rhomboidal prism, . 481
" 66. Oblique six sided prism, . 481
" 67. Double six sided pyramid, . 481
" 68. Pyramidal six sided prism, . 481
" 69. Modified rhombic octahedron, . 480
" 70. Regular six sided prism, . 481
" 71. Do. with truncated basal edges, 481
" 72. Do. with truncated corners, . 481
" 73. Obtuse double six sided pyramid, 481
" 74. Scalene octahedron, . . 481
" 75. Rhombohedron, . . 481
" 76. Six sided prism with four edges bevelled, . . 481
" 77, 78. Natural situation of two rhombohedrons, . 482
" 79. Grouping of crystallizations, . 482
" 80-87, 90, 91. Forms of ground jewels, . 486, 512
" 88, 89. Crystalline formations, . 482
" 90, 91. See 80, &c., . . 486
" 92, 93. Crystalline structure, . 482

PLATE 33.

Minerals and their Crystalline Forms.

Fig. 1. Meteoric iron, . . . 487
" 2. Iron pyrites, . . . 495
" 3, 4. Sulphur, . . . 485
" 5-10. Native bismuth, . . 488
" 6-11. Galena, . . . 493
" 7. Weidmannstedtian figures, . 487
" 8. Sulphate of lead, . . 493
" 9. Native silver, . . . 487
" 10. See 5, . . . 488
" 11. See 6, . . . 493

Fig. 12. Arborescent native silver, . 487
" 13. Native copper, . . 488
" 14. Native gold, . . . 487
" 15. Pyrites in calcareous spar, . 495
" 16. Filiform native silver, . 487
" 17. Galena on quartz, . . 493
" 18. Arsenical pyrites, . . 496
" 19. Galena on calcareous spar, . 493
" 20. Galena in cubes, . . 493
" 21. Selenid of mercury, . . 493
" 22. Crystallization of iron pyrites, . 496
" 23. Molybdenite, . . . 496
" 24. Native copper, . . 488
" 25. Native antimony, . . 489
" 26-29. Sulphur, . . . 484
" 30. Native silver, . . . 487
" 31. Antimony, . . . 489
" 32-36. Gold, galena, &c., 487, 493
" 37. Sulphuret of copper, . . 495
" 38. Antimony, . . . 489
" 39, 47. Antimonial silver, . . 490
" 40-45. Gold, 40 and 42, Silver, . 487
42, 43, Diamond, . 485
" 46. Diamond, . . . 485
" 47. See 39, . . . 490
" 48. Copper pyrites, . . . 495
" 49, 50. Glance cobalt, . . 492
" 51. Diamond, Grey copper ore, 485, 496
" 52, 53, 56, 59. Grey copper ore, . 496
" 54, 55. Glance cobalt, . . 492
" 56. See 52, . . . 496
" 57, 58, 60. Glance cobalt, . , 492
" 59. See 52, . . . 492
" 60. See 57, . . . 492
" 61-63. Native mercury, . . 488
" 64. Glance cobalt, . . . 492

PLATE 34.

Minerals and their Crystalline Forms.

Fig. 1. Micaceous iron ore, . . 498
" 2, 3. Quartz, . . . 499
" 4. Tourmaline, . . . 506
" 5. Hematite, . . . 498
" 6. Datholite, . . . 501
" 7. Pyrolusite, . . . 500
" 8. Tin ore, . . . 499
" 9. Fibrous brown hematite, . 498
" 10. Rutile, . . . 500
" 11. Scaly hematite, . . 498
" 12. Andalusite, . . . 503
" 13. Asbestos, . . . 531
" 14. Stilbite, . . . 506
" 15. Analcime, . . . 506
" 16. Mesotype, . . . 506
" 17. Apophyllite, . . . 502
" 18. Chabazite, . . . 506
" 19. Tin ore in granite, . . 499
" 20. Reniform hematite, . . 498
" 21, 22. Silica, . . . 499
" 23, 25. Oxyde of iron, . . 498
" 24. Manganite, . . . 500
" 25. See 23, . . . 498
" 26. Braunite, . . . 500
" 27. Red copper ore, . . 501

Fig. 28. Apophyllite, . . . 502
" 29. Hausmannite, . . . 500
" 30. Sapphire, . . . 501
" 31. Oxyde of iron, . . 498
" 32. Anatase, . . . 500
" 33. Red copper ore, . . 501
" 34. Tourmaline, . . . 506
" 35. Augite, . . . 502
" 36. Quartz, . . . 499
" 37. Oxyde of tin, . . 499
" 38. Corundum, . . . 501
" 39, 40. Arsenious acid, . . 501
" 41. Picrosmine, . . . 502
" 42. Oxyde of tin, . . 499
" 43. Rutile, . . . 500
" 44. Oxyde of copper, . . 501
" 45. Nepheline, . . . 505
" 46. Scapolite, . . . 505
" 47. Staurotide, . . . 503
" 48, 53. Idocrase, . . . 504
" 49. Beryl, . . . 504
" 50. Thomsonite, . . . 505
" 51. Silica, . . . 499
" 52. Augite, . . . 502
" 53. See 48, . . . 504
" 54. Chondrotite, . . . 502
" 55. Humboldtite, . . . 503
" 56. Various silicates, . . 501
" 57. Emerald, . . . 504
" 58. Euclase, . . . 504
" 59. Natrolite, . . . 505
" 60. Dichroite, . . . 505
" 61. Oxyde of copper, . . 501
" 62. Prehnite, . . . 505
" 63. Epistilbite, . . . 506
" 64. Garnet, . . . 504
" 65. Albite, . . . 506
" 66. Chabazite, . . . 506
" 67. Pyroxene, . . . 502
" 68, 69. Beryl, . . . 504
" 70. Staurotide, . . . 503
" 71. Iolite, . . . 505
" 72. Silica, . . . 499
" 73. Datholite, . . . 501
" 74. Olivine, . . . 502
" 75. Hornblende, . . . 503
" 76. Feldspar, . . . 506

PLATE 35.

Minerals and their Crystalline Forms.

Fig. 1. Spodumene, . . . 507
" 2. Feldspar twin crystal, . . 507
" 3. Sphærosiderite, . . . 508
" 4. Natrolite, . . . 505
" 5. Harmotome, . . . 506
" 6. Green garnet, . . . 504
" 7. Strontianite, . . . 508
" 8, 10, 11, 14, 16-22, 24, 25, 27-29, 31-37, 40, 41, 43-47, 49. Various forms of arragonite and calcareous spar, . 508
" 9. Topaz, . . . 503
" 10, 11. See 8, . . . 508
" 12, 30, 38, 39, 42, 48, Boracite, 509

Fig. 13, 23. Stalactite, ... 507
" 14. See 8, ... 508
" 15. Opake beryl, ... 504
" 16–22. See 8, ... 508
" 23. See 13, ... 507
" 24, 25. See 8, ... 508
" 26. Feldspar, ... 507
" 27–29. See 8, ... 508
" 30. See 12, ... 509
" 31–37. See 8, ... 508
" 38, 39. See 12, ... 509
" 40, 41. See 8, ... 508
" 42. See 12, ... 509
" 43–47. See 8, ... 508
" 48. See 12, ... 509
" 49. See 8, ... 508

PLATE 36.

Minerals and their Crystalline Forms.

Fig. 1, 2, 4, 6, 8–10, 13. Sulphate of
baryta, ... 509
" 3. Double spar, ... 508
" 4. See 1, ... 509
" 5. Wavellite, ... 510
" 6. See 1, ... 509
" 7, 20. Strontianite, ... 508
" 8–10. See 1, ... 509
" 11. Thorns coated with salt, . . 510
" 12. Cypoum, ... 535
" 13. See 1, ... 509
" 14. Spathic iron, ... 508
" 15. Wolfram, ... 510
" 16, 24, 25. Alum, ... 511
" 17. Sulphate of soda, ... 511
" 18. Sulphate of ammonia, . . 511
" 19, 34, 35. Copperas, ... 510
" 20. See 7, ... 508
" 21. White lead ore, ... 509
" 22. Yellow lead ore, ... 510
" 23. Sulphate of zinc, ... 510
" 24, 25. See 16, ... 511
" 26, 36, 41, 43, 47, 48. Saltpetre, . 511
" 27. Green vitriol, ... 509
" 28. Sulphate of potassa, . . 511
" 29, 37. Calcareous spar, . . . 508
" 30. Rocksalt, ... 510
" 31. Karstenite, ... 509
" 32. Fluor spar, ... 510
" 33, 40. Sulphates of alkalies, . . 510
" 34, 35. See 19, ... 510
" 36. See 26, ... 511
" 37. See 29, ... 508
" 38, 39, 42, 44, 46, 49. Phosphates of
alkalies, ... 511
" 40. See 33, ... 510
" 41. See 26, ... 511
" 42. See 38, ... 511
" 43. See 26, ... 511
" 44. See 38, ... 511
" 45. Sulphate of iron, . . . 509
" 46. See 38, ... 511
" 47, 48. See 26, ... 511
" 49. See 38, ... 511

PLATE 37.

Fig. 1–59. Fossils of the transition slate, . 578
" 60–72. Fossils of the carboniferous
period, ... 585
a–f. Buckland's representation of
animals of the Lias, . . 605

PLATE 38.

Fig. 1, 2. Fossils of the Copper Slate Formation, ... 590
" 3–11. Fossils of the Rock Salt Formation, ... 592
" 12–67. Fossils of the Jura, . . 600
" 68. Section of the Wirksworth cave, 620

PLATE 39.

Fig. 1–45. Fossils of the Cretaceous System, ... 609
" 46–50. Fossils of the Tertiary Period, 620
" 51–80. Skeleton of Hydrarchos har-
lani, ... 623
" 81–87. Illustrating the formations of
veins of ores, . . . 560

PLATE 40.

Fig. 1–3, 11–22. Fossils of the Tertiary
Period, ... 620
" 4–9. Fossils of the Rock Salt Formation, ... 595
" 10. Plesiosaurus macrocephalus
(Jura), ... 605
" 11–22. See 1.

PLATE 41.

Fig. 1–10. Fossil remains of Arachnida,
&c. (Tertiary), . . . 621
" 11–27. Fossils of the Jura, . . 600
" 28. Fossil Irish elk (Tertiary), . 623
" 29. Dinotherium giganteum (Tert.), . 621
" 30. Missourium theristocaulodon
(Tert.), ... 623
" 31, ab. Batrachoid tracks (Rock Salt), 596
" 32. Birds' tracks in Connecticut
(Rock Salt), ... 595
" 33. Scull of Hyæna spelæa (Tert.), 623
" 34. Scull of Ursus spelæus (Tert.), 623
" 35. Pterodactylus crassirostris (Jura), 605
" 36. Human skeleton from Guada-
loupe (fossil in Limestone), 624

PLATE 42.

Fig. 1–12. Fossils of the Tertiary, . 620
" 13–23. Do. do. Cretaceous, 609
" 24–31. Do. do. Jura, . 600
" 32–40. Do. do. Rock Salt, . 595
" 41–56. Do. do. Carboniferous, . 585
" 57–66. Do. do. Transition Slate, 578

PLATE 43.

Fig. 1–3. Illustrating the formation of valleys, ... 554
" 4–6. Ill'g the formation of rock beds, 555
" 7–9, 12. Ill'g stratification, . 551
" 10, 11. Penetration of various rocks
in volcanic regions, . . 557

Fig. 12. See 7.
" 13–15. Illustrating the relation of
stratification to mountain
masses, ... 552
" 16–19. Ill'g subordinate strata, . 558
" 20, 21. Ill'g disseminated and imbed-
ded ores, ... 561
" 22–25. Ill'g the cleavage of rocks, . 550
" 26. Table mountain at the Cape of
Good Hope, . . . 578

PLATE 44.

Fig. 1. The valley of Pyrmont, . 553
" 2–5, 12–14. Illustrating the relation
of stratification to mountain
masses, ... 553
" 6, 7. Tertiary basin of Paris, 555, 598, 616
" 8. Dunes on the sea shore, . . 626
" 9. Section of a volcanic cone, . 638
" 10. Mont Blanc chain, . . 554
" 11. Mountains in the vicinity of
Bärschwyl, . . . 554
" 12–14. See 2.
" 15. Fissures in the earth in Calabria, 646
" 16. Circular cavities in the plain of
Rosarno, ... 646
" 17. Crater of the Geyser in Iceland, . 646
" 18. Volcano of Eyafiël in Iceland, . 647

PLATE 45.

Fig. 1. Illustrating valleys of disruption, . 553
" 2. Extinct volcanic district in
Auvergne, ... 546
" 3. Section of Judæa and the Dead
Sea, ... 549
" 4. Vesuvius in the time of Pliny, . 641
" 5. Vesuvius as seen at present, . 641
" 6. Mount Etna, ... 647
" 7. Campi Phlegræi near Naples, . 647
" 8. Chart of the Bay of Naples, . 644
" 9. Volcanic chart of Etna, . . 647
" 10. Volcanic chart of Iceland, . 646
" 11. Map of the vicinity of Lake Titicaca, in Peru, . . . 549
" 12. Section of the mountains around
the lake, ... 549

GLOSSARY.

Basalt Boden, Basaltic soil.
Bugt, Bay.
Busen von Neapel, — von Salerno, Bay of
Naples, — of Salerno.
Cyclopen Inseln, Cyclops Islands.
Die Flegreischen Felder, The Phlegræan fields.
Fiorden, The inlet.
Island, Iceland.
Längenthal im Trachyt, Long valley in the
trachyte formation.
Lava Ströme, Lava streams.
Neapel, Naples.
Nord Cap, North Cape.
Œ, Island.
Passhöhe, Height of the pass.
Polarkreis, Arctic circle.

See, Lake.
Vesuv, Vesuvius.

PLATE 46.

Special Geognosy.

Fig. 1–3. Silurian system, . . . 576
" 4–6. Devonian system, . . . 577
" 7, 8. Carboniferous group, . . 583
" 9, 10. Copper slate formation, . 587
" 11. Rock salt formation, . . 591
" 12–16. Jura formation, . . . 596
" 17. Cretaceous system, . . . 606
" 18. Upper tertiary, . . . 616
" 19. Erratic boulder, . . . 619

GLOSSARY.

Aufgeschw. Land, Deposited ground.
Braunschweig, Brunswick.
Bunter Sandstein, Variegated sandstone.
Donau, Danube.
Ebbe Geb., Ebbe Mountains.
Egge Geb., Egge Mountains.
Geb. v. Charolais, Mountains of Charolais.
Harz Gebirge, Hartz Mountains ; — und Thürin-
ger Wald, Hartz and Thuringian Mountains.
Hochwald, High forest (mountain tract).
Jura Gebirg, Jura Mountains ; — -kalk, Jurassic
Limestone.
Kohlengebirge, Carboniferous formation.
Kohlenkalk, Carboniferous limestone.
Kohlensandstein, Carboniferous sandstone.
Kreide, Chalk.
Laacher See, Lake Laach.
Porphyr, Porphyry.
Quadersandstein, Freestone.
Rhein, Rhine.
Rheinisches Uebergangsgebir, Rhenish transition
rock.
Rothhaar Geb., Rothhaar Mountains.
Schuttland, Conglomerate.
Steink. Gebilde, Carboniferous formation.
Tertiär, Tertiary.
Teutoburger Wald, Teutoburg forest.
Todtliegendes, Red sandstone.
Trias, Rock salt formation.
Trier, Treves.
Uebergangskalk, Transition limestone.
Vogel Geb., Vogel Mountains.
Vogesen sandstein, Vosges sandstone.
Vulcan Gebilde ; — Gerölle, Volcanic forma-
tion ; — rubble.
Weser Geb., Weser Mountains.

PLATE 47.

PAGE
Fig. 1. Volcanic chart of the world, . 640
(Also chart of the winds, 374,
glossary at pl. 29.)
" 2. Chart of European volcanoes, . 640
" 3. Volcanic chart of Lower Italy, . 640
" 4. Crater of Kiraüea, . . . 641
" 5. Crater on the Island of Hawaï, . 641
" 6. Landscape from the Southern Continent, ... 641
" 7. Profile of mountains in the Old
World, ... 648

Fig. 8. Profile of mountains in the New World, ... 648
" 9, 10. Charts of hurricanes, . . 377

GLOSSARY.

Ægatische In., Ægatian Islands.
Atlantischer Ocean, Atlantic Ocean.
Canal von Malta, Maltese Channel.
Deutschland, Germany.
Frankreich, France.
Grosse Antillen, The larger West India Islands.
Indischer Ocean, Indian Ocean.
Kleine Antillen, The smaller West India Islands.
Liparische In., Liparian Islands.
Lissabon, Lisbon.
Meerb. v. Taranto, Bay of Taranto.
Mittellåndisches Meer, Mediterranean Sea.
Mozambique Kanal, Mozambique Channel.
Neapel, Naples.
Nord Amerika, North America.
Sicilien, Sicily.
Spanien, Spain.
Str. von Messina, Strait of Messina.
Türkei, Turkey.
Tyrrhenisches Meer, Tyrrhenian Sea.
Venedig, Venice.
Vesuv, Vesuvius.
Wien, Vienna.

PLATE 49.

Fig. 1. *Coup d'œil* of the normal masses, 628
" 2. Illustrating the theory of springs and Artesian wells, . 626
" 3. Section of the Artesian well of Grenoble, . . . 628
" 4. Interior of a boring shed, . . 629
" 5–14. Boring tools, . . . 627

PLATE 49.

Fig. 1. Interior of the crater on the Island of Hawaï, . . . 641
" 2. Coral island in the Pacific Ocean, 624
" 3. Rock groups on the Faroe Islands, ... 629
" 4. Natural bridge of Icomonzo in Columbia, . . . 630
" 5. Glacier sources of the Rhine, . 627
" 6. Trachyte columns in the Siebengebirge, ... 630
" 7. Basaltic groups on the Island of Staffa, ... 550
" 8. Fissured clay slate on the Lahn, . 575
" 9. Cleft variegated sandstone near Kreuznach, Germany, . 592

PLATE 50.

Fig. 1. The Geyser of Iceland, . . 646
" 2. Submarine volcanic eruption, . 646
" 3. Air volcano of Turbaso in Columbia, ... 647
" 4. The volcanic Island of Ferdinandea, ... 645
" 5. Crater of the same, . . . 646
" 6. Crater of the Krabla in Iceland, . 642
" 7. Crater of Etna in Sicily, . . 640
" 8. Niagara Falls, . . . 630

Fig. 9. The Dal Elf Fall in Sweden, . 630

PLATE 51.

Fig. 1. Primitive forest of Brazil, . 626
" 2. Lake of Keswick, Cumberland, England, . . . 548
" 3. Arch of rock on Cape Parry, . 630
" 4. The fresh water cave, Isle of Wight, England, . . 629
" 5. The Blackgang cave on the Isle of Wight, . . . 630
" 6. Basalt rocks on the Island of Tahiti, . . . 637
" 7. The Grotto del Cane near Naples, 646
" 8. The grotto of Jupiter on the Island of Naxos, Greece, . . 551

PLATE 52.

Fig. 1. Icebergs of the antarctic regions, . 630
" 2. Sandstone cave in Sicily, . . 592
" 3. Lava arch in Iceland, . . 642
" 4. Burning mountain near Duttweiler, . . . 639
" 5. Cascade of Teverone near Tivoli, 624
" 6. Basalt columns on the Island of Staffa, . . . 637
" 7. Upright tree stems found in carboniferous formations, . 587
" 8. Island of Staffa with Fingal's cave, . . . 551
" 9. Section of the cavern of Gailenreuth in the Hartz, . . 620

PLATE 53.

Fig. 1. The Grotte des Demoiselles in France, . . . 575
" 2. The Dunold Mill Cave, Lancashire, England, . . . 626
" 3. The cave of Montserrat in Catalonia, Spain, . . . 575
" 4. Porphyry mountain near Kreuznach, Germany, . . 634
" 5. The Lurley rock on the Rhine, . 575
" 6. The Rhonetrichter (*Perte du Rhone*), France, . . 630
" 7. Serpentine rocks near Lizard Point, Cornwall, England, . . 629
" 8. Clay slate strata on the coast of Scotland, . . . 551
" 9. Submarine section of the Straits of Gibraltar, . . . 544
" 10. Do. do. between Tarifa and Alcazar, Spain, . . 544
" 11–13. Illustrating the cleavage of rocks, . . . 550
" 14. Ill'g subordinate beds, . . 558

BOTANY

PLATE 54.

Figs. 1–15. Jussieu's Classification of Plants, types of classes, . 54
" 16. Ustilago segetum, . . 60
" 17. Uredo phaseoli, . . 60
" 18. Tuber cibarium, truffle, . 60
" 19. Bovista gigantea, . . 60
" 20. Morchella esculenta, morel, . 60
" 21. Polyporus perennis, . . 60
" 22a. Boletus umbellatus, . . 60
" 22b. Boletus edulis, edible mushroom, . . . 60
" 23. Hydnum auriscalpium, . 60
" 24. Cantharellus cibarius, . 60
" 25. Agaricus fimetarius, . . 60
" 26. Agaricus campestris, champignon, 60
" 27. Agaricus procerus, . . 60
" 28. Agaricus muscarius, toadstool, . 60
" 29. Cladonia pyxidata, . . 61
" 30. Parmelia parietina, . . 61
" 31. Cetraria islandica, Iceland moss, 61
" 32. Rochella tinctoria, . . 61
" 33. Usnea florida, . . . 61
" 34. a, Conferva bombycina ; b, C. rivularis ; c, C. flaccida ; d, C. glomerata, . . 58
" 35. Sphærococcus coronopifolius, . 58
" 36. Laminaria digitata, . . 59
" 37. Laminaria saccharina, . 59
" 38. Fucus vesiculosus, . . 59
" 39. Spagnum acutifolium, Peat-moss, 63
Fig. 40. Polytrichum juniperinum, . 63
" 41. Climacium dendroides, . 63
" 42. Anthoceros punctatus, . 62
" 43. Gymnoscyphus repens, . 62
" 44. Marchantia polymorpha, . 62
" 45. Pilularia globulifera, . 64
" 46. Salvinia natans, . . 64
" 47. Marsilea quadrifolia, . 64
" 48. Ceterach leptophylla, . 66
" 49a. Polypodium vulgare, . 65
" 49b. Ceterach officinarum, . 66
" 50. Aspidium filix mas, . . 65
" 51. Asplenium trichomanes, . 65
" 52. Scolopendrium officinarum, . 65
" 53. Lomaria spicans, . . 65
" 54. Adiantum capillus veneris, . 65
" 55. Osmunda regalis, . . 65
" 56. Botrychium lunaris, . . 65
" 57. Ophioglossum vulgatum, . 65
" 58. Lycopodium clavatum, . 64
" 59. Equisetum limosum, . 66

PLATE 55.

Fig. 1. Potamogeton natans, . . 73
" 2. Arum maculatum, wake robin, . 74
" 3. Zostera marina, . . 73
" 4. Acorus calamus, . . 73
" 5. Typha latifolia, cat-tail, . 73

Fig. 6. Eriophorum angustifolium, . 72
" 7. Cyperus officinalis, . . 72
" 8. Saccharum officinale, sugar cane, 68
" 9. Oryza sativa, rice, . . 70
" 10. Bambusa arundinacea, bamboocane, . . . 69
Centre figure: Musa sapientum, banana tree (German : Banana oder Feigenbaum), . . . 83

PLATE 56.

Fig. 1. Cocos nucifera, cocoa palm, . 77
" 2. Phœnix dactylifera, date palm, . 77
" 3. Sagus farinifera, sago palm, . 77
" 4. Cycas circinalis, sago tree, . 88
" 5. Dracæna braziliensis, . 79
" 6. Aloë arborescens, . . 79
" 7. Areca catechu, areca palm, . 77
" 8. Zamia elliptica, . . 88
" 9. Papyrus antiquorum, . . 72

PLATE 57.

Fig. 1. Dracæna draco, dragon's blood, 79
" 2. Luzula pilosa, woodrush, . 77
" 3. Commelyna tuberosa, . 75
" 4. Colchicum autumnale, . 78
" 5. Veratrum album, sneezewort, . 79
" 6. Fritillaria imperialis, crown imperial, . . . 80
" 7. Erythronium dens canis, dog's tooth, . . . 80
" 8. Agave americana, century plant, 81
" 9. Phormium tenax, New Zealand flax, . . . 80
" 10. Scilla maritima, squill, . 79

PLATE 58, 59.

Fig. 1. Amaryllis formosissima, daffodil lily, . . . 81
" 2. Narcissus pseudo-narcissus, daffodil, . . . 81
" 3. Crocus sativus, saffron, . 82
" 4. Iris germanica, iris, . . 82
" 5. Musa paradisiaca, plantain, . 83
" 6. Curcuma zedoaria, turmeric, . 84
" 7. Zingiber officinale, ginger, . 84
" 8. Vanilla aromatica, vanilla, . 85
" 9. Nymphæa lotus, . . 199
" 10. Aristolochia clematis, birthwort, 102
" 11. Aristolochia sipho, Dutchman's pipe, . . . 102
" 12. Aristolochia serpentaria, Virginia snake root, . . 102
" 13. Elæagnus angustifolia, . 105
" 14. Daphne mezereum, mezereon, . 104
" 15. Camphora officinarum, camphor tree, . . . 107
" 16. Cinnamomum zeylanicum, cinnamon tree, . . . 107
" 17. Laurus nobilis, victor's laurel, . 107
" 18. Cinnamomum cassia, cassia tree, 107

PLATE 60, 61.

Fig. 1. Protea speciosa, sugar-bush, . 105
" 2. Banksia serrata, . 105
" 3. Myristica moschata, nutmeg, . 106
" 4. Rheum palmatum, rhubarb, . 108
" 5. Beta vulgaris, common beet, . 110
" 6. Celosia cristata, cock's comb, . 110
" 7. Plantago major, common plantain, 111
" 8. Mirabilis longifolia, . 111
" 9. Plumbago europæa, toothwort, . 112
" 10. Anagallis arvensis, pimpernel, . 112
" 11. Dodecatheon integrifolium, American cowslip, . . 113
" 12. Cyclamen europæum, sow-bread, 112
" 13. Lysimachia vulgaris, loose-strife, 112
" 14. Veronica officinalis, speedwell, 117
" 15. Pedicularis palustris, lousewort, . 117
" 16. Lathræa squamaria, tooth-wort, 117

PLATE 62.

Fig. 1. Ruellia formosa, . . . 114
" 2. Acanthus mollis, bear's claw, . 114
" 3. Olea europæa, olive, . . 126
" 4. Jasminum officinale, . . 126
" 5. Vitex agnus castus, . . 114
" 6. Betonica officinalis, betony, . 115
" 7. Galeopsis tetrahit, hemp nettle, . 115
" 8. Digitalis purpurea, purple foxglove, . . . 116
" 9. Calceolaria corymbosa, slipperwort, . . . 116
" 10. Verbascum thapsus, mullein, . 116
" 11. Nicotiana tabacum, tobacco, . 118

PLATE 63.

Fig. 1. Hyoscyamus niger, henbane, . 118
" 2. Datura stramonium, jimson weed, 118
" 3. Atropa belladonna, belladonna, . 118
" 4. Solanum dulcamara, climbing nightshade, . . 118
" 5. Capsicum annuum, cayenne pepper, . . 118
" 6. Borago officinalis, borage, . 119
" 7. Exogonium purga, jalap plant, . 120
" 8. Polemonium cœruleum, Jacob's ladder, . . 121
" 9. Jacaranda tomentosa, . 122
" 10. Bignonia leucoxylon, . . 122
" 11. Gentiana pneumonanthe, common gentian, . . 122
" 12. Spigelia marilandica, pinkroot, . 123
" 13. Nerium oleander, oleander, . 124

PLATE 64.

Fig. 1. Cynanchum vincetoxicum, celandine, . . 125
" 2. Asclepias cornuti, swallowwort, 125
" 3. Mimusops dissecta, . . 127
" 4. Styrax benzoin, benzoin tree, . 129
" 5. Ledum palustre, marsh tea, . 131
" 6. Erica filamentosa, cape heath, . 131
" 7. Campanula trachelium, . 132

Fig. 8. Lobelia fulgens, . . 132
" 9. Lactuca virosa, poison lettuce, . 139
" 10. Cynara scolymus, artichoke, . 139
" 11. Carthamus tinctorius, safflower, 139
" 12. Serratula tinctoria, saw wort, . 139
" 13. Tanacetum vulgare, tansy, . 139

PLATE 65.

Fig. 1. Artemisia absinthum, wormwood. . . 139
" 2. Dipsacus fallonum, cardoon, . 140
" 3. Rubia tinctoria, madder, . 142
" 4. Coffea arabica, coffee, . 142
" 5. Lonicera caprifolium, woodbine, 142
" 6. Aralia nudicaulis, sarsaparilla. . 144
Fig. 7. Œnanthe fistulosa, dead tongue, 147
" 8. Cicuta virosa, water hemlock, . 147
" 9. Æthusa cynapium, fool's parsley, 147
" 10. Chærophyllum temulum, cow parsley, . 147
" 11. Conium maculatum, hemlock, . 147
" 12. Sium latifolium, water parsley, . 147

PLATE 66.

Fig. 1. Clematis erecta, creeping climber, 203
" 2. Anemone hortensis, garden anemone, . 203
" 3. Pulsatilla fratensis, pasque flower, 203
" 4. Ranunculus acris, crowfoot, . 203
" 5. Adonis vernalis, bird's eye, . 203
" 6. Helleborus niger, black hellebore, 203
" 7. Aquilegia vulgaris, columbine, . 203
" 8. Aconitum stœrkianum, helmet flower, . . 203
" 9. Papaver somniferum, poppy, . 198
" 10. Chelidonium majus, celandine, . 198
" 11. Sinapis alba, white mustard, . 197
" 12. Capparis spinosa, caper plant, . 195
" 13. Reseda luteola, dyer's rocket, . 195
" 14. Paullinia pinnata, paulinia, . 181
" 15. Æsculus pavia, small buckeye, . 181

PLATE 67.

Fig. 1. Acer pseudo-platanus, white maple, . . . 182
" 2. Malpighia urens, . . 183
" 3. Hypericum perforatum, . 185
" 4. Garcinia cambogia, . 184
" 5. Citrus medica, citron, . 185
" 6. Thea chinensis, tea plant, . 186
" 7. Swietenia mahogoni, mahogany tree, . . 180
" 8. Vitis vinifera, wine grape, . 179
" 9. Geranium sanguineum, cranesbill, . . 178
" 10. Oxalis acetocella, wood-sorrel, 177
" 11. Gossipium herbaceum, cotton plant, . . 190
" 12. Theobroma cacao, cacao tree, . 178

PLATE 68.

Fig. 1. Magnolia grandiflora, . . 201
" 2. Illicium anisatum, star anise, . 201
" 3. Anona squamosa, anona, . 201
" 4. Cocculus lacunosus, . 200
" 5. Berberis vulgaris, barberry, . 200
" 6. Tilia grandiflora, lime tree, . 187
" 7. Bixa orellana, arnotto tree, . 194
" 8. Helianthemum vulgaris, . 194
" 9. Guaiacum officinale, . 175
" 10. Diptamus albus, white dittany, . 175
" 11. Dianthus caryophyllus, carnation 191
" 12. Saponaria officinalis, soapwort, . 191
" 13. Camellia japonica, camelia, . 186

PLATE 69.

Fig. 1. Sedum acre, stone crop, . . 151
" 2. Saxifraga granulata, stone-break, 149
" 3. Cereus hexagonus, six-edged cactus, . . 150
" 4. Tamarix germanica, tamarisk, . 192
" 5. Mesembryanthemum rubrocinctum, fig-marigold, . 151
" 6. Œnothera biennis, evening primrose, . . 157
" 7. Epilobium angustifolium, willowherb, . . 157
" 8. Santalum myrtifolium, . 102
" 9. Melaleuca cajeput, cajeput tree, 158
" 10. Melaleuca fulgens, fiery cajeput, 158
" 11. Eugenia pimenta, allspice, . 158
" 12. Caryophyllus aromaticus, clovetree, . . 158
" 13. Melastoma malabathricum, . 159

PLATE 70.

Fig. 1. Lythrum salicaria, . . 161
" 2. Mespilus germanicus, medlar, . 165
" 3. Rosa moscata, musk rose, . 164
" 4. Potentilla anserina, silver weed, 164
" 5. Amygdalus communis, sweet almond, . . 165
" 6. Acacia vera, gum arabic tree, . 168
" 7. Cassia lanceolata, senna, . 169
" 8. Tamarindus indica, tamarind tree, . . 169
" 9. Hæmatoxylon campechianum, logwood, . . 169
" 10. Coronilla varia, sicklewort, . 168
" 11. Phaseolus vulgaris, kidney bean, 168
" 12. Genista tinctoria, dyer's greenwood, . . 168
" 13. Indigofera anil, anil, . 168
" 14. Glycyrrhiza glabra, . 168

PLATE 71.

Fig. 1. Anacardium occidentale, cashew nut, . . 170
" 2. Rhus cotinus, smoke tree, . 170
" 3. Pistacia terebinthus, turpentine tree, . . 170
" 4. Juglans regia, English walnut, . 91
" 5. Euonymus europæus, spindle tree, 172
" 6. Ilex aquifolium, European holly, 128

Fig. 7. Rhamnus catharticus, buckthorn, 171
" 8. Euphorbia cyparissias, wolf's milk, 100
" 9. Euphorbia officinarum, spurge, . 100
" 10. Siphonia elastica, caoutchouc tree, . . 100
" 11. Cucumis citrullus, water melon, 155
" 12. Momordica balsamina, balsam apple, . . 156
" 13. Bryonia alba, white bryony, . 756
" 14. Carica papaya, West India pawpaw, . . 155
" 15. Cucumis melo, . 155

PLATE 72.

Fig. 1. Ficus carica, fig tree, . 98
" 2. Artocarpus incisa, breadfruit, . 98
" 3. Morus nigra, black mulberry, . 98
" 4. Humulus lupulus, hops, . 98
" 5. Cannabis sativa, hemp, . 98
" 6. Piper nigrum, black pepper, . 94
" 7. Castanea vesca, chestnut, . 93
" 8. Quercus tinctoria, black oak, . 93
" 9. Liquidambar styraciflua, sweet gum, . . 93
" 10. Taxus baccata, European yew, . 90
" 11. Juniperus communis, common juniper, . . 90
" 12. Cupressus sempervirens, European cypress, . 90
" 13. Larix cedrus, European cedar, . 90

PLATE 73.

Fig. 1. Botanical chart, . . . 51
" 2. Chart of the Chinese and Indian cotton region, . 51
" 3. Chart of the American region of the sugar cane, coffee, &c. 51
" 4. Chart of the *vertical* distribution of plants in Asia, . 51
" 5. The same of America, . 52
" 6. The same of Europe, . 52
" 7. The same of the Canary Islands, 52
" 8. The same of the frigid zone of Europe, . . 52

GLOSSARY.

Ægypten, Egypt.
Aleuten, Aleutian Islands.
Algerien, Algeria.
Amazonenstrom, Amazon River.
Anden Gebirge, the Andes.
Arabien, Arabia.
Aral S., Lake Aral.
Asien, Asia.
Atlantischer Ocean, Atlantic Ocean.
Australien, Australia.
Azorische In., the Azores.
Bahama In., Bahama Islands.
Baumwolle, Cotton.
Bonin In., Bonin Islands.
Brasilien, Brazil.
Californien, California.
Canarische In., Canary Islands.
Cap der guten Hoffnung, Cape of Good Hope.

Cap Horn, Cape Horn.
Cap Verdische In., Cape Verde Islands.
Caraibisches M., Caribbean Sea.
Carolinen In., Caroline Islands.
Caspisches M., Caspian Sea.
Chinawälder, Bathbark forests.
Deutschland, Germany.
Falklands In., Falkland Islands.
Feuerland, Terra del Fuego.
Frankreich, France.
Freundschafts In., Friendly Islands.
Gallopagos In., Gallopagos Islands.
Gerste u. Hafer, barley and oats.
Gewürznelken, cloves.
Grönland, Greenland.
Grossbritannien, Great Britain.
Grosser oder Stiller Ocean, Pacific Ocean.
Habesch, Habesh,
Himmalaya Geb., Himmalaya Mountains.
I. Island, Iceland.
I. Karafta oder Sachalin, Island of Karafta or Sachalin.
Indisches Meer, Indian Ocean.
Irland, Ireland.
Kaffee, coffee.
Kaschmir, Cashmere.
Kurilen, Kurile Islands.
Ladronen In., Marian Islands.
Mais, Indian corn.
Malediven In., Maldive Islands.
Mandschurei, Manchooria.
Marañon od. Amazonenstrom, Amazon River.
Marianen od. Ladronen In., Marian Islands.
Mb. v. Mexico, Gulf of Mexico.
Mendana's Arch., Mendana's Archipelago.
Mittel Amer., Central America.
Mittelländisches Meer, Mediterranean Sea.
Mongolei, Mongolia.
Moskau, Moscow.
Muscatbaum, nutmeg tree.
N. Gran., New Grenada.
Neufundland, Newfoundland.
Neu Guinea, New Guinea.
Neu Seeland, New Zealand.
Nord Amerika, North America.
Norwegen, Norway.
Nubien, Nubia.
Ost Indien, East India.
Patagonien, Patagonia.
Pfeffer, pepper.
Reis, rice.
Roggen, rye.
Russisches Amerika, Russian America.
Russland, Russia.
Sandwichs In., Sandwich Islands.
Schiffer In., Navigators' Islands.
Schwarzes M., Black Sea.
Schweden, Sweden.
Sibirien, Siberia.
Sklaven S., Slave Lake.
Spanien, Spain.
Süd Amerika, South America.
Thee, tea.
Toisen, toises, (1t.=6 feet.)

Türkei, Turkey.
Vanille, vanilla.
Vereinigte Staaten, United States.
Vulc. v. Aconcagua, Volcano of Aconcagua.
Weitzen, wheat.
West Indien, West Indies.
Wüste Sahara, Desert of Sahara.
Wüste Schamo oder Gobi, Desert of Shamo or Gobi.
Zeichenerklärung für fig. 1, 2, u. 3., Explanation of the marks in figs. 1, 2, and 3.
Zimmt, cinnamon.
Zucker, sugar.

ZOOLOGY

PLATE 74.

Classification.

Fig. 1. Monas, animalcule, . . . 213
" 2. Monocerca, do. . . 213
" 3. Spongia, sponge, . . 213
" 4. Hydra, naked polypi, . . 213
" 5. Diphies, medusa, . . . 214
" 6. Velella, nautilus, . . 214
" 7. Sipunculus, tube worm, . 214, 246
" 8. Holothuria, sea jelly, . . 214
" 9. Ligula, strapworm, . . 214
" 10. Nemertes, cordworm, . 214, 353
" 11. Botryllus, sea grape, . . 214
" 12. Ostrea, oyster, . . . 214
" 13. Chiton, sea cockroach, . . 214
" 14. Fissurella, fissure shell, . . 214
" 15. Vermetus, worm shell, . . 214
" 16. Strombus, screw shell, . . 214
" 17. Carina, keel shell, . . 214
" 18. Bulla, wood digger, . . 214
" 19. Phyllidium, leaf shell, . 214, 284
" 20. Tritonium, triton, . 214, 283
" 21. Limnæus, mud shell, . . 214
" 22. Clio, whale louse, . . 215
" 23. Octopus, polypus, . . 215
" 24. Hirudo, leech, . . . 215
" 25. Aphrodite, sea mouse, . . 215
" 26. Amphitrite, . . . 215
" 27. Anatifa, duck muscle, . . 215
" 28. Cancer, crab, . . . 216
" 29. Squilla, shrimp, . . 216
" 30. Talitrus, sea flea, . . 216
" 31. Cyamus, whale louse, . . 216
" 32. Oniscus, cheslip, . . 216
" 33. Cyclops, water flea, . . 216
" 34. Caligus, fish louse, . . 216
" 35. Aranea, spider, . . . 216
" 36. Chelifer, . . . 216
" 37. Scolopendra, . . . 217
" 38. Lepisma, book worm, . . 217
" 39. Pediculus, louse, . . 217
" 40. Pulex, flea, . . . 217
" 41. Carabus, ground beetle, . . 217

Fig. 42. Forficula, earwig, . . . 217
" 43. Cimex, bedbug, . . . 217
" 44. Libellula, dragon fly, . . 217
" 45. Tenthredo, tailed wasp, . . 217
" 46. Vanessa, butterfly, . . 217
" 47. Stomoxys, autumn fly, . . 217
" 48. Petromyzon, lampereel, . . 217
" 49. Squalus, shark, . . . 217
" 50. Raja, ray, . . . 217
" 51. Acipenser, sturgeon, . . 217
" 52. Orthagoriscus, moon fish, . 218
" 53. Hippocampus, sea horse, . 218
" 54. Anguilla, eel, . . . 218
" 55. Pleuronectes, sole, . . 218
" 56. Merlangus, whiting, . . 218
" 57. Cyprinus, chub, . . 218
" 58. Xiphias, swordfish, . . 218
" 59. Salamandra, salamander, . . 218
" 60. Rana, frog, . . . 218
" 61. Vipera, viper, . . . 218
" 62. Boa, boa constrictor, . 218
" 63. Anguis, adder, . . . 218
" 64. Ophisaurus, . . . 218
" 65. Chirotes, . . . 218
" 66, 67. Chalcides, . . . 218
" 68. Bipes, . . . 218
" 69. Anolis, . . . 218
" 70. Scincus, . . . 218
" 71. Tilicua, . . . 218
" 72. Chamæleo, chameleon, . . 218
" 73. Ptyodactylus, . . . 218
" 74. Basiliscus, basilisk, . . 218
" 75. Iguana, guana, . . 218
" 76. Draco, dragon, . . 218
" 77. Agama, . . . 218
" 78. Stellio, stellion, . . 218
" 79. Lacerta, lizard, . . . 218
" 80. Tejus, . . . 218
" 81. Crocodilus, crocodile, . . 218
" 82. Plesiosaurus, . . . 218
" 83. Ichthyosaurus, . . . 218
" 84. Chelonia, sea tortoise, . . 218
" 85. Testudo, land tortoise, . . 219
" 86. Anas, duck, . . . 219
" 87. Sula, dodo, . . . 219
" 88. Pelecanus, pelican, . . 219
" 89. Procellaria, petrel, . . 219
" 90. Podiceps, diver, . . 219
" 91. Phœnicopterus, flamingo, . 219
" 92. Rallus, water rail, . . 219
" 93. Scolopax, snipe, . . 219
" 94. Ardea, heron, . . . 219
" 95. Grus, crane, . . . 219
" 96. Otis, bustard, . . . 219
" 97. Struthio, ostrich, . . 219
" 98. Gallus, cock, . . . 219
" 99. Crax, curassow, . . . 219
" 100. Columba, pigeon, . . 219
" 101. Psittacus, parrot, . . 219
" 102. Picus, woodpecker, . . 219
" 103. Buceros, rhinoceros bird, . 219
" 104. Merops, bee-eater, . . 219
" 105. Sitta, nut-pecker, . . 219
" 106. Alauda, lark, . . . 219

Fig. 107. Cypselus, sea swallow, . . 219
" 108. Pica, magpie, . . . 219
" 109. Otus, owl, . . . 219
" 110. Vultur, vulture, . . . 219
" 111. Milvus, kite, . . . 219
" 112. Balæna, whale, . . . 219
" 113. Cervus, deer, . . . 219
" 114. Bos, ox, . . . 219
" 115. Camelus, camel, . . . 219
" 116. Equus, horse, . . . 219
" 117. Sus, hog, . . . 219
" 118. Elephas, elephant, . . 219
" 119. Ornithorhynchus, duckbilled platypus, . . . 219
" 120. Manis, pangolin, . . . 219
" 121. Bradypus, sloth, . . . 219
" 122. Lepus, rabbit, . . . 219
" 123. Sciurus, squirrel, . . . 219
" 124. Castor, beaver, . . . 219
" 125. Mus, mouse, . . . 219
" 126. Didelphys, kangaroo, . . 219
" 127. Phoca, seal, . . . 219
" 128. Mustela, marten, . . . 219
" 129. Viverra, civet, . . . 219
" 130. Felis, cat, . . . 219
" 131. Hyæna, hyena, . . . 219
" 132. Canis, dog, . . . 219
" 133. Ursus, bear, . . . 219
" 134. Erinaceus, hedgehog, . . 219
" 135. Vespertilio, bat, . . . 219
" 136. Pteropus, rousset, . . . 219
" 137. Lemur, maki, . . . 219
" 138. Hapale, ouistiti, . . . 219
" 139. Simia, monkey, . . . 219
" 140. Homo, man, . . . 219

PLATE 75.

Fig. 1. Monas lens, . . . 227
" 2. Proteus diffluens, . . . 228
" 3. Bursaria vesiculosa, . . 228
" 4. Cryptomonas ovata, . . 228
" 5. Trachelocerca olor, . . 228
" 6. Trachelocerca viridis, . . 229
" 7. Vibrio anguillula, . . . 227
" 8. Cyclidium glaucoma, . . 228
" 9. Paramecium compressum, . 229
" 10. Chilodon cucullatus, . . 228
" 11. Gonium pectorale, . . 227
" 12. Bursaria truncatella, . . 228
" 13. Urocentrum turbo, . . 228
" 14. Trichodina cometa, . . 228
" 15. Volvox globator, . . . 227
" 16. Rotifer vulgaris, . 229, 308
" 17. Opercularia articulata, . . 228
" 18. Stentor mylleri, . . . 228
" 19. Melicerta ringens, . . 229
" 20. Carchesium polypinum, . . 228
" 21. Hydra grisea, . . . 231
" 22. Hydra fusca, . . . 231
" 23. Hydra viridis, . . . 231
" 24. Virgularia juncea, . . . 241
" 25. Pennatula granulosa, . . 240
" 26. Pennatula phosphorea, . 240
" 27. Pennatula grisea, . . . 241

Figs. 28, 29. Tubularia coronata, . . 231
" 30. Sertularia polyzonalis, . . 231
" 31. Sertularia falcata, . . . 231
" 32. Thuaria thuia, ... 231
" 33. Sertularia abietina, . . 231
" 34. Sertularia operculata, . . 231
" 35. Corallina rubens, . . . 221
" 36. Flabellaria opuntia, . . 221
" 37. Penecillus penecillus, . . 221
" 38. Corallina officinalis, . . 221
" 39. Tubularia sultana, . . . 231
" 40. Tubularia campanularia, . . 231
" 41. Acetabulum mediterraneum, . 231
" 42. Tubularia indivisa, . . 231
" 43. Flustra foliacea, . . . 258
" 44. Spongia fistularis, . . 221
" 45. Spongia officinalis, . . 220
" 46. Alcyonium ficiforme, . . 241
" 47. Alcyonium palmatum, . . 241
" 48. Gorgonia flabellum, . . 241
" 49. Gorgonia verrucosa, . . 241
" 50. Gorgonia cerataphyta, . . 241
" 51. Antipathes spiralis, . . 240
" 52. Coralium nobile, . . . 241
" 53. Isis hippuris, . . . 241
" 54. Flustra, ... 258
" 55. Pocillopora polymorpha, . . 249
" 56. Retepora, ... 258
" 57. Eschara, ... 258
" 58. Oculina virginea, . . . 240
" 59. Oculina gemmascens, . . 240
" 60. Madrepora prolifera, . . 240
" 61. Porites porites, . . . 240
" 62. Astrea astroites, . . . 239
" 63. Explanaria ananas, . . 240
" 64. Meandrina labyrinthica, . . 239
" 65. Fungia fungites, . . . 239
" 66. Tubipora musica, . . . 241
" 67. Teredo navalis, . . . 263
" 68. Sabella ventilabrum, . . 305
" 69. Vermetus lumbricalis, . . 289
" 70. Serpula glomerata, . . 304
" 71. Aspergillum javanum, . 256, 264
" 72. Serpula arenaria, . . . 304
" 73. Dentalium elephantinum, . . 286
" 74. Dentalium politum, . . 286
" 75. Dentalium entalis, . . 286
" 76. Patella granatina, . . . 285
" 77. Patella saccharina, . . 285
" 78. Calyptraea sinensis, . . 286
" 79. Patella laciniosa, . . . 285
" 80. Fissurella graeca, . . . 285
" 81. Ancylus lacustris, . . . 294
" 82. Emarginula fissura, . . 285
" 83. Pileopsis hungarica (Trochidae), 289
" 84. Neritina crepidularia, . . 290
" 85. Patella vulgata, . . . 285
" 86. Haliotis tuberculata, . . 289
" 87. Neritina fluviatilis, . . 290
" 88. Natica canrena, . . . 293
" 89. Sigaretus haliotideus, . . 292
" 90. Melania amarula, . . . 287
" 91. Limnea auricularia, . . 294
" 92. Limnea stagnalis, . . . 294

Fig. 93. Bulimus decollatus fasciatus, . 295
" 94. Bulimus decollatus albus, . . 295
" 95. Paludina vivipara, . . . 287
" 96. Janthina ianthina, . . . 289
" 97. Helix nemoralis, . . . 295
" 98. Helix pomathia, . . . 295
" 99. Turbo nautileus, . . . 289
" 100. Clausilia perversa, . . 295
" 101. Scalaria dathrus, . . . 287
" 102. Scalaria scalaris, . . . 287
" 103. Turbo cochlus, . . . 289
" 104. Delphinula delphinus, . . 289
" 105. Telescopium indicator, . . 288
" 106. Trochus solaris, . . . 289
" 107. Trochus magus, . . . 289
" 108. Solarium perspectivum, . . 289
" 109. Cerithium vertagus, . . 288
" 110. Pleurotoma babylonia, . . 290
" 111. Murex ramosa, . . . 290
" 112. Murex haustellum, . . 290
" 113. Murex tribulus, . . . 290
" 114. Strombus lentiginosus, . . 291
" 115. Pterocera chiragra, . . 291
" 116. Rostellaria rectirostris, . . 291
" 117. Terebra maculata, . . 292
" 118. Purpura lapillus, . . . 290
" 119. Harpa ventricosa, . . . 291
" 120. Baccinum undatum, . . 290
" 121. Cassidoria echinophora, . . 291
" 122. Oliva ispidula, . . . 292
" 123. Mitra episcopalis, . . 292
" 124. Mitra papalis, . . . 292
" 125. Oliva porphyria, . . . 292
" 126. Oliva maura, . . . 292

PLATE 76.

Fig. 1. Auricula midae, . . . 295
" 2. Ovula volva, ... 292
" 3. Bulla physis, . . . 284
" 4. Ovula ovum, ... 292
" 5. Cypraea moneta, . . . 292
" 6. Cypraea mauritiana, . . 292
" 7. Cypraea arabica, . . . 292
" 8. Conus aurantiacus, . . 291
" 9. Conus summus, . . . 291
" 10. Conus cedo nulli, . . . 291
" 11. Conus textillis, . . . 291
" 12. Conus marmoreus, . . 291
" 13. Spirula spirula, . . . 298
" 14. Nautilus beccari, . . . 299
" 15. Nautilus calcar, . . . 299
" 16. Nautilus pompilius, . . 298
" 17. Argonauta argo, . . . 297
" 18. Pinna obeliscus, . . . 270
" 19. Pinna rudis, ... 271
" 20. Avicula margaritifera, . . 267
" 21. Mytilus cygneus, . . . 270
" 22. Mytilus bidens, . . . 270
" 23. Terebrata caput serpentis, . 259
" 24. Crania craniolaris, . . . 259
" 25. Ostrea cristigalli, . . . 265
" 26. Malleus malleus, . . . 267
" 27. Pecten corallinus, . . . 260
" 28. Pecten pallium ducale, . . 266

Fig. 29. Pecten maximus, . . . 266
" 30. Perna ephippium, . . . 267
" 31. Arca senilis, ... 271
" 32. Arca noae, ... 271
" 33. Tridacna gigas, . . . 276
" 34. Isocardia corallina, . . 277
" 35. Spondylus gaederopus, . . 267
" 36. Venus mercenaria, . . . 278
" 37. Cytherea dione, . . . 279
" 38. Donax rugosa, . . . 278
" 39. Donax scripta, ... 278
" 40. Mactra solidissima, . . 262
" 41. Hemicardium cardissa, . . 277
" 42. Cardium echinatum, . . 277
" 43. Cyclas, ... 277
" 44. Tellina radiata, . . . 278
" 45. Solen vagina, ... 263
" 46. Solen siliqua, ... 263
" 47. Unio complanatus, . . . 272
" 48. Mya pictorum, . . . 262
" 49. Pholas pusillus, . . . 263
" 50. Pholas dactylus, . . . 263
" 51. Pollicipes mitella, . . . 305
" 52. Lepas anatifa, ... 305
" 53. Coronula, ... 306
" 54. Balanus psittacus, . . . 306
" 55. Chiton squamosus, . . . 285
" 56. Holopus rangii, . . . 242
" 57. Encrinus radiatus, . . 242
" 58. Pentacrinus osteria, . . 242
" 59. Oreaster turritus, . . . 243
" 60. Asterias aurantiaca, . . 243
" 61. Astrogonium granulare, . . 243
" 62. Ophiolepis scolopendrina, . . 243
" 63. Astrophyton caput medusae, . 243
" 64. Ophiurus asterias, . . . 243
" 65. Stellonia rubens, . . . 243
" 66. Solaster papposa, . . . 243
" 67. Spatangus purpureus, . . 245
" 68. Clypeaster rosacea, . . 245
" 69. Echinus cidaris, . . . 245
" 70. Cidaris diadema, . . . 245
" 71. Cidaris esculentus, . . . 245
" 72. Lucernaria quadricornis, . . 239
" 73. Thaumantias cymbaloidea, . 234
" 74. Aurelia aurita, . . . 234
" 75. Octopus octopodius, . . 296
" 76. Loligo loligo, ... 298
" 77. Sepia officinalis, . . . 298
" 78. Clio borealis, ... 281
" 79. Scyllaea pelagica (Tritoniidae), 273
" 80. Lernaea branchialis, . . 308
" 81. Lernaea cyprinacea, . . 308
" 82. Terebella conchilega, . . 305
" 83. Porpita nuda, . . . 234
" 84. Velella spirans, . . . 234
" 85. Cucumaria frondosa, . . 246

PLATE 77

Fig. 1. Physalia physalis, . . . 234
" 2. Thetis fimbria, . . . 283
" 3. Salpa maxima, ... 259
" 4. Pedicellaria, ... 221

Fig. 5. Actinia undata, . . . 238
" 6. Actinia senilis, . . . 238
" 7. Ascidia lepadiformis, . . 258
" 8. Ascidia venosa, . . . 258
" 9. Nais serpentina, . . . 302
" 10. Nais proboscidea, . . . 301
" 11. Phyllodoce stellifera, . . 303
" 12. Nereis tubicola, . . . 303
" 13. Amphitrite reniformis, . . 305
" 14. Spio filicornis, . . . 303
" 15. Aphrodite aculeata, . . 303
" 16. Doris papillosa, . . . 283
" 17. Doris argo, ... 283
" 18. Aplysia depilans, . . . 284
" 19. Limax agrestis, . . . 295
" 20. Limax empiricorum, . . 295
" 21. Limax fuscus, . . . 295
" 22. Malacobdella grossa, . . 301
" 23. Nephelis octoculata (Hirudinidae), . . . 300
" 24. Clepsina complanata, . . 301
" 25. Haemopis vorax, . . . 301
" 26. Hirudo officinalis, . . . 301
" 27. Sipunculus saccatus, . . 246
" 28. Sipunculus nudus, . . . 246
" 29. Echinococcus veterinorum suis, . 248
" 30. Cysticercus cellulosae, . . 249
" 31. Taenia cateniformis, . . 249
" 32. Bothriocephalus latus, . . 249
" 33. Taenia solium, . . . 249
" 34. Ligula cingulum, . . . 249
" 35. Planaria cornuta, . . . 250
" 36. Distoma hepaticum, . . 250
" 37. Lumbricus variegatus, . . 302
" 38. Lumbricus terrestris, . . 302
" 39. Echinorhynchus gigas, . . 251
" 40. Trichocephalus dispar, . . 251
" 41. Ascaris lumbricoides, . . 251
" 42. Oxyuris vermicolaris, . . 251
" 43. Filaria medinensis, . . 252
" 44. Lumbricus aquaticus, . . 302
" 45. Filaria papillosa, . . . 252
" 46. Argas fischeri, . . . 328
" 47. Argas savignii, . . . 328
" 48. Chelifer beauvoisii, . . 329
" 49. Galeodes phalangium, . . 329
" 50. Galeodes araneoides, . . 329
" 51. Scorpio europaeus, . . . 330
" 52. Buthus afer, ... 330
" 53. Epeira imperialis, . . . 332
" 54. Tetragnatha argyra, . . 334
" 55. Theridion denticulatum, . . 333
" 56. Argyroneta aquatica, . . 333
" 57a. Uloborus walcnaerius, . . 334
" 57b. Gasteracantha armata, . . 333
" 58. Mygale avicularia, . . . 332
" 59. Epeira diadema, . . . 332
" 60. Pallene brevirostris (Pycnogonidae), . . . 325
" 61. Chelifer cancroides, . . 329
" 62. Phalangium opilio, . . . 329
" 63. Phalangium aegyptiacum, . 329
" 64. Hydrachna abstergens, . . 328
" 65. Hydrachna despiciens, . . 328

Fig. 66. Ixodes annulatus, . . 327
" 67. Ixodes americanus, . . 327
" 68. Sarcoptes scabiei, . . 326
" 69. Gamasus coleopterorum, . 327
" 70. Acarus siro, . . . 326
" 71. Ixodes orbiculatus, . . 327
" 72. Pulex penetrans, . . 352
" 73. Pulex irritans, . . . 352
" 74, 75. Nirmidæ, . . . 351
" 76. Phthirius pubis, . . 351
" 77. Pediculus capitis, . . 351
" 78. Podura nivicola, . . 349
" 79. Podura villosa, . . 349
" 80. Smynthurus fimetarius, . 349
" 81, 84. Machilus polypoda, . 350
" 82, 83. Lepisma saccharina, . 350
" 84. See 81.
" 85. Melophagus ovis, . . 400
" 86. Hippobosca equina, . . 400
" 87. Bombylius major, . . 397
" 88. Dioctria ater, . . . 397
" 89. Asilus cabroniformis, . 397
" 90. Conops macrocephala, . 398
" 91. Stomoxis calcitrans, . . 398
" 92, 93. Empidæ, . . . 397
" 94. Anopheles bifurcatus, . 397
" 95. Culex nemorosus, . . 897
" 96. Culex pipiens, . . . 397
" 97. Tabanus tropicus, . . 397
" 98. Tabanus bovinus, . . 397
" 99—109. Muscidæ, . . 398
" 110. Clitellaria ephippium, . 397
" 111. Volucella pellucens, . . 398
" 112. Scæva pyrastri, . . 398
" 113. Crysotoxum vespiformis, . 398
" 114. Eristalis tenax, . . . 398
" 115. Helophilus pendulus, . . 398
" 116. Leptis vermileo, . . 398
" 117. Stratiomys chamæleon, . 397
" 118. Chironomus plumosus, . 397
" 119. Anisomera nigra, . . 397
" 120. Ctenophora elegans, . . 397
" 121. Psychoda phalænoides, . 397
" 122. Mycetophila cericea, . . 397
" 123. Bibio marci, . . . 397
" 124. Mycetophila mirabilis, . 397
" 125. Cephalemyia ovis, . . 399
" 126, 127. Gasterophilus equi, . 399
" 128. Œstrus tarandi, . . 399
" 129. Œstrus bovis, . . . 399

PLATE 78.
Fig. 1, 2. Cancerinæ, . . . 322
" 3. Thalamita natator, . . 322
" 4. Gecarcinus lateralis, . . 321
" 5. Gelasimus annulipes, . . 321
" 6. Ocypoda arenaria, . . 321
" 7. Philyra scabriuscula, . . 321
" 8. Dorippe sima, . . . 321
" 9. Ranina serrata, . . . 321
" 10. Pagurus diogenes, . . 321
" 11. Palinurus guttatus, . . 320
" 12. Scyllarus æquinoctialis, . 320
" 13. Stenopus hispidus, . . 320

Fig. 14. Callianassa uncinata, . . 320
" 15. Squilla maculata, . . 318
" 16. Gonodactylus stylifer, . 318
" 17. Phyllosoma stylicornis, . 318
" 18. Orchestia fischeri, . . 318
" 19. Ancylomera hunteri, . . 319
" 20. Cymadocea armata, . . 316
" 21. Sphæroma serratum, . . 316
" 22. Porcellio granulatus, . . 317
" 23. Caprella acuminifera, . . 317
" 24. Cyamus ovalis, . . . 317
" 25. Aprus canceriformis, . . 313
" 26. Branchipus pisciformis, . 313
" 27. Cyclops communis, . . 311
" 28. Phyllophora cornuta, . . 311
" 29. Ergasilus sieboldi, . . 311
" 30. Lernæa polycolpus, . . 309
" 31. Achtheres percarum, . . 310
" 32. Pycnogonum litterale, . 325
" 33. Nymphon gracile, . . 325
" 34. Limullus moluccanus, . . 315
" 35. Nemesia cellicola, . . 333
" 36. Segestria perfida, . . 333
" 37. Lycosa tarentula, . . 333
" 38. Lycosa melanogaster, . . 333
" 39. Hersilia caudata, . . 333
" 40. Chersis savinii, . . . 333
" 41. Salticus formicarius, . . 333
" 42. Eripus heterogaster, . . 333
" 43. Arcys lanceolarius, . . 333
" 44. Latrodectus malmignatus, . 333
" 45. Nyssa timida, . . 333, 334
" 46. Tegenaria domestica, . . 333
" 47. Lachesis perversa, . . 334
" 48. Uloborus walenærius, . . 334
" 49. Argyroneta aquatica, . . 333

PLATE 79.
Fig. 1. Mutilla europæa, . . . 378
" 2. Apterogyna occidentalis, . 378
" 3—9. Formicidæ, . . . 378
" 10. Bombus lapidarius, . . 380
" 11. Bombus muscorum, . . 380
" 12. Megachile sementaria, . . 380
" 13. Bombus terrestris, . . 380
" 14. Xylocopa violacea, . . 380
" 15. Nomada variegata, . . 380
" 16. Eucera longicornis, . . 380
" 17. Megachile centuncularis, . 380
" 18. Apis mellifica, . . . 380
" 19. Vespa maculata, . . . 379
" 20. Polistes paritum, . . 380
" 21. Vespa vulgaris, . . . 380
" 22. Vespa crabro, . . . 380
" 23. Leucospis dorsigera, . . 376
" 24. Chrysis cyanea, . . . 376
" 25. Chrysis aurata, . . . 376
" 26. Chrysis ignita, . . . 376
" 27. Pompilus cœruleus, . . 377
" 28. Pompilus viaticus, . . 377
" 29. Crabro cribrarius, . . 376
" 30. Pelopæus spirifex, . . 377
" 31. Ammophila sabulosa, . . 377
" 32, 33, 36—39. Ichneumonidæ, . 375

Figs. 34, 35. Chalcididæ, . . . 376
" 36—39. See 32.
" 40. Rhyssa persuasoria (Ichneumo-
        nidæ), ... 375
" 41. Urocerus spectrum, . . 375
" 42. Urocerus gigas, . . . 375
" 43. Lophyrus juniperi, . . 375
" 44. Nematus capreæ, . . . 375
" 45. Cimbex americana, . . 375
" 46. Tenthredinidæ, . . . 374
" 47. Cimbex variabilis, . . 375
" 48—53. Cinipidæ, . . . 375
" 54. Mantispa pagana, . . 372
" 55. Raphidia ophiopsis, . . 372
" 56. Termes fatalis, . . . 370
" 57. Bittacus tipularia, . . 372
" 58. Panorpa communis, . . 372
" 59. Ascalaphus barbarus, . . 372
" 60. Myrmeleon libelluloides, . 372
" 61. Myrmeleon formicarius, . 372
" 62—64. Hermerobiidæ, . . 372
" 65. Hydropsyche plumosa, . . 373
" 66. Phryganea striata, . . 373
" 67. Perla bicaudata, . . . 371
" 68. Limnophilus rhombica, . 373
" 69. Phryganea grandis, . . 373
" 70—72. Ephemeridæ, . . 371
" 73. Agrion puella, . . . 472
" 74. Calepteryx virgo, . . 372
" 75. Libellula depressa, . . 372
" 76. Æschna grandis, . . . 372
" 77. Pterophorus pentadactyla, . 383
" 78. Coccyx resinosa, . . . 384
" 79. Carpocapsa pomonella, . 384
" 80. Hercyna paliotalis, . . 384
" 81. Tinea granella, . . . 383
" 82. Plutella xylostella, . . 383
" 83. Gallerea cereana, . . . 383
" 84. Tinea pellionella, . . 383
" 85. Lemmatophila salicella, . 383
" 86. Hyponomeuta evonymella, . 383
" 87. Hyponomeuta pedella, . . 383
" 88. Hypena rostralis, . . 384
" 89. Botys verticalis, . . . 384
" 90. Sciaphila literata, . . 384
" 91. Tortrix viridana, . . . 384
" 92. Halias prasinana, . . 384
" 93—102. Geometridæ, . . 384
" 103—123, 129, 136. Noctuidæ, 384, 385
" 124. Callimorpha jacobææ, . . 385
" 125. Arctia fuliginosa, . . 385
" 126. Arctia matronula, . . 385
" 127. Arctia dominula, . . 385
" 128. Pygæra bucephala, . . 385
" 129. See 103.
" 130—135, 137—151. Bombycidæ, . 385
" 136. See 103.

PLATE 80.
Fig. 1. Lasiocampa quercus, . . 385
" 2. Dendrolimus pini, . . 385
" 3. Odonestis potatoria, . . 385
" 4—7. Bombycidæ, . . . 385
" 8. Zygæna filipendula, . . 386

Fig. 9. Sesia fuciformis, . . . 387
" 10—21. Sphingidæ, . . 386, 387
" 22. Hesperia malvarum, . . 388
" 23—50. Papilionidæ, . . 387, 388
" 51. Thrips phisapus, . . . 370
" 52. Lecanium illicis, . . . 390
" 53. Lecanium hesperidum, . . 390
" 54. Coccus cacti, . . . 389
" 55. Psylla alni, . . . 390
" 56. Dorthesia urticea, . . 390
" 57, 59. Aphidæ, . . . 390
" 58. Chermes ulmi, . . . 390
" 59. See 57.
" 60. Pyrrhocoris apterus, . . 393
" 61. Coryzus hyoscyami, . . 393
" 62. Cydnus biguttatus, . . 393
" 63. Pentatoma juniperinus, . 393
" 64. Pentatoma baccarum, . . 393
" 65. Acanthosoma hæmorrhoidalis, . 393
" 66. Cimex rufipes, . . . 393
" 67. Acanthia lectularia, . . 392
" 68. Ranatra linearis, . . . 391
" 69. Nepa cinerea, . . . 391
" 70. Neucoris cimicoides, . . 391
" 71. Belostoma grandis, . . 391
" 72. Corixa striata, . . . 391
" 73. Notonecta glauca, . . 391
" 74. Aphrophora spumaria, . . 390
" 75. Cicada fraxini, . . . 390
" 76. Fulgora candelaria, . . 390
" 77. Fulgoria laternaria, . . 390
" 78. Œdipoda stridula, . . 370
" 79. Œdipoda cærulescens, . . 370
" 80. Œdipoda migratoria, . . 370
" 81. Acridium cristatum, . . 370
" 82—85. Locustidæ, . . . 369
" 86—88. Gryllidæ, . . . 369
" 89. Phyllium siccifolium, . . 368
" 90. Mantis religiosa, . . 368
" 91. Empusa gongylodes, . . 368
" 92. Cyphocrana gigas, . . 368
" 93. Blatta orientalis, . . 367

PLATE 81.
Upper Division.
Fig. 1—3. Forficulidæ, . . . 367
" 4—6. Brachelytra, . . . 359
" 7. Meloë proscarabæus, . . 363
" 8. Lytta vesicatoria, . . 363
" 9. Blaps mortisaga, . . . 364
" 10. Tenebrio molitor, . . 364
" 11—16. Carabidæ, . . . 357
" 17. Dyticus marginalis, . . 357
" 18. Hydrophilus piceus, . . 358
" 19—21. Mordellidæ, . . 363
" 22. Buprestis mariana, . . 362
" 23. Euchroma gigas, . . . 362
" 24. Buprestis chrysostigma, . 362
" 25. Elaphrus riparius (Carabidæ), . 357
" 26—29. Cicindela, . . . 357
" 30—33. Elateridæ, . . . 362
" 34. Malachius æneus, . . 362
" 35—38. Cantharis, . . . 363

Fig. 39. Lycus sanguineus.
" 40. Pyrochroa coccinea, . . . 363
" 41, 42. Lampyridæ, . . . 362
" 43. Necydalis cærulea.
" 44—61. Longicornia, . . . 365
" 62—64. Clerida, . . . 362
" 65—76. Rhincophora, . . 364
" 77—79. Bruchus.
" 80—101. Trimera, . . . 366
" 102, 103. Nitidulidæ, . . . 359
" 104. Silpha thoracica, . . . 359
" 105, 106. Necrophorus, . . 359
" 107, 108. Anthrenus, . . . 359
" 109. Byrrhus pilula (Byrrhidæ), . 360
" 110. Gyrinus natator, . . . 111
" 111. Ptinus fur.
" 112. Anobium pertinax, . . . 362
" 113. Apate capucinus.
" 114. Hylesinus piniperda.
" 115, 116. Bostrichus, . . . 345
" 117, 118. Dermestes, . . . 359
" 119—123. Hister, . . . 360
" 124. Lucanus, ... 360
" 125—127. Cetoniadæ, . . . 360
" 128—131. Melolonthidæ, . . 360
" 132, 136—144. Scarabæidæ, . . 360
" 133—135. Aphodiidæ, . . . 360
" 136—144. See 132.
" 145—148. Dynastidæ, . . . 360

Lower Division.

Fig. 1. Alosa vulgaris, shad, . . 413
" 2. Clupea harengus, herring, . 413
" 3. Engraulis encrasicholus, anchovy, 412
" 4. Harengula sprattus, sprat, . 413
" 5. Thymallus vulgaris, greyling, 416
" 6. Cobitis fossilis, mudfish, . 420
" 7. Exoglossum barbatula, ground-
ling, ... 420
" 8. Rhombus vulgaris, brill, . 424
" 9. Platessa flesus, fluke, . . 423
" 10. Zeus faber, dory, . . . 431
" 11. Lota vulgaris, burbot, . . 423
" 12. Trachinus draco, sea cat, . 426
" 13. Xiphias gladius, swordfish, . 430
" 14. Amodytes tobianus, sand-eel.
" 15. Syngnathus ophidion, sea serpent, 436
" 16. Syngnathus acus, sea-needle, . 436
" 17. Pegasus draco, sea-dragon, . 437
" 18. Lumpus anglorum, lump sucker, 433
" 19. Diodon punctatus, sticklebag, 436
" 20. Tetraodon lagocephalus, star
belly, ... 436
" 21. Centriscus scolopax, trumpet fish, 433
" 22. Aluteres monoceros, unicorn fish, 435
" 23. Lophius piscatorius, widegap, 434
" 24. Acipenser ruthenus, caviar sturgeon, ... 442
" 25. Acipenser sturio, sturgeon . 442
" 26. Sphyrna malleus, hammer-headed
shark, ... 445
" 27. Spinax acanthias, thorn-hound, 446
" 28. Petromyzon fluviatilis, lamprey, 411

Fig. 29. Seps chalcides, bronze colored
lizard, ... 477
" 30. Scincus cyanurus, scink, . . 477
" 31. Plestiodon aldrovandii, . . 477
" 32. Triton cristatum, eft, . . 460
" 33. Draco dandini, flying dragon, . 483
" 34. Rana temporaria, yellow frog, . 462
" 35. Hyla viridis, tree or green frog, . 463
" 36. Bufo calamita, toad, . . 464
" 37. Bombinator igneus, glistering
toad, ... 463
" 38. Pelobatus fuscus, water toad, . 483
" 39. Testudo geometrica, tortoise, . 491
" 40. Testudo græca, mosaic tortoise, 491
" 41. Cistudo europæa, European tortoise, ... 492
" 42. Emys picta, terrapin, . . . 492
" 43. Sphargis coriacea, leather turtle, 493

PLATE 82.

Fig. 1. Aspidophorus cataphractus,
pogge, ... 427
" 2. Pristis antiquorum, saw fish, . 446
" 3. Esox lucius, pike, . . . 417
" 4. Perca fluviatilis, perch, . . 424
" 5. Anguilla vulgaris, eel, . . 411
" 6. Gasterosteus aculeatus, stickle-
back, ... 427
" 7. Salmo fario, salmon trout, . 415
" 8. Holocanthus tricolor, tricolor, . 432
" 9. Synanceia horrida, dragon's head, 427
" 10. Labrax lupus, bass, . . . 425
" 11. Solea vulgaris, sole, . . . 424
" 12. Platessa limanda, dab, . . 423

PLATE 83.

Fig. 1. Holocentrum longipinne, red
perch, ... 426
" 2. Acanthurus gemmatus, gem fish, 432
" 3. Amphacanthus corallinus, coral
perch, ... 433
" 4. Sphyræna spet, barracuda pike, . 426
" 5. Scorpæna scropha, dragon's head, 427
" 6. Naucrates ductor, pilot fish, . 431
" 7. Trigla lyra, piper, . . . 426
" 8. Thynnus vulgaris, tunny, . . 430
" 9. Scomber vulgaris, mackerel, . 430
" 10. Acerina cornua, ruffe, . . 426
" 11. Cepola rubescens, band fish, . 432
" 12. Dactylopterus volitans, flying
fish, ... 426

PLATE 84.

Fig. 1. Carcharius verus, shark, . . 445
" 2. Coryphæna hippuris, dolphin, . 431
" 3. Echineis remora, sucking fish, . 424
" 4. Chondrostoma nasus, broad snout, 418
Fig. 5. Cottus gobio, bullhead, . . 427
" 6. Gobio fluviatilis, gresling, . 419
" 7. Alburnus lucidus, bleak, . . 418
" 8. Acanthurus chirurgus, lancet-
tail, ... 432
" 9. Chætodon auriga, angel, . . 432
" 10. Barbus vulgaris, barbel, . . 419

" 11. Cyprinus carpio, carp, . . 419
" 12. Tinca vulgaris, tench, . . 419
" 13. Anabas scandens, climbing perch, 429

PLATE 85.

Fig. 1. Morrhua vulgaris, codfish, . 422
" 2. Merlangus vulgaris, whiting, . 423
" 3. Raia batis, skate, . . . 447
" 4. Trachinus vividus, weever, . 426
" 5. Blennius viviparus, guffer, . 434
" 6. Ophiocephalus striatus, ophidion, 429
" 7. Mullus barbatus, mullet, . . 426
" 8. Dipterodon capensis, Cape-dipter-
odon, ... 432
" 9. Amphiprion bifasciatus, amphiprion, ... 432
" 10. Scolopsides vosmari.
" 11. Trachypterus spinolæ, trachypterus, ... 432
" 12. Cyprinus auratus, gold-fish, . 419

PLATE 86.

Fig. 1. Deirodon nasutus, green snake, . 475
" 2. Tropidonotus natrix, ringed snake, 474
" 3. Trigonocephalus lanceolatus, cop-
perhead, ... 471
" 4. Naia tripudians, cobra di capello, 471
" 5. Boa constrictor, . . . 473
" 6. Phrynosoma cornuta, horned frog, 482

PLATE 87.

Fig. 1. Anguis fragilis, slow worm, . 476
" 2. Vipera berus, viper, . . . 471
" 3. Cerastes cornutus, horned viper, . 471
" 4. Xiphosoma caninum, dog boa, . 473
" 5. Crotalus horridus, rattlesnake, . 470
" 6. Seps chalcides, scink, . . 477

PLATE 88.

Fig. 1. Siren lacertina, siren, . . 456
" 2. Necturus lateralis, water-puppy, . 456
" 3. Chamæleo vulgaris, chamæleon, . 483
" 4. Platydactylus guttatus, gecko, . 484
" 5. Uroplatus fimbriatus, flat headed
salamander, . . . 485
" 6. Lophyrus furcata, lophyrus, . 482
" 7. Crocodilus lucius, alligator, . 487
" 8. Crocodilus vulgaris, crocodile, . 487

PLATE 89.

Fig. 1. Salamandra maculata, salamander, ... 460
" 2. Triton tœniatum, brook salamander, ... 460
" 3. Draco dandini, flying dragon, . 483
" 4. Scincus officinalis, scink, . . 477
" 5. Basiliscus mitratus, basilisk, . 482
" 6. Iguana tuberculata, guana, . 482
" 7. Lacerta viridis, lizard, . . 481

PLATE 90.

Fig. 1. Bufo viridis, green toad, . . 464
" 2. Engystoma ovale, S. Amer. toad, . 464
" 3. Dactelythra capensis, Cape toad, . 464
" 4. Pipa americana, Guiana toad, . 464

" 5. Rana esculenta, frog, . . 462
" 6. Hyla viridis, tree or green frog, . 463
" 7. Achrochordus javanica, Java
snake, ... 472
" 8. Platurus laticaudis, India water
snake, ... 471
" 9. Elaps corallinus, coral snake, . 474
" 10. Typhline cuvierii, blind scink, . 477
" 11. Chelonia mydas, green turtle, . 493
" 12. Cistudo europæa, land tortoise, . 492
" 13. Testudo geometrica, India tortoise, ... 491

PLATE 91.

Fig. 1. Podiceps cristatus, crested grebe, 591
" 2. Podiceps minor, little grebe, . 591
" 3. Colymbus glacialis, loon, . . 591
" 4. Sterna nigra, sooty tern, . . 593
" 5. Larus eburneus, ivory gull, . 593
" 6. Pelecanus crispus, hairy pelican, 594
" 7. Cygnus olor, mute swan, . . 589
" 8. Cygnus ferus, hooper swan, . 589
" 9. Oidemia americana, scoter, . 590
" 10. Anas crecca, teal, . . . 590
" 11. Procellaria capensis, Cape pigeon, 593
" 12. Diomedia exulans, white alba-
tross, ... 592
" 13. Aptenodytes patagonica, Patagonian penguin, . . . 592
" 14. Fratercula arctica, puffin, . 591
" 15. Alca torda, razor-billed auk, . 591

PLATE 92.

Fig. 1. Carbo cormoranus, cormorant, . 595
" 2. Eudytes cristatus, crested penguin, ... 592
" 3. Tachypetes aquilus, frigate pelican, ... 595
" 4. Phæton æthereus, tropic bird, . 593
" 5. Plotus anhinga, snake bird, . 594
" 6. Sula bassana, booby, . . 595
" 7. Anser segetum, bean goose, . 588
" 8. Anas boschas, mallard, . . 590
" 9. Anas galericulata, mandarin
duck, ... 590
" 10. Merges cucullatus, hooded mer-
ganser, ... 591
" 11. Larus argentatus, herring gull, . 593
" 12. Sterna hirundo, sea swallow, . 593

PLATE 93.

Fig. 1. Charadius auratus, plover, . . 582
" 2. Vanellus cristatus, lapwing, . 582
" 3. Grus cinerea, crane, . . . 583
" 4. Platalea leucorrhodia, roseate
spoon-bill, . . . 584
" 5. Ardea purpurea, purple heron, . 584
" 6. Egretta candidissima, snowy
heron, ... 584
" 7. Ciconia alba, white stork, . . 584
" 8. Gallinago major, snipe, . . 586
" 9. Limosa rufa, rufous godwit, . 585
" 10. Recurvirostra avocetta, avocet, . 585

Fig. 11. Phænicopterus ruber, scarlet flamingo, ... 588
" 12. Ardea ralloides, pigmy heron, . 584

PLATE 94.

Fig. 1. Struthio camelus, ostrich, . . 581
" 2. Otis tarda, great bustard, . 581
" 3. Otis tetrax, smaller bustard, . 581
" 4. Balearica pavonina, crowned crane, ... 583
" 5. Botaurus stellaris, bittern, . 584
" 6. Ibis alba, white ibis, . . 585
" 7. Numenius arcuatus, curlew, . 585
" 8. Totanus calidris, sandpiper, . 586
" 9. Parra indica, Indian jacana, . 587
" 10. Fulica americana, coot, . . 587
" 11. Porphyrio hyacinthinus, hyacinth gallinule, ... 587
" 12. Heliornis surinamensis, sun bird, 591
" 13. Totanus ochropus, green sand-piper, ... 586

PLATE 95.

Fig. 1. Casuarius galeatus, cassowary, . 581
" 2. Palamedea cornuta, horned screamer, . . . 586
" 3. Ibis cristatus, crested ibis, . 585
" 4. Tringa rufescens, rufous sand-piper, ... 586
" 5. Glareola torquata, pratincole, . 582
" 6. Himantopus albicollis, stilt, . 585
" 7. Cinclus interpras, turnstone, . 583
" 8. Rallus aquaticus, dusky rail, . 587
" 9. Rallus crex, corn crake, . 587
" 10—11. Gallus domesticus, common fowl, ... 577
" 12. Meleagris gallopavo, turkey, . 577
" 13. Numida meleagris, guinea fowl, 578
" 14. Pterocles alchata, desert grouse, 580
" 15. Turnix dactylisonans, quail, . 579

PLATE 96.

Fig. 1. Tetrao urogallus, cock of the woods, . . . 579
" 2. Tetrao tetrix, moor cock, . 580
" 3. Perdix cinerea, grey partridge, . 578
" 4. Perdix rubra, red partridge, . 578
" 5. Pavo cristatus, peacock, . . 575
" 6. Phasianus colchicus, pheasant, . 576
" 7. Phasianus pictus, golden pheasant, 576
" 8. Argus giganteus, argus pheasant, 576
" 9. Tragopan hastingsii, golden breasted horned pheasant, . 576
" 10. Crax rubra, red curassow, . 574
" 11. Lophortyx californicus, California partridge, . . . 579
" 12. Columba livia, rock pigeon, . 572
" 13. Columba œnas, blue-backed dove, 572
" 14. Goura cruenta, ground pigeon, . 573
" 15. Columba turtur, turtle dove, . 572

PLATE 97.

Fig. 1. Cacatua sulphurea, yellow-crest-ed cockatoo, . . . 567
" 2. Psittacus erythacus, grey African parrot, ... 566

Fig. 3. Palæornis malaccensis, Malacca parrot, ... 566
" 4. Palæornis alexandri, redheaded parrot, ... 566
" 5. Psittacus melanocephalus, black-headed parrot, . . . 567
" 6. Trogon curucui. curucui, . 527
" 7. Trogon viridis, green curucui, . 527
" 8. Bucco macrorhynchus, puff-bird, . 527
" 9. Monasa tranquilla, S. Amer. puff-bird, . . . 527
" 10. Capito viridiauranthius, green and orange barbet, . . 567
" 11. Pogonias sulcirostris, grooved-bill barbet, . . . 567
" 12. Pteroglossus aracari, long-tailed aracari, ... 565
" 13. Ramphastus tucanus, largebilled toucan, ... 565

PLATE 98.

Fig. 1. Platycercus viridis, green parrot, 566
" 2. Ara ararauna, blue and yellow maccaw, ... 566
" 3. Ara militaris, military maccaw, . 566
" 4. Lorius domicellus, lory, . . 566
" 5. Picus villosus, hairy woodpecker, 567
" 6. Picus cayennensis, Cayenne wood-pecker, ... 567
" 7. Gecinus viridis, green wood-pecker, ... 568
" 8. Picus major, large wookpecker, . 567
" 9. Yunx torquilla, wry neck, . 567
" 10. Pica caudata, magpie, . . 556
" 11. Corvus monedula, jackdaw, . 555
" 12. Corvus corax, raven, . . 555
" 13. Corvus cornix, hooded crow, . 555

PLATE 99.

Fig. 1, 3. Garrulus glandarius, jay, . 544
" 2. Nucifraga caryocatactus, nut-cracker, ... 556
" 3. See Fig. 1.
" 4. Paradisea minor, bird of paradise, 531
" 5. Paradisea regia, king paradise bird, ... 531
" 6. Paradisea superba, superb para-dise bird, . . . 531
" 7. Paradisea sexsetacea, six shafted paradise bird, . . 531
" 8. Trochilus moschitus, ruby topaz humming bird, . . 533
" 9a. Trochilus ornatus, magnificent humming bird, . . 533
" 9b. Trochilus colubris, humming bird, 533
" 10. Trochilus delalandii, De La-lande's humming bird, . 533
" 11. Trochilus minimus, smallest humming bird, . . 533
" 12. Trochilus cristatus, crested humming bird, . . 533
" 13. Trochilus macrourus, swallow tailed humming bird, . 533
" 14. Buphaga africana, beefeater, . 558
" 15. Sturnella ludoviciana, American lark, ... 558

Fig. 16. Icterus baltimore, Baltimore oriole, ... 559

PLATE 100.

Fig. 1. Sturnus vulgaris, starling, . . 558
" 2. Loxia pityopsittacus, parrot cross-bill, ... 563
" 3. Coccothraustes vulgaris, haw-finch, ... 560
" 4ab. Fringilla canaria, canary bird, 561
" 5. Fringilla cannabina, red poll, . 561
" 6. Fringilla domestica, house-spar-row, ... 561
" 7. Sylvia hippolais, willow wren, . 541
" 8. Oriolus galbula, oriole, . . 547
" 9. Merula vulgaris, blackbird, . 546
" 10. Merula saxatilis, rock thrush, . 546
" 11. Pastor roseus, rose colored star-ling, ... 558
" 12. Merula viscivorus, missel thrush, 546
" 13. Merula iliaca, redwing, . . 546
" 14. Merula musica, song thrush, . 546

PLATE 101.

Fig. 1. Trochilus granatinus, garnet humming bird, . . 533
" 2. Pyrrhula europea, bullfinch, . 563
" 3. Spermophila crassirostris, thick-billed finch, . . 563
" 4. Coccothraustes chloris, green finch, ... 560
" 5. Fringilla senegala, senegal finch, 561
" 6. Fringilla amaduva, amaduvat, . 561
" 7. Vidua regia, king widow bird, . 560
" 8. Vidua erythrorhynchus, red-billed widow bird, . . 560
" 9. Carduelis spinus, siskin, . . 561
" 10. Carduelis elegans, goldfinch, . 561
" 11. Calliste tatao, seven-colored tana-ger, ... 561
" 12. Fringilla cœlebs, chaffinch, . 561
" 13. Emberiza hortulana, ortolan, . 562
" 14. Emberiza schœniculus, reed bun-ting, ... 562
" 15. Emberiza citrinella, yellow-hammer, ... 562
" 16. Rupicola aurantia, cock of the rock, ... 551
" 17. Muscicapa grisola, grey fly-catcher, ... 550
" 18. Muscicapa albicollis, white-necked flycatcher, . . 550
" 19. Muscicapa regia, king of the fly-catchers, . . . 550
" 20. Ampelis carnifex, scarlet-crested chatterer, . . . 552
" 21. Ampelis cortinga, banded chat-terer, ... 552

PLATE 102.

Fig. 1. Trochilus albicollis, white-necked humming bird, . . 534
" 2. Certhia familiaris, brown creeper, 536
" 3. Parus cristatus, crested tit, . 544
" 4. Parus major, titmouse, . . 544

" 5. Alauda calandria, field lark, . 562
" 6. Alauda cristata, crested lark, . 562
" 7. Alauda arvensis, skylark, . . 562
" 8. Acanthiza campestris, hedge war-bler, ... 543
" 9. Cæreba cyanea, blue creeper, . 532
" 10, 11. Phœnicura, redstarts, . . 541
" 12. Phœnicura suecica, blue throated Swedish redstart, . . 541
" 13. Erythaca rubecula, robin, . . 541
" 14. Menura superba, lyre bird, . 538
" 15. Dicrurus forficatus, fork-tailed drongo, ... 552
" 16. Cracticus varius, black and white shrike, . . 553
" 17. Vauga curvirostris, hooked-bill shrike, ... 552
" 18. Laniarius barbarus, Barbary shrike, ... 553
" 19. Laniarius collurio, red-backed shrike, ... 553
" 20. Laniarius exubitor, butcher bird, 553

PLATE 103.

Fig. 1. Buceros erythrorhynchus, red-billed hornbill, . . 564
" 2. Buceros rhinoceros, rhinoceros hornbill, . . . 564
" 3. Halcyon atricapilla, black capped kingfisher, . . . 528
" 4. Ceryle javanicus, Java kingfisher, 529
" 5. Alcido ispida, common king-fisher, ... 528
" 6. Caprimulgus europæus, goat-sucker, ... 524
" 7. Hirundo rustica, swallow, . 522
" 8. Cypselus melba, black martin, . 523
" 9. Tyrannus severus, Cayenne fly-catcher, . . . 549
" 10. Milvulus forficatus, South Amer. flycatcher, . . . 549
" 11. Parus ater, pine tit, . . 543
" 12. Regulus auricapillus, golden crested wren, . . 541
" 13. Philomela luscinia, nightingale, . 539
" 14. Curruca hortensis, garden warb-ler, ... 541
" 15. Curruca atricapilla, blackcap warbler, . . . 541
" 16. Phœnicura ruticilla, common redstart, . . . 541
" 17. Motacilla boarula, grey wagtail, 545
" 18. Saxicola œnanthe, wheatear, . 541

PLATE 104.

Fig. 1. Strix flammea, European barn owl, ... 515
" 2. Otus brachyotus, short eared owl, 515
" 3. Otus wilsonianus, long-eared owl, ... 515
" 4. Bubo maximus, grand duke, . 517
" 5. Falco peregrinus, wandering falcon, ... 505
" 6. Falco œsalon, merlin, . . 506
" 7. Milvus regalis, kite, . . 510

" 8. Buteo vulgaris, common buzzard, 507
" 9. Gyps fulvus, griffin vulture, . 501
" 10. Sarcoramphus papa, king vulture, 503
" 11. Sarcoramphus gryphus, condor, . 502

PLATE 105.

Fig. 1. Aquila chrysaëtos, golden eagle, . 507
" 2. Archibuteo niger, black buzzard, . 507
" 3. Pandion ossifragus, osprey, . . 509
" 4. Haliaëtus albicilla, sea eagle, . 508
" 5. Astur palumbarius, goshawk, . 511
" 6. Accipiter nisus, sparrow hawk, . 511
" 7. Falco subutes, hobby, . . 506
" 8. Falco alaudarius, kestril, . . 506

PLATE 105, b.

Chart of the migrations of fishes and birds
(Weltkarte in Mercator's Projection zur
Uebersicht der jährlichen Wanderungen
der hauptsächlichsten Gattungen der
Fische und Vögel), ... 497

GLOSSARY.

Aleuten In., Aleutian Islands.
Amazonenstrom, Amazon River.
Arabien, Arabia.
Arabisches M., Arabian Sea.
Asien, Asia.
Atlantischer Ocean, Atlantic Ocean.
Behringsstrasse, Behring's Straits.
Baffins Meer, Baffin's Bay.
Californien, California.
Canarische In., Canary Islands.
Cap der guten Hoffnung, Cape of Good Hope.
Capstadt, Capetown.
Cap Verds In., Cape Verde Islands.
Caspisches Meer, Caspian Sea.
Donau, Danube.
Felsen Geb., Rocky Mountains.
Fensterschwalben, Domestic swallows.
Feuerland, Terra del Fuego.
Freundschafts In., Friendly Islands.
Gesellschafts In., Society Islands.
Gr. Bären See, Great Bear Lake.
Grönland, Greenland.
Grossbritannien, Great Britain.
Grosser Ocean, Pacific.
Häringe, Herrings.
Hudsons Meer, Hudson's Bay.
I. Melville, Melville Island.
Indisches Meer, Indian Ocean.
Lissabon, Lisbon.
Makrelen, Mackerel.
Meerb. v. Bengalen, Bay of Bengal.
Meerb. v. Mexico, Bay of Mexico.
Mongolei, Mongolia.
Neuseeland, New Zealand.
Neu Sibirien, New Siberia.
Nord Amerika, North America.
Nördliches Eismeer, Arctic Sea.
Patagonien, Patagonia.
Raben u. Kräken, Ravens and crows.
Rauchschwalben, Barn swallows.
Russisch Amerika, Russian America.

Schiffer In., Navigators' Islands.
Schleiereulen, Barn owls.
Schwarzes Meer, Black Sea.
Sibirien, Siberia.
Sklavensee, Slave Lake.
Staare u. Amseln, Starlings and blackbirds.
Süd Amerika, South America.
Uferschwalben, Bank swallows.
Vereinigte Staaten, United States.
Versammlungs- u. Abzugspunkt, Place of meet-
ing and departure.
Wachteln, Quails.
Warschau, Warsaw.
West Indien, West Indies.
Wien, Vienna.
Wüste Sahara, Desert of Sahara.
Zeichenerklärung, Explanation of the marks.

PLATE 106.

Fig. 1. Balæna mysticetus, Greenland
whale, ... 625
" 2, 3. Physeter macrocephalus, sperm
whale, ... 627
" 4. Delphinus delphis, dolphin, . 629

PLATE 107.

Fig. 1, 2. Cervus elaphus, stag, . . 654
" 3. Cervus dama, fallow deer, . . 655
" 4. Cervus capreolus, roebuck, . 653
" 5. Lepus timidus, hare, . . 661
" 6. Lepus cuniculus, rabit, . 661
" 7, 8. Bos taurus, common ox, . 658
" 9. Ovis aries, sheep, . . 657
" 10. Capra hircus, goat, . . 656
" 11. Sciurus vulgaris, squirrel, . 676

PLATE 108.

Fig. 1. Camelus bactrianus, two-humped
camel, ... 651
" 2. Camelus dromedarius, dromedary, 651
" 3. Camelopardalis girafa, giraffe, . 651
" 4. Moschus moschiferus, musk, . 652
" 5. Antilope dorcas, gazelle, . . 655
" 6. Antilope redunca, antilope of
Senegal, ... 655

PLATE 109.

Fig. 1. Bison americanus, buffalo, . 657
" 2. Bos bubalus, Indian buffalo, . 658
" 3. Rupicapra tragus, chamois, . 656
" 4. Antilope scripta, Cape-elk, . 655
" 5. Auchenia alpaca, paco, . . 651
" 6. Auchenia lama, lama, . . 651
" 7. Auchenia vicunna, vicunna, . 651
" 8, 9. Tarandus furcifer, reindeer, . 654
" 10. Cervus alces, eland, . . 654
" 11. Siberian horse, . . . 648

PLATE 110.

Fig. 1. Equus zebra, zebra, . . 648
" 2. Equus asinus, ass, . . 648
" 3. Equus mulus, mule, . . 648
" 4. Equus caballus, horse, . . 647
" 5. Norman team horse, . . 648
" 6. Arabian mare and colt, . . 647

" 7. Arabian stallion, . . . 647

PLATE 111.

Fig. 1. Tapir indicus, tapir, . . . 642
" 2. Hyrax syriacus, daman, . . 644
" 3. Dicotyle labiatus, peccary, . . 645
" 4. Porcus babyrussa, Asiatic hog, . 646
" 5. Sus domesticus, domestic hog, . 645
" 6. Sus scropha, wild hog, . . 645
" 7. Phacochœrus æthiopicus, wart
hog, ... 646
" 8. Hippopotamus amphibius, hippopotamus, ... 640
" 9. Elephas indicus, Indian elephant, 643

PLATE 112.

Fig. 1. Ornithorhynchus anatinus, duckbilled platypus, . . 608
" 2. Echidna aculeata, porcupine ant-
eater, ... 608
" 3. Manis pentadactyla, pangolin, . 609
" 4. Myrmecophaga didactyla, two-
toed ant-eater, . . 610
" 5. Myrmecophaga jubata, great ant-
eater, ... 610
" 6. Chlamydophorus truncatus, Chili
armadillo, . . . 611
" 7. Dasypus sexcinctus, six-girdled
armadillo, . . . 611
" 8. Dasypus novemcinctus, nine-
girdled armadillo, . . 611
" 9. Bradypus didactylus, sloth, . 614
" 10. Bradypus tridactylus, aï, . 614
" 11ab. Halmaturus laniger, rufous
kangaroo, . . . 617
" 12ab. Halmaturus dorsalis, ashy kangaroo, . . . 617
" 13. Didelphys murina, Brazilian opossum, ... 622
" 14. Didelphys virginiana, Virginia
opossum, . . . 622
" 15. Nasua rufa, brown coati, . . 687

PLATE 113.

Fig. 1. Chinchilla lanigera, chinchilla, . 662
" 2a. Cavia cobaya, Guinea pig, . 662
" 2b. Lagomys alpinus, pika, . 660
" 3a. Cercolabes villosus, Brazil
porcupine, . . . 664
" 3b. See 16 (mistake of the engraver's).
" 4. Hystrix cristatus, European porcupine, . . . 665
" 5. Halamys caffer, Cape jerboa, . 670
" 6. Mus sylvaticus, field mouse, . 669
" 7. Mus rattus, black rat, . . 669
" 8. Mus musculus, common mouse, 668
" 9. Cricetus vulgaris, hamster, . 669
" 10. Myoxus glis, dormouse, . 671
" 11. Arctomys alpinus, marmot, . 673
" 12, 13. Pteromys volucella, flying
squirrel; . . . 672
" 14. Sciurus carolinensis, grey squirrel, 676
" 15. Sciurus maximus, Malabar squirrel, ... 673

Fig. 16. Lutra vulgaris, European otter, . 690
" 17. Talpa europæa, European mole, 677
" 18. Erinaceus europæus, European
hedgehog, . . . 679

PLATE 114.

Fig. 1. Castor fiber americanus, beaver, . 671
" 2. Phoca vitulina, seal, . . 684
" 3. Trichechus rosmarus, walrus, . 637
" 4. Felis domesticus, cat, . . 695
" 5. Felis domesticus angorensis,
Angora cat, . . . 695
" 6. Hyæna striata, striped hyena, . 694
" 7. Canis aureus, jackal, . . 693
" 8. Canis lupus, wolf, . . 693
" 9. Canis familiaris pastoreus, shep-
herd's dog, . . . 692
" 10. Lutra canadensis, Canada otter, 690
" 11. Ursus maritimus, white polar
bear, ... 686

PLATE 115.

Fig. 1. Felis leo, lion, ... 695
" 2. Felis tigris, tiger, . . . 695
" 3. Felis leopardus, leopard, . . 695
" 4. Felis onca, jaguar, . . . 695
" 5. Felis pardus, panther, . . 695
" 6. Lynx europæus, lynx, . . 695

PLATE 116.

Fig. 1. Vulpes fulvus, red fox, . . 693
" 2. Meles vulgaris, badger, . . 687
" 3. Mustela martes, marten, . . 689
" 4. Mustela foina, beech marten, . 689
" 5. Mustela putorius, polecat, . . 689
" 6. Putorius furo, ferret, . . 689
" 7. Putorius vulgaris, weasel, . 689
" 8. Putorius erminea, ermine, . 689
" 9. Ursus arctos, brown bear, . . 686
" 10. Ursus americanus, black bear, . 686
" 11. Canis familiaris sibericus, Siberian
dog, ... 693
" 12. Canis familiaris, domestic dog, . 692
" 13. Canis familiaris molossus, bull
dog, ... 692
" 14. Canis familiaris leporarius, grey-
hound, . . . 692
" 15. Canis familiaris normanus, chase
dog, ... 693
" 16. Canis familiaris vertagus, badger
dog, ... 693

PLATE 117.

Fig. 1. Galeopithecus rufus, flying lemur, 697
" 2. Plecotus timoriensis, long-eared
bat, ... 681
" 3. Vespertilio noctula, common bat, 682
" 4. Vespertilio serotinus, serotine bat, 682
" 5. Vespertilio murinus, European
bat, ... 682
" 6. Rhinolophus ferrum equinum,
horse-shoe bat, . . 681
" 7. Megaderma lyra, broadwinged
bat, ... 681
" 8. Vampyrus spectrum, vampire, . 681

Fig. 9. Pteropus vulgaris, roussette, . 683
" 10. Otolicnus senegalensis, galago, . 697
" 11. Lemur pusillus, fox-nosed maki, 697
" 12. Lemur macao, maki, . 697
" 13. Cynocephalus maimon, mandrill, 700
" 14. Cercopithecus diana, holoway, . 701
" 15. Hylobates agilis, agile gibbon, . 701

PLATE 118.

Fig. 1. Rhinocerus indicus, Indian rhinoceros, ... 641
" 2, 3. Cebus capucinus, capucin, . 699
" 4. Macacus cynomolgus, hare-
lipped monkey, . . 700
" 5. Cercopithecus ruber, patras, 701
" 6. Cercopithecus griseus, grey patras, 701
" 7. Macacus silenus, maned maca-
que, ... 700
" 8. Cynocephalus sphinx, baboon, . 700
" 9. Inuus ecaudatus, Barbary ape, . 700
" 10. Troglodytes niger, chimpanse, . 701
" 11. Pithecus satyrus, orang outang, . 701

ANTHROPOLOGY AND SURGERY

PLATE 119.

Figs. 1—9. Varieties of Mankind, . 714
" 10—12. Facial angles, . . . 714
Centre figure. Chart of the five races of Blumen-
bach.

GLOSSARY.

I. Kaukasische oder Weisse Race, Caucasian
or White Race.
II. Mongolische oder Gelbe Race, Mongolian or
Yellow Race.
III. Æthiopische oder Schwarze Race, Ethio-
pian or Black Race.
IV. Amerikanische oder Kupferfarbige Race,
American or Copper-colored Race.
V. Malayische oder Olivenfarbige Race, Malay
or Olive-colored Race.
F. 1 bis 4. Grundzüge (Typus) der Kaukasi-
schen Race, Figs. 1—4. Types of
the Caucasian Race.
Figur 5. Grundzüge der Mongolischen Race,
Fig. 5. Type of the Mongolian
Race.
Figur 6. Grundzüge der Æthiopischen Race,
Fig. 6. Type of the Ethiopian
Race.
F. 7, 8. Grundzüge der Kupferfarbigen Race,
Figs. 7, 8. Type of the Copper-
colored Race.
Figur 9. Grundzüge der Olivenfarbigen Race,
Fig. 9. Type of the Olive-colored
Race.

Afghanen, Afghans.
Algonkiren, Algonkins.
Araber, Arabs.
Azteken, Azteks.
Berbern, Berbers.
Birmanen, Birmans.
Bucharen, Bucharians.
Caffern, Caffres.
Californier, Californians.
Canadier, Canadians.
Caraiben, Caribbeans.
Celten, Celts.
Chaldäer, Chaldæans.
Chinesen, Chinese.
Cinbebassen, Cinbebasses.
Colombier, Colombians.
Eleuten, Aleutians.
Eskimos, Esquimaux.
Ethiopier, Ethiopians.
Fellatas, Fellatah.
Finnen, Finns.
Germanen, Germans.
Gothen. Goths.
Hindus, Hindoos.
Hottentotten, Hottentots.
Iberier, Iberians.
Jakuten, Yacoots.
Japanesen, Japanese.
Jukaghiren, Youkaghirs.
Kalmücken, Calmucks.
Kamtschadalen, Kamskadales.
Kaukasier, Caucasians.
Kirghisen, Kirghese.
Koriälen, Koreans.
Kosaken, Cossacks.
Kriks, Creek Indians.
Lappen, Laplanders.
Letten, Lethonians.
Madagassen, Madagassees.
Mandschus, Manchoos.
Mauren, Moors.
Mongolen, Mongols.
Neger, Negroes.
Negritos, Negritoes.
Neuseeländer, New Zealanders.
Osagen, Osages.
Osmanen, Osmanli.
Ostiaken, Ostiaks.
Patagonen, Patagonians.
Pelasger, Pelasgians.
Perser, Persians.
Samojeden, Samoeids.
Sius, Sioux Indians.
Slaven, Slavonians.
Soyten, Soyetes.
Tibetaner, Thibetans.
Tschucktschen, Tchoukches.
Tungusen, Tungus.
Wogulen, Voguls.

PLATE 120.

Figs. 1—21. Illustrating the psychological
relations of the brain (Phre-
nology), ... 825

PLATE 121.

Figs. 1—19. The bones of the head, . 719

PLATE 122.

Figs. 1—31. Anatomy of the bones, . 717

PLATE 123.

Figs. 1—50. Anatomy of the bones, . 717

PLATE 124.

Figs. 1—14. Anatomy of the ligaments, . 717
" 15—17. Anatomy of the muscles, . 750

PLATE 125.

Figs. 1—18. Anatomy of the ligaments, . 717
" 19, 20. Anatomy of the muscles, . 750

PLATE 126.

Figs. 1—19. Anatomy of the ligaments, . 717
" 20, 21. Anatomy of the muscles, . 750

PLATE 127.

Figs. 1—15. Anatomy of the muscles, . 750

PLATE 128.

Figs. 1—19. Anatomy of the muscles, . 750

PLATE 129.

Figs. 1—22. Anatomy of the fasciæ, . 752
" 23—26. Anatomy of the integuments, . 851
" 27—30. Organs of mastication and
deglutition, . . 890
" 31—38. Organs of respiration and
voice. . . . 882

PLATE 130.

Figs. 1—21. Anatomy of the organs of
digestion, . . . 889

PLATE 131.

Figs. 1—45. Anatomy of the eye, . . 867

PLATE 132.

Figs. 1—25. Anatomy of the ear, . . 859
" 26—45. Anatomy of the nose, . 856

PLATE 133.

Figs. 1—13. Anatomy of the vascular
system, ... 782

PLATE 134.

Figs. 1—13. Anatomy of the vascular system, ... 782

PLATE 135.

Figs. 1—17. Anatomy of the vascular system, ... 782

PLATE 136.

Figs. 1—16. Anatomy of the vascular system, ... 782

PLATE 137.

Figs. 1—21. Anatomy of the brain and
nerves, . . . 810

PLATE 138.

Figs. 1—14. Anatomy of the nerves, . 810

PLATE 139.

Figs. 1—35. Various surgical operations, . 909

PLATE 140.

Figs. 1—90. Various surgical instruments, 909

GEOGRAPHY AND PLANOGRAPHY

PLATE 1.

Physical map of Europe, ... 4

PLATE 2, 3.

Mountain and river systems of Central Europe, ... 5
See also Austria, 79 ; Prussia, 82 ; Germany, 84 ; Netherlands, 59.

PLATE 4.

Physical map of Asia, ... 10

PLATE 5.

Physical map of Africa, ... 13

PLATE 6.

Physical map of North America, . . 15

PLATE 7.

Physical map of South America, . . 15

PLATE 8.

I. Map of the world according to Hero-
dotus, ... 21
II. Map of the world according to Strabo, 23
III. " " " Ptole-
my, ... 23
IV. Map of the world known to the An-
cients, ... 21
V. Wind-chart of Aristotle, . . . 24
VI. " " Vitruvius, . . . 24

PLATE 9.

The kingdom of Alexander the Great, . 24

PLATE 10.

Roman Empire under Constantine the Great, 24

PLATE 11.

Europe in the time of Charlemagne, . . 32

PLATE 12.

Europe at the time of the Crusades, . . 35

PLATE 13.

Europe before the French Revolution of
1789, ... 42

PLATE 14.

Europe as it is at present, ... 48

PLATE 15, 16.

The railroads of Central Europe, . . 89

PLATE 17.

The Austrian Empire, . . . 79

PLATE 18.

Prussia, ... 82

PLATE 19.

Denmark, Sweden, and Norway, . 65, 67

PLATE 20.

Great Britain and Ireland, . . . 61

PLATE 21.

Spain and Portugal, . . . 50, 48

PLATE 22.

France, ... 53

PLATE 23.

Switzerland, ... 56

PLATE 24.

Italy, ... 75

PLATE 25.

Russia, ... 69

PLATE 26.

The Turkish Empire, . . 72, 94

PLATE 27.

Greece, ... 74

PLATE 28.

Asia, ... 93

PLATE 29.

Africa, ... 101

PLATE 30.

North America, ... 108

PLATE 31.

South America, ... 115

PLATE 32.

Australia, ... 19, 118

PLATE 33.

London, ... 123

PLATE 34.

Paris and environs, ... 123

PLATE 35.

Fortifications of Paris, . . . 123

PLATE 36.

Constantinople, ... 133

PLATE 37.

St. Petersburg, ... 135
Warsaw, ... 138

PLATE 38.

Berlin, ... 140

PLATE 39.

Vienna, ... 143

PLATE 40.

Lisbon, ... 148
Naples, ... 150

PLATE 41.

Rome, ... 152
Milan, ... 155

PLATE 42.

Madrid, ... 157
Saragossa, ... 159
Barcelona, ... 160

PLATE 43.

Copenhagen, ... 161
Stockholm, ... 162
Antwerp, ... 163
Amsterdam, ... 165

PLATE 44.

Leghorn, ... 167
Florence, ... 168
Ancona, ... 170
Modena, ... 171

GLOSSARY TO THE GEOGRAPHICAL MAPS.

Abasgia, Abkhas.
Abassien, Abassi (tribe in North Africa).
Abbitibes, Abbitibbe River.
Abdera, Adra.
Abrincate, Abrincafui.
Abyssinien, Abyssinia.
Acci, Guadix.
Achalziche, Akalzike.
Achen, Aix la Chapelle.
Acincum, Buda Pest.
Adagk, Island Adack.
Admiralitäts Is., Admiralty Islands.
Adrianopel, Adrianople.
Adriatisches Meer, Adriatic Sea.
Adulis, St. Gothard.
Ægadische In., the islands of Levanso, Favignana, and Maritimo (the ancient Ægades).
Ægäisches Meer, Archipelago.
Aegypten, Egypt.
Ægyptische Schöne wovon 18⅘ *a. d. Gr.*, Egyptian miles 18⅘ to a degree.
Ælana, Akaba.
Æmona, Laybach.
Æquat. d. ewigen Schnees, Equator of perpetual snow.
Æquatorgrenze d. Schneefalles, Equatorial boundary of snow.
Æquatorialgrenze d. europ. tropn. Getreides, Equatorial boundary of European tropical grain.
Æquatorialgr. des ewigen Schnees, Equatorial boundary of perpetual snow.
Æthiopien, Ethiopia.
Æthiopisches Meer, Ethiopian Sea.
Agrigentum, Girgenti.
Aguja Sp., Cape Aguya.
Akjerman, Akerman.
Alands In., Aland Islands.
Alanen, Alani.

Albanien, Albany.
Albaracin, Albarracin.
Albersche, Alberche River.
Albis, Elbe River.
Albufeira, Albufera.
Albufera See, Lake Albufera.
Alemannen, Alemanni.
Aleschki, Aleshki.
Aleuten Inseln, Aleutian Islands.
Alexandrien, Alexandria.
Algesiras, Al Gezira.
Algier, Algiers.
Alpen 1200 *t. mittlere Höhe*, Alps 1200 toises mean height.
Alpen Gebirge, the Alps.
Alpes Bastarnicæ, Lower Alps.
Alpes Rhætiæ, Rhætian Alps.
Alsen, Isle of Als.
Alt Californien, Upper California.
Alter Molo, Old pier.
Amassera, Amasserah.
Amboser Hochland, Ambose Highlands.
Amenis, Ameni Island.
Amiranten I., Amirante Islands.
Amisia, Ems River.
Ammonia, Hargiah.
Ancyra, Angora.
Andalusien, Andalusia.
Andamanen, Andaman Islands.
Andes von Peru, the Andes of Peru.
Andes von Quito, the Andes of Quito.
Andöe, Island of Andoen.
Andros mit Hafen, Andros with port.
Anemurium, Cape Anamour.
Angeln, Angli.
Anten, Antæ (Sarmatian tribe).
Antinoe, Enseneh.
Antwerpen, Antwerp.
Anurigrammum, Anurajapoera.
Aornus, Ohund.
Aosta Thal, Aosta Valley.
Apeliotes (Ost), Southeast trade-wind.
Apenninen Geb., the Apennines.
Apulien, Apulia.
Aquæ Sextiæ, Aix.
Aquitanien, Aquitania.
Arabien, Arabia.
Arabische Wüste, Arabian Desert.
Arab. Mb., Arabian Gulf.
Arabisches od. Persisches Meer, Arabian or Persian Sea.
Arachosia, S. E. Cabul.
Arachotus, Lora River.
Aral See, Aral Sea.
Aran, Karabagh.
Araxes, Aras River.
Arbela, Arbay.
Archangelsk, Archangel.
Archipel von Neu Britannia, Archipelago of New Britain.
Archipel der Niedrigen Inseln, Low Islands.
Archipelagus, Archipelago.
Ardennen, Ardennes.
Arelate, Arles.

Argolische In., Archipelago of Nauplia.
Argelis, Argellez.
Argentoratum, Strasbourg.
Argonnen Wald, the Argonne Forest.
Aria, Khorasan.
Aria See, Lake of Zarrah.
Ariaspæ, Ariaspes (inhabitants of Aria, in ancient Drangiana, in Persia).
Ariminum, Rimini.
Armenier, Armenians.
Armoricum, ancient Aquitania (S. W. France).
Arnheim, Arnhem.
Aroe, Patras.
Arsanus, Murad River.
Arsinoe, Suez.
Art. Magazin, Artillery Arsenal.
Aru In, Aroo Islands.
Arvernum, Auvergne.
Asiatisches Russland, Asiatic Russia.
Asiatisches Sarmatn., Asiatic Sarmatia.
Asow, Azov.
Asowsches Meer, Sea of Azov.
Assomtion, Asuncion.
Assyrn., Assyria.
Asta, Asti.
Asturica, Astorga.
Asturien, Asturias.
Athabasca S., Lake Athapescow.
Athen, Athens.
Athenæ, Athens.
Athribis, Tel Atrib.
Atlantischer Ocean, Atlantic Ocean.
Atschin, Acheen.
Attalia, Adalia.
Attici, Inhab. of Attica.
Augila, Augela.
Aug. Turinorum, Turin.
Aug. Vindelicorum, Augsburg.
Augustodunum, Autun.
Aulona, Valona.
Auster (Süd), South Wind.
Australien, Australia.
Austral. Busen, Gulf of Australia.
Austrasien, Empire of Chlodwig.
Avalites, Zeyla.
Avalitischer G., Bay of Zeyla.
Aventicum, Avenche.
Avernum, Lake Averno.
Azania, Ajan.
Azorische Inseln, Portugiesisch, the Azores, Portuguese.
Azowsches Meer, Sea of Azov.

B. von Athen od. v. Ægina, Bay of Athens or of Ægina.
B. von Nauplia od. v. Argos, Bay of Nauplia or of Argos.
Babadagh, Baba Dag.
Bagistanus, Beesitoon.
Bagous Geb., Bagous Mountains.
Bahama Inseln, Bahama Islands.
Bai u. Dorf Catalan, Bay and village of Catalan.
Baiern, Bavaria.
Baikal S. u. Geb., Baikal Lake and Mountains.

Baireuth, Bayreuth.
Bairischer Wd., Bavarian Forest.
Baktrien, Bactriana.
Balearen, Balearic Islands.
Baleares, Balearic Islands.
Balearischer Canal, Balearic Channel.
Balkan Geb., Balkan Mountains.
Balkasch S., Lake Balkash.
Baltica, Sweden.
Banasa, Meheduma.
Banater Geb., Banat Mountains.
Banater Milit. Grenze, Military frontier of the Banat.
Banks Land, Banks' Island.
Barcelonnetti, Barceloneta.
Barcino, Barcelona.
Baschkiren, Bashkirs.
Bass Strasse, Bass's Strait.
Bassistis, Bashnia.
Baumwolle, Cotton.
Baumwolle u. Reis, Cotton and Rice.
Bayrische Alpen, Bavarian Alps.
Bayrisches Hochland, Bavarian Highlands.
Behrings Meer, Behring's Strait.
Behrings Meer od. Meer von Kamtschatka, Behring's Strait or Kamtschatkian Sea.
Belgien, Belgium.
Belice, Belici River.
Belochrobaten, Belochrobati (Slavonian tribe).
Belzoi See, Lake Belzoi.
Berenike, Bengazi.
Berg Andros, Mount Andros.
Berkley Sund, Berkeley Sound.
Bermudas od. Sommer I., Bermudas or Somers Islands.
Berner Alpen, Bernese Alps.
Bernstein Küste, Amber Coast.
Bessarabien, Bessarabia.
Bieler S., Lake of Biel.
Bjelos See, Lake Biellos.
Biled-ul-gerid, od. Dattelland, Biled-ul-gerid, or Land of Dates.
Biscayscher Meerbusen, Bay of Biscay.
Bithynien, Bithynium.
Blaue Bge., Blue Mountains.
Bodensee, Lake of Constance.
Böhmische Höhe, Bohemian Highlands.
Böhmischer Kessel, Bohemian Basin.
Bogen Indianer, Strongbow Indians (tribe of the Chippeways).
Bolzoi, oder Grosser See, Bolzoi or Large Lake.
Boreas (Nord), North Wind.
Borysthenes, Pripet River.
Borysthenes (Danapris), Dniepr River.
Bosnien, Bosna.
Bostra, Boszra.
Bothnischer Busen, Gulf of Botnia.
Bracara, Braga.
Brasilien, Brazil.
Brasilische Gebirge, Brazil Mountains.
Brasilische Strömung, Brazil Current.
Brasilisches Guyana, Brazil Guyana.
Braunschweig, Brunswick.
Brede Bugt, Bay of Brede.
Brienzer S., Lake of Brienz.

Brigantium, Briançon.
Britannien, Gr. Britain.
Britisches Guyana, British Guyana.
Brivates Haf, Bay of Brest.
Brüssel, Brussels.
Brundisium, Brindisi.
Brundusium, Brindisi.
Bucephala, Ihylum.
Bucharest, Bukarest.
Bucharien, Bokhara.
Buchweitzen, Buckwheat.
Bucinarische In. Buccinarian Islands.
Bulgaren, Bulgari (tribe on the lower Danube).
Burdigala, Bordeaux.
Burgunder, Burgundians.
Busen von Bengalien, Bay of Bengal.
Busen von Cadix, Bay of Cadiz.
Busen Carpentaria, Bay of Carpentaria.
Busen v. Danzig, Bay of Dantzig.
Busen von Lepanto oder von Korinth, Gulf of Lepanto or of Corinth.
Busen v. Lion, Gulf of Lyons.
Busen v. Lübeck, Bay of Lubeck.
Busen von Panama, Bay of Panama.
Busen von Taranto, Gulf of Taranto.
Busen von Tehuantepec, Gulf of Tehuantepec.
Busen von Triest, Gulf of Trieste.
Busen von Venedig, Bay of Venice.
Byblos, Djebail.
Byzacium, Tunis.
Byzant., Constantinople.

C. d. guten Hoffnung, Cape of Good Hope.
C. Horner Strömung, Cape Horn Current.
Cabillonus, Chalons.
Cæsar Augusta, Saragossa.
Cætobriga, Setobal.
Cajeta, Gaeta.
Caledonien, Caledonia.
Caledonischer Canal, Caledonian Canal.
Calvadosfelsen, Calvados Rocks.
Canal oder La Manche, the British Channel.
Canal u. Strömung v. Mozambique, Channel and current of Mozambique.
Canal von Yucatan, Channel of Yucatan.
Canarische Inseln, Canary Islands.
Candriaces, Nugor River.
Canopus, Aboukir.
Cantabrisches Geb. 600 *t.,* Santillanos Mountains 600 toises.
Cantal G., Cantal Mountains.
Cap Strom, Cape current.
Cap u. Ins. Breton, Cape and Island of Breton.
Cappadocien, Cappadocia.
Capsa, Wataras.
Capstadt, Cape Town.
Capverdische Inseln, Cape Verde Islands.
Caraibisches Meer, Caribbean Sea.
Caralis, Cagliari.
Carenisches Gebirge, Sutherland Highlands.
Carmania, Kerman.
Carpathus, Scarpanto.
Carteja, Ocana.
Carthaginiensis Sinus, Gulf of Tunis.
Carthago, Carthage.

Carthago nova, Cartagena.
Casp. Engpässe, Caspian or Caucasian passes.
Caspisches Meer, Caspian Sea.
Caspisch. See liegt 33 *t. unter d. Niveau d. Oceans,* Caspian Sea, lies 33 toises lower than the level of the ocean.
Caspische See, Caspian Sea.
Cassiterides Ins., Scilly Islands.
Catalonien, Catalonia.
Celænæ, Dingla.
Cerasus, Keresoun.
Cevennen, Cevennes Mountains.
Chalifat der Abassiden, Caliphate of the Abassides.
Charolais Geb. Charolles Mountains.
Chemnis, Ekhmin.
Cherson, Kherson.
Chersonesus, Cape Razatin.
Cheviot Gebirge, Cheviot Hills.
Chile, Chili.
China Wälder, Bathbark Forests.
Chinesisches Meer, Chinese Sea.
Chios, Scio.
Choco Kette, Choco Mountain Chain.
Chorasmia See, Lake Kharasm.
Chorasmii, Kharasm.
Churhessen, Electoral Hesse.
Cibalis, Palanha.
Cilicia, Itshili ; *Die Cilicischen Thore,* the Passes of Itshili.
Cimbrische Halb I., Cimbrian Peninsula (Jutland).
Clearwater See, Clearwater Lake.
Cnossus, Macritichos.
Colchis, Mingrelia.
Colchischer G., Gulf of Mingrelia.
Colonia, Cologne.
Comana, Bostan.
Comer S., Lake of Como.
Comum, Como.
Conimbriga, Coimbra.
Constantinopel, Constantinople.
Constantinopolis, Constantinople.
Constanz, Constance.
Cooks Strasse, Cook's Strait.
Cophas, Guadel.
Cophes, Ghizni River.
Coptos, Ghouft.
Corcyra, Corfu.
Cordofan, Kordofan.
Corduba, Cordova.
Corps unter Hephæstion, Corps under Hephæstion.
Croatien, Croatia.
Croatische Militair Grenze, Croatian military frontier.
Curene, Kuren.
Curland, Courland.
Cydonia, Canea.
Cynopolis, Nesle Sheik Hassan.
Cypern, Cyprus.
Cyrene, West Barca.
Cyropolis, Enzellee.
Cyrus, Politica.
Cythere, Citria.
Cyzicus, Kyzik.

Dacia, Hungary and Transylvania.
Daenemark, Denmark.
Dakien, Dacia (Hungary).
Dalmatien, Dalmatia.
Dampfschiffe von Triest der Œstn. Lloyd Ges., Steamers of the Austrian Lloyd Company from Trieste.
Dänen, Danes.
Danubius, Danube River.
Danzig, Dantzig.
Daphne, Daia.
Dardanellen Schlösser, Palaces at the Dardanelles.
Dardanellen Str., Dardanelles.
Darnis, Derna.
Das Alpen Gebirge, the Alps.
Das Po Thal, the Po Valley.
Daurisches Alpenland, the Da Oural Alps (branch of the Oural Mountains).
Davis Strasse, Davis's Strait.
Delphi, Castri.
Dembo Hochland, Dembo Highlands.
D'Entrecasteaux Spitze, Point d'Entrecasteaux.
Der Normannen Reiche, the Norman Empires.
Der Spiegel des todten Meeres liegt 220 *t. tiefer als der Ocean,* the surface of the Dead Sea lies 220 toises below the level of the ocean.
Der Wash, the Wash.
Dergh See, Lake Derg.
Dertosa, Tortosa.
Deutsche Meilen 15 *auf den Grad,* German miles 15 to the degree.
Deutsche unter Kaiser Friedrich II., Germans under Emperor Frederick II.
Deutsches Kaiserreich, German Empire.
Deva, Ayas.
Die Aleuten od. Catharinas Archipel, the Aleutian Islands or Catharine's Archipelago.
Die Aleutischen Inseln, the Aleutian Islands.
Die Azoren, the Azores.
Die bekannte Welt des Alterthums, the world known to the Ancients.
Die Carolinen, the Caroline Islands.
Die 3 *Oder Mündn.,* the three mouths of the Oder.
Die Eols Grotten, the Grottoes of Æolus.
Die grosse osteuropäische Ebene in welcher kein Punkt die Höhe von 180 *t. erreicht,* the large East-European plain, in which no point reaches the height of 180 toises.
Die Nord See oder das deutsche Meer, the North Sea or the German Sea.
Die Ostsee, oder das Baltische Meer, the Baltic.
Die Philippinen, the Philippine Islands.
Die Schweiz, Switzerland.
Die sieben Kuhfirsten, the Seven Cowridges.
Diemtiger Th., Diemtig Valley.
Dinarisches Alpen Gebirg, Dinarian Alps (on the lower Danube).
Dio Adelphi (Die 2 *Brüder),* Dio Adelphi (The Two Brothers).
Dioscorides I., Island of Socotra.
Dioscurias, Iskuria.

District diesseits der Donau, District north of the Danube.

District diesseits der Theiss, District west of the Theiss.

District jenseits der Donau, District beyond the Danube.

District jenseits der Theiss, District beyond (east of) the Theiss.

Dobrudscher, Dobrodje.

Donau, Danube.

Donaumündungen, Mouths of the Danube.

Donauwörth, Donauwerth.

Donische Kosaken, Cossacks of the Don.

Dora Baltea, Doria Baltea River.

Drapsaea, Bamian.

Drontheim, Trondheim.

Dschebil el Kamar od. Mond Geb., Gebel Komri, or Mountains of the Moon.

Düna, Dvina River.

Dünkirchen, Dunkirk.

Durius, Douro River.

Durovernum, Canterbury.

Eblana, Dublin.

Eboracum, York.

Ebro Mündung, Mouth of the Ebro.

Ebusus, Iviza.

Eisenbahnen, Railroads.

Eisenbahnkarte von Mitteleuropa, Railroad chart of Central Europe.

Eismeer, Arctic Ocean.

Eisstarre Sand u. Morast Fläche, Frozen Sand and Swamp Plain.

Elusa, Eauze.

Emerita Aug., Merida.

Emirat v. Cordova, Emirate of Cordova.

Enara See, Lake Enara.

Engländer unter Richard Löwenherz, the English under Richard Cœur de Lion.

Engl. Colonien am Schwanflusse, K. Georg's Sund und N. S. Wales, English Colonies on Swan River, King George's Sound, and New South Wales.

Englische Meilen 69 22/100 auf den Grad, English miles, 69 22/100 to the degree.

Engpass v. Kaipha, Pass of Kaipha.

Ephesus, Ayasaluk.

Epidaurus, Ragusa Vecchia.

Epirus, Albania.

Eregli, Erekli.

Erklärung der Zahlen, Explanation of the figures.

Erne See, Erne Loch.

Erymanthus, Mount Olonos.

Eskimos, Esquimaux.

Esthland, Esthonia.

Euböa, Negropont.

Euphrat, Euphrates.

Europa vor der Französischen Revolution, Europe before the French Revolution.

Europa zur Zeit der Kreuzzüge, Europe during the Crusades.

Europa zur Zeit Karls des Grossen, Europe at the time of Charlemagne.

Europäisch Sarmatien, European Sarmatia.

Europäische Besitzungen in Nord Guinea, European possessions in North Guinea.

Europäisches Russland, European Russia.

Europäisches Scythien, European Scythia.

Fadejewski, Fadevskoi.

Fær.Œer, Faro Islands.

Falklands Ins., Falkland Islands.

Falsche Bai, Bay of Falso.

Faltschi, Faltsi.

Fan Œ., Fano I.

Favonius (West), West Wind (Zephyr).

Feuerland, Terra del Fuego.

Finnischer Busen, Gulf of Finland.

Fischereien von Agoutinitza, Fisheries of Agoutinitza.

Fittre See, Bahr Fittre.

Flachs u. Hanf, Flax and Hemp.

Flandern, Flanders.

Flavia Cäsariensis, Central England.

Flaviobriga, Bilbao.

Flavionavia, Laviana.

Flevus, Flevo, Zuyder Zee.

Florentia, Florence.

Florenz, Florence.

Franken, Franconia.

Frankfurt, Frankfort.

Fränkisches Italien, Frankish Italy.

Fränkisches Plateau, Franconian plateau.

Frankreich, France.

Französ. Guyana, French Guyana.

Französische Lieues 25 auf den Grad, French leagues 25 to the degree.

Franzosen unter Philipp August, The French under Philip Augustus.

Franzosen unter Ludwig IX., The French under Louis IX.

Freiburg, Freeburg.

Freie Indianer, Free Indians.

Freundschafts oder Tonga In., Friendly or Tonga Islands.

Friedens Fl., Peace River.

Frobischer Str., Frobisher's Strait.

Fuchs Ins., Fox Islands.

Fünen, Fyen.

Fuglæ, Bird Island.

Fürstm. Benevent, Principality of Benevento.

Fürstenthum Neuenburg, Principality of Neuenburg.

Gabæ, Chavos.

Gades, Cadiz.

Gaditanum, Gibraltar.

Galætia, Anadolia.

Galicien, Galicia.

Galizien, Galicia.

Gallien, Gallia (France).

Gallische Wegestunden wovon 50 auf den Grad, Gallic miles 50 to the degree.

Gangischer oder Indischer Golf, Bay of Bengal.

Garamantes, Fezzaneers and Tibboo (tribe).

Garda See, Lake of Garda.

Gaugamela, Kamalis.

Gaulos, Island of Goza.

Geb. v. Granada, Granada Mountains.

Gebirge von Auvergne, Mountains of Auvergne.

Gedros, Mekran.

Gelbes Meer, Yellow Sea.

Genf, Geneva.

Genfer See, Lake of Geneva.

Gent, Ghent.

Genua, Genoa.

Geographen B., Geographer's Bay.

Geogr. Meilen 15 auf den Grad, Geographical miles 15 to the degree.

Gepiden, Gepidæ (tribe).

Germanen, Germans.

Germanien, Germany.

Germanische Meer, North Sea.

Germanische Tiefebene, German Low Plain.

Gerste, Barley.

Gerste, Hafer, Roggen, Barley, Oats, Rye.

Gerste, Roggen, Kartoffeln und Buchweitzen, Barley, Rye, Potatoes, and Buckwheat.

Gesellschafts In., Society Islands.

Gesoriacum, Boulogne.

Geten, Getæ (tribe).

Gletscher, Glacier.

Glückliches Arabien, Arabia Felix.

Gogana, Congoon.

Göksschai See, Lake Gokshai.

Goldener Chersonesus, Golden Khersonesus (Malaya).

Gordium, Sarilar.

Gorsunia, Atchicola.

Gothen, Goths.

Gr. Bären See, Great Bear Lake.

Gr. Minsh oder Caledonisches Meer, Great Minsh or Caledonian Sea.

Gr. Sclaven S., Great Slave Lake.

Grampian Gebirge, Grampian Mountains.

Graubündner Alpen, Grison Alps.

Griechenland, Greece.

Griechisches Italien, Greek Italy.

Grönland, Greenland.

Gross Britannien und Ireland, Great Britain and Ireland.

Gross Phrygia, Phrygia Major.

Gross Russland, Great Russia.

Grosse Antillen, the larger Antilles (West India Islands).

Grosse Eskimos, Great Esquimaux.

Grosser Atlas, Mount Atlas.

Grosser oder Stiller Ocean, Pacific Ocean.

Grossherz. Hessen, Grand Duchy of Hesse.

Grüne Berge, Green Mountains.

Grünes Vorgebirge, Cape Verde.

Gürtel des Getreides, Zone of the grains.

Gürtel ohne Cultur, Zone without cultivation.

Guräus, Kamah River.

H. I. or *Halbinsel* stands for " Peninsula" before the respective names.

Haag, the Hague.

Habesch, Habesh.

Hadrianopolis, Adrianople.

Hæmus, Balkan Mountains.

Haf. v. or *Hafen von* stands for "Port of" before the respective names.

Hafer, Oats.

Hafer u. Gerste, Oats and Barley.

Hafer u. Weitzen, Oats and Wheat.

Halbinsel Methana, Peninsula of Dara (Methana).

Halicarnassus, Boodroom.

Haliez oder Galizien, Galicia.

Han Hai (Südl. Meer), South Sea.

Harz Gb., Harz Mountains.

Hasen Ind., Hare Indians.

Haupt Æquatorial Strömung, Principal equatorial current.

Haupstadt, Capital.

Hebräische Stadien wovon 750 a. d. Gr., Hebrew stadia 750 to the degree.

Hebriden oder Western Inseln, Hebrides or Western Islands.

Hecatompylos, Danghan.

Hedschas, Hedjas.

Heiliges Vgb., Promontorium Sacrum.

Heliopolis, Baalbec.

Hellas, Greece.

Hellespontus, Dardanelles.

Helsingör, Elsinore.

Heniochi, Tribe in Armenia.

Hermopolis, Eshmounein.

Hermunduren, Hermunduri (tribe in central Germany).

Herodots Erdtafel, Herodotus's Map of the World.

Heruler, Heruli (tribe in North Germany).

Herzogl. Sächsische Länder, Saxon Duchies.

Herzogthum, Duchy.

Hibernien, Hibernia.

Hinter Rhein, Hind Rhine (one of the rivulets tributary to the Rhine).

Hippo Regius, Bona.

Hispalis, Seville.

Hispanien, Spain.

Hoch Alp, High Alp.

Hoch Sudan, Soudah Mountains.

Hochland von Africa, Highlands of Africa.

Hohe Tatarei, Tartar Highlands.

Hoher Atlas, Mount Atlas.

Hügelgruppe v. Sandomir, Group of Hills of Sandomir.

Hunds Ribben Ind, Dogrib Indians.

Hunigaren oder Ungrier, Hungarians.

Hydruotes, Ravee River.

Hypanis, Kuban River.

Hyphasis, Beyah River.

Hyrcania, Gyrgaun.

Hyrkanisch. Meer, Caspian Sea.

I., Ia., Ins., or *Insel* stands for "Island" before the respective names.

I. Helgoland, Island of Heligoland.

I. Kângurah, Kangaroo Island.

I. u. Stadt Cayenne, Island and Town of Cayenne.

Jacobs Thal, Jacob's Valley.

Jadera, Zarah.

Japanisches Meer, Sea of Japan.

Jasygien, Jassygia.

Jaxartes, Sihon River.

Jazygen (Sarmaten), Sarmatians.

Ibenes, Ebro River.

Iberia, Georgia.
Ichthyophagen, Fish-eaters.
Iconium, Konia.
Jenseits d. Ganges, Beyond the Ganges.
Jenseits d. Imaus, Beyond the Altai.
Jernis, Dunkerrin.
Illyricum, Illyria.
Illyrien, Illyria.
Im Sommer 15°, In the summer 66 degrees F.
Im Winter 5°, In the winter 43 degrees F.
Imandra See, Lake Imandra.
Imaus Geb., Altai Mountains.
Indischer Ocean, Indian Ocean.
Indsche Burun, Cape Indjeh.
Indus Mündn., Mouths of the Indus.
Ins. unter d. Winde, Caribbean Islands.
Ins. d. günen Vorgebirges, Cape Verde Islands
Jomanes, Jumna River.
Jonische Inseln, Ionian Islands.
Joppe, Yaffa.
Joux See, Lake Joux.
Ipsus, Ipsilihissar.
Irgis, Irghiz River.
Irische See, Irish Sea.
Irland, Ireland.
Irtisch, Irtish River.
Is, Hit.
Isca, Exe River.
Island, Iceland.
Issedones, Mongolian tribe.
Ister (Donau), Danube.
Ister Mündn., Mouths of the Danube.
Italien, Italy.
Jülich, Juliers.
Jüten, Jutlanders.
Juliobriga, Reynosa.
Julische Alpen, Carnic or Julian Alps.
Jura Geb., Jura Mountains.
Jura Sund, Jura Sound.
Juvavia, Saltzburg.

K. Charlotte S., Queen Charlotte's Sound.
Kärnthen, Carinthia.
Kaiser Canal, Emperor's Canal.
Kaiserthum Œsterreich, Empire of Austria.
Kalmüken, Calmucks.
Kamische Bulgaren, Kama Bulgarians.
Kanäle, Canals.
Kanal von Bristol, Bristol Channel.
Kaptschak, Cabjak (tribe in Bokhara).
Karafta oder Sachalin, Caraphta or Sachalin.
Karazubazar, Kara Soo.
Karchedon, Carthage.
Karischer B., Bay of Caria.
Karmanien, Kerman.
Karolinen, Caroline Islands.
Karpathen 2000 *t. mittl. Höhe,* Carpathian Mountains 2000 toises mean height.
Karpathen Geb., Carpathian Mountains.
Karpathisches Waldgebirge, Carpathian Forest.
Kartagena, Cartagena.
Karthago, Carthage.
Kartoffeln u. Hafer, Potatoes and Oats.
Kartoffeln u. Buchweitzen, Potatoes and Buckwheat.

Kaspisches Meer, Caspian Sea.
Kattegat, Cattegat.
Kaukasien, Caucasia.
Kaukasus Gebirge, Caucasian Mountains.
Kaukasische Steppe, Caucasian Steppes.
Keine Bäume ab. Graswuchs, No trees but grass.
Kelten, Celts.
Kemi See, Lake Kemin.
Kgn. Charlotte I., Queen Charlotte's Island.
Kimbrischer Cherson, Cimbrian Chersonesus (Jutland).
Kjölen Gebirge, Koelen Mountains.
Kirchenstaat, Papal States.
Kirgisen Horde, Kirghis Horde.
Kirghisen Steppe, Kirghis Steppes.
Kizil Ermak, Kizil Irmak River.
Kl. Antillen, Little Antilles (Caribbean Islands).
Kl. Karpathen, Little Carpathians.
Kl. Kumanien, Kis Kunsag.
Klein Phrygia, Phrygia Minor.
Klein Russland, Little Russia (Russian Province).
Kleinasien, Asia Minor.
Kleine Kirgisen Horde, Little Kirghis Horde.
Koblenz, Coblentz.
Köln, Cologne.
Kön. Georg Sund, King George's Sound.
König. Georg's I., King George's Islands.
Königin Charlotte Sund, Queen Charlotte's Sound.
Königreich stands for "kingdom" before the respective names.
Konäguen, Tribe of Esquimaux.
Kong Gebirge, Mountains of Kong.
Kopenhagen, Copenhagen.
Kosaken, Cossacks.
Krakau, Cracow.
Krym, Crimea.
Kuba, Cuba.
Kupfer Ind., Copper Indians.

L. I. Sund, Long Island Sound.
Ladoga See, Lake Ladoga.
Lakeneig, Lakeneigh.
Laminium, Alambra.
Lamose, Lamusa River.
Lampsacus, Lamsaki.
Lanai, Tribe in North Germany.
Lancerote, Lancerota Island.
Land der Finnen, Land of the Finns.
Land der kleinen Eskimos, Land of the dwarf Esquimaux.
Larice, Lack.
Lauriacum, Lorch.
Lausitzer Gebirg, Lusatian Mountains.
Leba See, Lake Leba.
Leman S., Lake Leman.
Leptis, Lebida.
Lerdalsöer, Lerdals Islands.
Lesbos, Mytilene.
Lessöewerk, Lessoe forge.
Leucas, Amaxiki.
Leuce, Island of Adasi.
Ljæchen, Bohemians.
Libyen, Africa.
Libysche Wüste, Libyan Desert.

Lieukieu In., Loo Choo Islands.
Ligeris, Loire River.
Liguria, Genoa.
Ligurisches Meer, Gulf of Genoa.
Likeio In., Loo Choo Islands.
Lilybæum, Boe.
Lindum, Lincoln.
Liptauer Alp, Liptau Alps.
Lissus, Allessio.
Lithauer, Lithuania.
Litus Saxonum, Coast of Sussex.
Litwanen, Lithuania.
Livadien, Livadia.
Liviner Thal, Livin Valley.
Livland, Livonia.
Livorno, Leghorn.
Lixus, Luccos River.
Loja, Loxa.
Lombardei, Lombardy.
Lomond S., Lake Lomond.
Londinum, London.
Longobarden, Longobardi (Lombards).
Lucentum, Alicante.
Luceria, Lucera.
Lüneburger Heide, Luneburg Heath.
Lüttich, Liège.
Lugdunensis, North West France.
Lugdunum, Leyden.
Lugovallum, Carlisle.
Lugumkloster, Lugum Convent.
Lulea See, Lake Lulea.
Lumnitz B., Mount Lomnitz.
Lusitania, Portugal.
Lutitschen, Luititsi or Wilzi (Tribe in North Germany).
Luzern, Lucerne.
Lycaonia, N. W. Karamania.
Lyon, Lyons.
Lystra, Illisera.

Maas, Meuse River.
Maasstäbe, Scales.
Macedonien, Macedonia.
Mackenzie In., Mackenzie's Islands.
Macquarie In., Macquarie's Island.
Madgyaren, Magyars.
Mähren, Moravia.
Mährische Höhe, Moravian Highlands.
Mælar See, Lake Mælar.
Maeotis See, Sea of Azov.
Magelhaens Strasse, Straits of Magallan.
Mahadia, Mahedia.
Mahrah, Mahran.
Mailand, Milan.
Mainz, Mayence, Maynz.
Mais und Weitzen, Indian Corn and **Wheat.**
Makarjew, Makariv.
Mal Ström, Malstrom.
Malaca, Malacca.
Malmö, Malmo.
Malmysch, Malmish.
Malouinen, Falkland Islands.
Mandeln, Almonds.
Mandschurei, Manchooria.
Manytsch, Manich River.

Maraniten, Maranites, tribe in Arabia Felix.
Marcomannen, Marcomanni, tribe in S. E. Germany.
Mare Adriaticum, Adriatic Sea.
Mare Caspium, Caspian Sea.
Mare Erythræum (Indisches Meer), Indian Ocean.
Mare Hyrcanum oder Casplum, Caspian Sea.
Mare Internum (Mittelländisches Meer), Mediterranean Sea.
Marea, El Khreit.
Margaret In., Margaret's Island.
Margus, Murghab River.
Marianen od. Ladronen, Marian Islands.
Marinestunden 25 *auf den Grad,* Marine leagues 25 to the degree.
Marisus, Maros River.
Marmara Meer, Sea of Marmora.
Marschall Inseln, Mulgrave Islands.
Marseille, Marseilles.
Martyropolis, Meia Farekin.
Mascarenen Inseln, Mascarenhas Islands (Mauritius, Bourbon, &c.).
Massaga, Massa.
Massilia, Marseilles.
Mater, Matter.
Mauritania, Algiers.
Mauritanien, Algiers.
Maxima Cæsariensis, Northern England.
Mb. v. Issus (Sinus Issilicus), Bay of Iskenderoon.
Meder, Medes (nation).
Mediolanum, Milan.
Medus, Abkuren River.
Meer Alpen, Maritime Alps.
Meer von Ochotsh, Sea of Okotsk.
Meer von Tarrakai, Gulf of Tartary.
Meerb. v. Californien, Gulf of California.
Meerb. v. Sues, Gulf of Suez.
Meerbusen von Mexico, Gulf of Mexico.
Meiningen, Meinungen.
Melgig Sumpf, Melgig Swamp.
Melitene, Malatia.
Memel od. Niemen, Meman River.
Memel Niederung, Tilsit Lowlands.
Memnis, Korkor Baba.
Memphis, Mangel Mousa, or Mit Raheni.
Meninx, Jerba Island.
Mergui In., Mergue Archipelago.
Meroe, Gibbainy.
Mesagna, Mesagne.
Mesembria, Missivri.
Mesopotamia, Al Gezira.
Messana, Messina.
Mettis, Metz.
Mexicanische Küstenströmung, Mexican Coast Current.
Miletus, Palatia.
Militär Colonien, Military Colonies.
Militair Grenze, Military Boundary.
Minius, Minho River.
Miö See, Lake Miœ.
Mioritz See, Lake Mioritz.
Mississippi Mündungen, Mouths of the Mississippi.
Mittelländisches Meer, Mediterranean Sea.

Mittlere Kirgisen Horde, Middle Kirghis Horde.
Mittlere Temperatur nach Celsius, Mean temperature according to Celsius.
Mittlere Temperatur nach Reaumur, Mean temperature according to Reaumur.
Mogontiacum, Mayntz.
Molukken, Molucca Islands.
Molukken Str., Molucca Passage.
Mond Gebirg, Mountains of the Moon.
Mongolei, Mongolia.
Monreale, Monreal.
Montagnes Noires, Black Mountains (Black Forest).
Mordwinen, Mordwines (tribe in Asiatic Russia).
Moreton C. u. B., Moreton Cape and Bay.
Moscha, Morebat.
Mosel, Moselle River.
Moskenasö, Mosken Island.
Moskau, Moscow.
Moskwa, Moskow.
Mosyneoci (tribe on the Black Sea).
Mozyr, Mozir.
Mühlhausen, Mulhouse.
München, Munich.
Mündung des Amazonen Stroms, Mouth of the Amazon River.
Mündung der Elbe, Mouth of the Elbe.
Mündung des Tajo, Mouth of the Tagus.
Murray Busen, Murray Firth.
Muthmassliche Grenze der den Alten bekannten Binnenländer von Afrika nach den Geographen Walkenaer und Gosselin, Probable boundary of the African inland known to the Ancients according to the geographers Walkenaer and Gosselin.
Mutina, Modena.

N. Schottl., North Scotland.
N. W. Ausflüsse des Æquatorial Stroms, Northwest termination of the Equatorial Current.
Nabathæer, Nabathæi (nation in Arabia).
Nadel Banck, Cape Agulhas.
Naissus, Nissa.
Namadus, Nerbuddah River.
Napeta, Mograt.
Narbona, Narbonne.
Narbonensis, Narbonne.
Nasamonen, Nasamones (tribe in West Barca).
Natal Küste, Natal Coast.
Navusa mit Hafer, Nausa, with port.
Nazareth Bank und Ins., Nazaret Bank and Island.
Neagh S., Lake Neagh.
Neapel (Neapolis), Naples.
Nelson Canal, Nelson Channel.
Nemausus, Nismes.
Nerbudda, Nerbuddah River.
Neu stands for "New" before the respective names.
Neu Californien, New California.
Neu Georgien, New Georgia.
Neu Helvetien, New Helvetia.
Neu Karthago, New Carthage.
Neu Scotia, Nova Scotia.
Neu Sibirien, New Siberia.

Neue Hebriden, New Hebrides.
Neue Saline, New Saltwork.
Neuenburg, Neufchatel.
Neuenburger S., Lake of Neufchatel.
Neustrien, Neustria (the part of France lying between the Meuse, Loire, and the Atlantic Ocean).
Nicasia, Island of Karos.
Nicobaren, Nicobar Islands.
Nicomedia, Izmid.
Nieder Canada, Lower Canada.
Nieder Ungarische Ebene, Lower Hungarian Plain.
Niederl. Guyana, Dutch Guyana.
Niederlande, Netherlands.
Niger, Niger River.
Nil, Nile River.
Nil Mündungen, Mouths of the Nile
Nilus, Nile River.
Nîmes, Nismes.
Niphates Geb., Sepan Mountains.
Nizza, Nice.
Norba Cæsaria, Alcantara.
Nördlicher Oceanus, Arctic Ocean.
Nördlicher Polarkreis, Arctic Circle.
Nördlicher Wolga Rücken, Northern Volga Ridge.
Nördliches Eismeer, Arctic Ocean.
Nord stands for "North" before the respective names.
Nord Afrikanische Strömung, North African Current.
Nord Albinger, North Albingians (tribe in Holstein).
Nord Georgien, North Georgia.
Nord Georgien I., North Georgia Island.
Nord See, North Sea.
Noricum, Styria, Salzburg, &c.
Norische Alpen, Noric Alps.
Normanische Inseln, Normandy Islands (Guernsey, Jersey, Alderney, Sark).
Northlined S., Northlined Lake.
Norwegen, Norway.
Notium Vgb., Mizen Head.
Nuba See, Nuba Lake.
Nuba Sumpf, Nuba Swamp.
Nubier, Nubians (tribe).
Nubische Wüste, Nubian Desert.
Numidien, Numidia (East Algiers).
Nursa, Norcia.
Nymegen, Nimegue.

Obdorisches Gebirge, Obdorsk Mountains (Northern extremity of the Oural Ms).
Ober See, Lake Superior.
Obi, Oby Island.
Obotriten, Obotrites (Vandal tribe in North Germany).
Oceanus Atlanticus, Atlantic Ocean.
Oceanus Germanicus, North Sea.
Ochus See, mit dem Kaspisches Meere früher wahrscheinlich zusammenhängend, Ochus Sea (Aral Sea), probably formerly connected with the Caspian Sea.
Odessus, Odessa.

Odyssus, Odessa.
Œ. L. v. Ferro, East longitude from the Island of Ferro.
Œ. L. v. Paris, East longitude from Paris.
Œca, Tripoli.
Œlbäume, Olive trees.
Œsterreich, Austria.
Œsterreichische Alpen, Austrian Alps.
Œsterreichische Landestheile, Austrian dependencies.
Œstl. Gats, Eastern Ghauts.
Œstliche Länge von Ferro, East longitude from the Island of Ferro.
Œstliche Länge von Paris, East longitude from Paris
Offene B., Open Bay.
Olisibon (Olisipo), Lisbon.
Olite, Olitte.
Olivenza, Olivenca.
Olympia, Miracca.
Olympische Stadien wovon 600 a. d. Grad, Olympic stadia, 600 to the degree.
Onega See, Onega Lake.
Ophiusa, Island of Formentera.
Orange od. Gariep, Orange or Gariep River.
Orangen, Oranges.
Orbelus, Mt. Gliubotin.
Orchoe, Bassora.
Oregon oder Felsen Gebirge, Rocky Mountains.
Oregon od. Columbia, Columbia River.
Orinoco Münd., Mouth of the Orinoco.
Orkaden, Orkney Islands.
Orscha, Orsha.
Orsowa, Orsova.
Ortles Sp., Ortler Spitz.
Ortospanum, Kandahar.
Osca, Huesca.
Osmanisches Asien, Ottoman Asia.
Osmanisches Reich, Ottoman Empire.
Ossa, Mount Kissovo.
Ossadiæ (tribe in India).
Ost stands for "East" before the respective names.
Ost Küste von Brasilien, East Coast of Brazil.
Ost Preussen, East Prussia.
Ost Pyrenäen, East Pyrenees.
Ost See, Baltic.
Ost Römisches Kaiserreich, East Roman Empire.
Ostphalen, Eastphalians (tribe of the Saxon nation).
Ostracine, Ras Straki.
Ostrogothen, Ostrogoths.
Othrys Gebirg, Othrys (Hellovo) Mountains.
Ottomaken, Ottomak Indians.
Oxus, Amoo River.
Oxyrynchus, Behenese.
Oxydraces, Oxydracæ (tribe in Moultan).
Ozark Gebirg, Ozark Mountains.

P. Gr. d. Getreides u. d. Zone d. Regens, Polar boundary of grain and of the zone of rain.
P. Gr. d. Weines u. d. europäisch. tropen. Getreides, Polar boundary of the grape vine and of European tropical grain.
Padua, Padova.
Padus, Po River.

Pæstum, Pesto.
Palästina, Palestine.
Palibothra (Palimbothra), Patna.
Palks Strasse, Palk's Straits.
Palmyra oder Tadmor, Palmyra or **Tadmor.**
Palus Mæotis, Sea of Azov.
Pamphylia, S. E. Anadolia.
Pandosia, Mendicino.
Pannonia, Hungary.
Pannonien, Hungary.
Panormus, Raphti.
Panticapæum, Kertch.
Paphlagonia, N. E. Anadolia.
Paphos, Baffa.
Parætonium, Al Bareton.
Parisii, nation in North France.
Paropanusus Geb., Hindoo Koosh.
Parthia, Province in Khorasan and N. E. Irak.
Parthiscus (Tibiscus), Theiss River.
Pasargadæ (Persepolis), Istakar.
Pastona, Pasten.
Patagonien, Patagonia.
Patagonische Kette, Patagonian Cordilleras.
Pax Julia, Beja.
Pella, Allahkilissia.
Pelopones, Morea.
Pelusium, Tineh.
Penninische Alpen, Pennine Alps.
Pentapolis, Chittagong.
Pentland Strasse, Pentland Firth.
Pergamus, Pergamo.
Pers. Golf, Gulf of Persia.
Persien, Persia.
Persische Parasangen, wov. 25 a. d. Gr., Persian Parasangs, 25 to the degree.
Persischer M. B., Gulf of Persia.
Peruanische Strömung, Peruvian Current.
Petschenegen, Petshenegs (Tartar tribe).
Peucetia, Terra di Bari.
Peuciner, Peucini (tribe in Galicia, &c.).
Phanagoria, Tmutarakan.
Pharsalus, Pharsala.
Pharselis, Tekrova.
Phazania, Fezzan.
Philippi, Filibah.
Philippinen, Philippine Islands.
Philippopel, Philippopolis.
Phocæa, Fokies.
Phryger, Phrygians (nation in Anadolia).
Physikalische Karte von Europa (— Afrika, — Asien, — Nord America, — Süd America), Physical map of Europe (— Africa, — Asia, — North America, — South America).
Pictavi (nation in Gallia Aquitania).
Picten, Picts (nation in Scotland).
Pielis See, Lake of Pielis.
Pindus Mn., Agrafa and Smocovo Mountains.
Pisidia, S. E. Anadolia.
Pithyusen (Pityusæ), Islands of Iviza, Formentera, &c.
Pityus, Soukoum.
Pitkarainen, Pitcairn's Island.
Plateau v. (or *von*) stands for "Plateau of" before the respective names.
Plateau von Ost Galizien, Plateau of East Galicia.

Plattkopf Indr., Flathead Indians.
Podolien, Podolia.
Polænen, Polænæ (Slavonic tribe).
Polargr. d. Bäume, Polar boundary of trees.
Polargr. d. Moose u. Beeren, Polar boundary of mosses and berries.
Polargr. d. Obstbaumes, Polar boundary of fruit trees.
Polargr. d. Œlbaumes, Polar boundary of the olive tree.
Polargr. d. Weinstocks, Polar boundary of the grape vine.
Polargrenze, Polar boundary.
Polargrenze d. Banane u. d. tropischen Getreides, Polar boundary of the banana and of the tropical grain.
Polargrenze des Getreides, Polar boundary of grain.
Polargrenze d. Palmen, Polar boundary of palm trees.
Polargrenze d. Weinstocks u. d. europäisch. trop. Getreides, Polar boundary of the grape vine and of the European tropical grain.
Polar Kreis, Arctic (or Antarctic) Circle.
Polen, Poland.
Polesiens Urwälder u. Sümpfe, Primitive forests and swamps of Polesia (now Minsk in Russia).
Pommern, Pomerania.
Pompelo, Pampeluna.
Pont. Eux. (Pontus Euxinus), Black Sea.
Pontinische In., Ponza Islands.
Pontus, N. E. Bulgaria.
Pontus Euxinus (Schwarzes Meer), Black Sea.
Porata, Pruth River.
Portland Sp., Portland Point.
Prag, Prague.
Prairien, Prairies.
Premnis, Cas. of Ibrim.
Pr. Holland, Prussian Holland (district in East Prussia).
Preussen, Prussia.
Preussische Landestheile, Prussian districts.
Preussische Höhe, Prussian Plateau.
Prophtasia (Prophthasia), Dookshak.
Propontis, Sea of Marmora.
Pskow, Pskov.
Psyllen, Psylli (tribe in N. Africa).
Ptolemäische Erdtafel, Map of the world according to Ptolemy.
Ptolemäische Stadien wovon 700 auf den Grad, Ptolemæan stadia 700 to the degree.
Pudosh, Pudog.
Pura, Pureg.
Purpur Ins., Purpureæ Insulæ (probably Salvage Islands).
Putea, Fuentes.
Putziger Wiek, Bay of Putzig.
Pyrenæi, Pyrenees.
Pyrenäen, Pyrenees.
Pyreneos Geb., Pyrenees.

Quaden, Quadi (nation in Hungary).
Quadra u. Vancouvers I., Vancouver's Island.
Querimbe, Querimba.

Rathenow, Rathenau.
Ratiaria, Arcer Palanka.
Rauhe Alp, Rauhe Alpe.
Rauraci, Tribe in Alsace.
Rch. d. Picten, Kingdom of the Picts.
Ree See, Lake Ree.
Regen Fluss, Rain River.
Regen S., Rain Lake.
Regenloses Gebiet, Rainless territory.
Regensburg, Ratisbon.
Reich der Aglabiten, Kingdom of the Aglabites (dynasty of Ibrahim ben Aglab).
Reich Alexanders des Grossen, Empire of Alexander the Great.
Reich der Bulgaren, Empire of the Bulgarians.
Reich der Chazaren, Empire of the Chazares (nation in East Russia).
Reich Karls d. Gr., Empire of Charlemagne.
Reich des Porus, Kingdom of Porus (in India).
Reich der Seleuciden, Kingdom of the Seleucidæ (dynasty of Seleucus).
Reich der Slaven, Empire of the Slavonians.
Reiche d. Angelsaxen, Anglo-Saxon Possessions.
Reiche d. Briten, Possessions of the Britons.
Reiche d. Dänen, Possessions of the Danes.
Reiche d. Scoten, Possessions of the Scots.
Reis und Kaffee, Rice and Coffee.
Reis und Mais, Rice and Indian Corn.
Republik Genua, Republic of Genoa.
Republik Venedig, Republic of Venice.
Reuss, Reuss.
Reval, Revel.
Rha (Wolga), Rha (Volga).
Rhätische Alpen, Rhætian Alps.
Rhagæ, Rha.
Rhein, Rhine River.
Rhein Bayern, Rhenish Bavaria.
Rhegium, Reggio.
Rheims, Reims.
Rhenus, Rhine.
Rhoda, Rosas.
Rhodanus, Rhone River.
Rhodus, Rhodes.
Rhön Gb., Hohe Rhœne Mountains.
Rhoxolanen, Rhoxolani (Sarmatian tribe).
Römisch Deutsches Kaiserreich, Romano-Germanic Empire.
Römische Meilen wovon 75 auf den Grad, Roman miles 75 to the degree.
Römisches Reich, Roman Empire.
Römisches Reich zur Zeit Constantins des Grossen, Roman Empire in the time of Constantine the Great.
Roggen, Gerste, Weitzen, Rye, Barley, Wheat.
Roggen u. Gerste, Rye and Barley.
Roggen und Weitzen, Rye and Wheat.
Rom, Rome.
Roma, Rome.
Rothes od. Erythräisches Meer, Red Sea.
Rothes Meer od. Arabischer Meerb, Red Sea.
Rotomagus, Rouen.
Roxolanen, Roxolani (Sarmatian tribe).
Rückkehr der Flotte unter Nearch, Return of the fleet under Nearchus.
Rücklaufende Strömung, Counter current.

Ruinen v. Babylon, Ruins of Babylon.
Ruinen von Carthago, Ruins of Carthage.
Ruinen v. Palmyra, Ruins of Palmyra.
Ruinen v. Susa, Ruins of Susa.
Rumanier, Rumini (tribe in Bulgaria, Moldavia, and Moravia).
Rusadir, Melilla.
Rusicada, Stora.
Ruspæ, Sbea.
Russische Werste 104 3 auf den Grad, Russian Wersts 104.3 to the degree.
Russisches America, Russian America.
Russlands beste Kornfelder, Russia's best grainfields.
Rusucurrum, Koleah.

Saas Thal, Saas Valley.
Sabier, Sabians (St. John the Baptist's disciples; sect in Persia).
Sachalites Golf, Bay of Seger.
Sachsen, Saxony.
Sächsische Schweiz, Saxonian Switzerland.
Saguntum, Murviedro.
Saima S., Lake Saim.
Saker, Sakr.
Salamis, Coulouri.
Salmantica, Salamanca.
Salomons Ins., Solomon Islands.
Salz Seen, Salt Lakes.
Salz Wüste, Salt Desert.
Sambus, Chumbul River.
Samojeden, Samoyedes.
Samoa oder Schiffer In., Navigators' Islands.
Samosate, Samisat.
Samsun, Samsoun.
Sandw. Cobi od. Hanhai, Desert of Cobi.
Sand Wüste, Sandy Desert.
Sangarius, Sakariah River.
Sarazenen, Saracens or Moors.
Sardes, Sart.
Sardica, Sophia.
Sardinien, Sardinia.
Sariphi Geb., Shar Mountains.
Sarmatæ, Sarmatians.
Sarmatien, Sarmatia.
Sarmatische Tiefebene, Sarmatian Lowland (East Prussia, Poland, and part of Russia).
Sarmatisches Meer, Sarmatian Sea (part of the Baltic).
Sarnia, Island of Guernsey.
Satala, Shaygran.
Sauromaten, Sarmatians.
Saxen, Saxony (Saxonians, Saxons).
Scandinavisches Meer, Scandinavian Sea.
Schetland In., Shetland Islands.
Schlangen Indr., Snake Indians.
Schlesien, Silesia.
Schloss v. Romelli, Romelli Castle.
Schnee Alp, Snowy Alps.
Schotland, Scotland.
Schwäbische Alp, Suabian Mountains.
Schwarzes Meer 52 t. tief, Black Sea 52 toises deep.
Schwarzw. (ald), Black Forest.

Schweden, Sweden.
Schweden, Norwegen und Dänemark, Sweden, Norway, and Denmark.
Schwedische Landestheile, Swedish districts.
Schweiz, Switzerland.
Sclaven K. (üste), Slave Coast.
Scodra, Scutari.
Scordisci, tribe in Slavonia.
Scythopolis, Bysan.
Scupi, Uskup.
Scylacium, Squillace.
See, Sea or Lake.
See Alpen, Maritime Alps.
See Alpen von Californien, Maritime Alps of California.
See Alpen der Nord West Küste, Maritime Alps of the N. W. Coast.
See Arsissa, Lake Van.
See Küsten Kette v. Venezuela, Sea coast mountain chain of Venezuela.
See Likari, Lake Likaris.
Seehunds B., Seal's or Shark's Bay.
Seeland, Zealand.
Seemeilen 20 auf den Grad, Sea miles 20 to the degree.
Segobriga, Segorbe.
Seliger S., Lake Seligero.
Selinus, Vostizza River.
Senegambien, Senegambia.
Senogallia (Lugdunensis quarta), Isle of France and Champagne.
Senus, Shannon River.
Septentrio (Nord), North.
Septimanen, Septimani (tribe in Languedoc).
Serbien, Servia.
Sesamus, Amasserah.
Setuval, Setubal.
Sevennen, Cevennes Mountains.
Seyschellen Ins., Seychelle Islands.
Shetland Inseln, Shetland Islands.
Shin See, Shin Lake.
Sicilia, Sicily.
Sidodona, Shenaas.
Sidon, Sayda.
Siebenbürgen, Transylvania.
Siebenbürgisches Plateau, Plateau of Transylvania.
Siena, Sienna.
Siga, Takumbreet.
Signia, Segni.
Sil, Sile River.
Simferopol, Taurida.
Simmen Thal, Simm Valley.
Singaglia, Sinigaglia.
Singara, Sinjar.
Singidunum, Belgrade.
Siniope, Sinub.
Sinus Arabicus, Red Sea.
Sirmium, Alt Schabacz.
Siscia, Sziszek.
Sitacus, Sita Rhegian River.
Sitife, Seteef.
Skagerak, Skager Rack.
Skagestrandsbugt u. Handelsted, Skager Beach Bay and Commercial Town.

Skandien (Scandia), Sweden.
Skythen, Scythians (nation).
Skythini (Scythini), probably Saracens in Armenia.
Slaven, Slavonians.
Slavonische Militair Grenze, Slavonian military frontier.
Slowenen, Wends (Slavonic nation).
Sogdiana, Great Bukaria.
Sogdianien (Sogdiana), Great Bukaria.
Solanus (Ost), East.
Soledad od. Ost I., Soledad or Eastern Island (Falkland Islands).
Soli, Mezetlu.
Soraben, Sorbi (Slavonic tribe).
Span. Mark, Spanish mark (modern Catalonia, Navarre, and part of Arragonia).
Spanien, Spain.
Speier, Speyer.
Spoletum, Spoleto.
St. Georgs Kanal, St. George's Channel.
St. Johann, St. John.
Staaten der Mexicanischen Union, States of the Mexican Union.
Staaten der Nordamerikanischen Union, States of the North American Union.
Staatenland, Staten Island (S. A.).
Stadt der Getæ, City of the Getæ.
Stalaktiden Grotte, Stalactite Grotto.
Steyermark, Styria.
Str. v. (Strasse von) stands for "Straits of" before the respective names.
Strabo's Erdtafel, Map of the World according to Strabo.
Strasse v. Calais, the British Channel.
Strom und Gebirgs-System von Mitteleuropa, River and Mountain System of Central Europe.
Südamerika, South America.
Süd Atlantische Strömung, South Atlantic Current.
Süd Cap, South Cape.
Süd Georgien, South Georgia.
Südl. Continent, Southern Continent.
Südl. Grenze des Weinstocks, Southern boundary of the grape vine.
Südliche Verbindungs Strömung, Southern Connecting Current.
Südlicher Polarkreis, Antarctic Circle.
Süd oder Neu Georgien, South or New Georgia.
Süd Schetland, New South Shetland.
Süd West, South West.
Sümpfe in gleicher Höhe m. d. Ocean, Swamps on a level with the ocean.
Sumpf, Swamp.
Sund, Sound.
Sunda See, Sea of Sunda.
Sunda Strasse, Straits of Sunda.
Susiana, Khuzistan and Louristan.
Swilly See, Lake Swilly.
Sybaris, Cochyle River.
Syracusa, Syracuse.
Syrdaria, Sir River.
Syrien, Syria.
Syrisch Arabische Wüste, Syro-Arabian Desert.

Syrische Wüste, Syrian Desert.
Syrtes, Gulf of Sidra.
Syrtika (Seli or Psylli), in Tripolis.

Tabor, Mt. Tor.
Tabraca, Tabarca.
Tacape, Cabes.
Tafelland von Armenien 250 t., Armenian Plateau 250 toises.
Tafelland von Iran 650 t. üb. d. Meere, Plateau of Iran 650 toises above the level of the sea.
Tafelland v. Mexico od. Anahuac, Plateau of Mexico or Anahuac.
Taifalen, Taifalæ (tribe on the Danube).
Tajo, Tagus River.
Tambow, Tambov.
Tamesis, Thames River.
Tanais (Danaber), Don River.
Tape, Bostam.
Tapes Ind., Tappe Indians.
Taprobana, Ceylon.
Tarnowitzer Höhe, Plateau of Tarnowitz.
Tarsus, Tersoos.
Tarum, Tarem.
Tatra Gebirg, Tatra Mountains (part of the Carpathian Ms.).
Taurica, Crimea.
Taurien, Tauria.
Taurischer Cherson, Crimea.
Taxila, Attock.
Tay Mündung, Firth of Tay.
Teate, Chieti.
Telmissus, Macry.
Tenerifa, Teneriffe.
Termessus, Schenet.
Teufels Inseln, Devil's Islands.
Thapsacus, Der.
Thebais, Upper Egypt.
Theben, Thebes.
Thebunte, Melhafa.
Themse, Thames River.
Therwinger, Thervingi (Gothic tribe).
Thessalonica, Salonica.
Thracia, Rumilia.
Thrakien (Thracia), Rumilia.
Thuner See, Lake of Thun.
Tiberis, Tevere River.
Tief Sudan, Low Soudan.
Tiefland von Afrika, Lowlands of Africa.
Tingis, Tangiers.
Tischit, Tisheet.
Titianus, Tezzano.
Titicaca See, Lake Titicaca.
Todtes Meer, Dead Sea.
Toletum, Toledo.
Tomi, Tomisvar.
Torneo See u. Elf, Tornea Lake and River.
Torres Strasse, Torres' Strait.
Toscana, Tuscany.
Toskanisches Hochland, Tuscan Highlands.
Transylvanische Alpen, Transylvanian Alps.
Trapezunt, Trebisonde.
Trapezus, Trebisonde.
Tremitische In., Tremiti Islands.
Tridentum, Trento.

Trier, Treves.
Triest, Trieste.
Trileucum, Ortegal.
Troglodyten, Troglodytes (tribe on the Red Sea).
Tschad See, Lake Tchad.
Tscheremissen, Tchermisses (Finnish tribe in Russian Asia).
Tscherkessien, Circassia.
Tschernomorische Kosaken, Cirnomorian Cossacks.
Tschuktschen, Tchookches (tribe in N. E. Asia).
Türkei, Turkey.
Türkisch Croatien, Turkish Croatia.
Tunes, Tunis.
Tungusen, Tungouski (nation in Asia).
Turini, Turin.
Turkmanen, Turcoman (Tartar tribe).
Tusculum, Frascati.
Tyana, Kiliss Hissar.
Tyras, Dniestr River.
Tyras Donaster, Dniestr River.
Tyroler Alpen, Tyrol Alps.
Tyrrhenen, Tyrrheni (Pelasgian tribe).
Tyrrhenisches Meer, Tyrrhenian Sea (part of the Mediterranean).
Tyrus, Soor.

Umgebung von Neu York, Vicinity of New York.
Unerforschte Alpengebirge, Unexplored Mountain Region.
Ungarisches Erzgebirge, Hungarian Erzgebirge.
Ungarn, Hungary.
Unterirdische Wasserleitung, Subterranean Aqueduct.
Unzugängliche Felsenküste, Inaccessible rocky coast.
Ural Gebirge, Oural Mountains.
Uralische Kosaken, Oural Cossacks.
Urumija See, Lake Uromija.
Usa, Ouse River.
Ursprung der Peruanischen Küsten Ström. kalten Wassers, Origin of the Peruvian cold water current.
Uzen, Cumanen oder Polowzer, Utses Camanes or Polovzi (Mongolian tribe).

Vandalen, Vandals (Gothic tribe).
Vanille u. Cacao, Vanilla and Cacao.
Vaterland des Kaffeebaumes, Country of the Coffee tree.
Veldidena, Wilden.
Venedicus Sinus, Gulf of Venice.
Venedig, Venice.
Venetæ, Venetes (tribe in Britany).
Veneten, Venetes (tribe in Britany).
Venetia, Venice.
Vereinigte Staaten, United States.
Verschiedene Ind. Stämme, Various Indian tribes.
Vesuv, Vesuvius.
Vgb. Comaria, Cape Comorin.
Vgb. Maceta, Cape Musseldom.
Vgb. Prionotus, Point Comol.
Vgb. Syagros, Cape Ras Vire.
Viadrus, Oder River.

Viennensis, Dauphiny.
Vierwaldstädter See, Lake of Lucerne.
Vindhy Kette, Vindhya Mountains.
Vindobona, Vienna.
Virunum, Waren.
Visurgis, Weser River.
Vogesen, Vosges Mountains.
Volhynien, Volhynia.
Volubilis, Pharaoh's Castle.
Vorder Rhein, Fore Rhine (one of the rivulets tributary to the Rhine).
Vorgeb Aromata, Cape Guardafui.
Vorgeb Simylla, Cape Simylla.
Votiaken, Wotyaks (Finnish tribe).

Wälder S., Lake of the Woods.
Wahabiten, Wahabites (Mahomedan sect).
Walachei, Walachia.
Waldai Geb., Waldai Mountains.
Walfisch B., Whale Bay.
Wallachisches Tiefland, Wallachian Lowlands.
Wallenstädter See, Lake of Wallenstadt.
Wan See, Lake Van.
Wanger Oge, Wanger Oog.
Warasdiner Geb., Warasdin Mountains.
Warschau, Warsaw.
Weichsel, Vistula River.
Weichsel Niederung, Vistula Lowlands.
Weisse Bai, White Bay.
Weisse Berge, White Mountains.
Weisse Bulgaren, White Bulgarians.
Weisses Meer, White Sea.
Weisses Vorgeb., Cape Blanc.
Weitzen, Gerste u. Hafer, Wheat, Barley and Oats.
Weitzen, Mais und Baumwolle, Wheat, Indian Corn and Cotton.
Weitzen u. Baumwolle, Wheat and Cotton.
Weitzen u. Reis, Wheat and Rice.
Wendekreis des Krebses, Tropic of Cancer.
Wendekreis des Steinbocks, Tropic of Capricorn.
Wenden, Wends (Slavonic tribe).
Wenern See, Lake Wenern.
Wesegothen, Visigoths (nation).
Weser Gb., Weser Mountains.
West Gats, West Ghauts.
West Indien, West Indies.
West Preussen, West Prussia.
West Pyrenäen, West Pyrenees.
West Russland, West Russia.
Wester W., Wester Wald.
Westliche Länge von Paris, W. Longitude from Paris.
Westphalen, Westphalia.
Wettern See, Lake Wettern.
Wien, Vienna.
Wilde Völker, Savage nations.
Windtafel der Griechen nach Aristoteles, Windchart of the Greeks according to Aristotle.
Windtafel der Römer nach Vitruvius, Windchart of the Romans according to Vitruvius.
Winipeg S., Winnipeg Lake.
Winipigoos S., Lake Winnipigoos.
Wogulen, Woguls or Uranfi (Finnish tribe).

Wolga, Volga River.
Wüste al Ahkaf, Desert Al Ahkaf.
Wüste Hochebene, Sandy Plateau.
Wüste Kharasm, Desert of Kharasm
Wüste Sahara, Desert of Sahara.
Wüste Sahel, Desert of Sahel.
Wüstes Arabien, Arabia Deserta.

Zacynthus, Zante.
Zadracasta, Goorgaun.
Zagrus Geb., Aiagha Mountains.
Zahn u. Elfenbein K., Ivory Coast.
Zalissa, Tiflis.
Zana See, Lake Zana.
Zembre S., Lake Zembe.
Zariaspa später Baetra (Zariaspa, later Baetra),
   Balkh.
Zeiton, Zeitoun.
Zenobia, Zelebi.
Zephyros (West), West wind.
Zerstückelung des Reiches, Dismembering of the
   Empire.
Zimmt, Muskatnuss u. Gewürznelke, Cinna-
   mon, Nutmeg, and Clove.
Zoromba, Dustee River.
Zucker, Sugar.
Zucker, Kaffee, Thee, Sugar, Coffee, Tea.
Zucker u. Kaffee, Sugar and Coffee.
Züricher See, Lake of Zurich.
Zug unter Gottfried von Bouillon, Crusade under
   Godfrey of Bouillon.
Zug unter Conrad III. u. Ludwig VII., Crusade
   under Conrad III. and Louis VII.
Zug unter Ludwig IX. v. Frankr., Crusade un-
   der Louis IX. of France.
Zug unter Friedrich Barbarossa, Crusade under
   Frederick Barbarossa.
Zug unter Kaiser Friedrich II., Crusade under
   Emperor Frederick II.
Zug unter Richard I. u. Phil. August, Crusade
   under Richard I. and Philip Augustus.
Zuyder See, Zuyder Zee.
Zwarte Bge., Black Mountains.
Zweibrücken, Bipont.
Zwischen 0° und 10°, Between 0° and 10°.

HISTORY
AND ETHNOLOGY

A. ANCIENT TIMES AND MIDDLE AGES (PLATES
   III. 1—39).

PLATE 1.

PAGE

Egypt.

Fig. 1. The court of the dead, . . 178
 " 2–4. Different trades, . . . 180
 " 5. Agriculture, ... 180
 " 6, 7. Hunting and fishing, . . 180
 " 8. Vintage, ... 180

Fig. 9. King in his chariot, . . . 179
 " 10. King on his throne, receiving presents, ... 179

PLATE 2.

Figs. 1–3. Egyptian costumes, . . 179
 " 4. Lybian costume, . . 179
 " 5. Chinese, . . . 181
 " 6–14. Assyrians, . . . 180
 " 15, 16. Medes, . . . 180
 " 16–20. Persians, . . . 180

PLATE 3.

Figs. 1–4. Egyptian features and head-
   dresses, from monuments, . 176
 " 5ab. Heads of male mummies, . 176
 " 6ab. Heads of female mummies, . 176
 " 7. Mummy with the inner fillets, . 178
 " 8. Mummy with the exterior cover, . 178
 " 9–11. Mummies with the coffins, . 178
 " 12. Coffin with its cover, . . 178
 " 13, 14. Embalmed animals, . . 178
 " 15, 16. Vases, . . . 179
 " 17–19. Large stone vases, . . 179
 " 20ab. Pitchers, . . . 179
 " 21, 22. Altars, . . . 179
 " 23, 24. Chairs, . . . 179
 " 25. Folding chair, . . . 179
 " 26, 27. Thrones, . . . 179
 " 28, 29. Lounge and footstool, . 179
 " 30. Knife, . . . 179
 " 31. Royal sceptre, . . . 179
 " 32, 33. Sphinxes, . . . 178
 " 34, 35. Obelisks, . . . 178
 " 36. Entrance to the Egyptian laby-
   rinth, . . . 176
 " 37–39. Indian pyramids, ground plan,
   elevation, and section, . 181
 " 40. Rock-tombs near Persepolis, . 180

PLATE 4.

Fig. 1. Carthaginian king, . . 182
 " 2. Mauritanian, . . . 182
 " 3. Persian woman, . . . 180
 " 4–6. Armenians, . . . 183
 " 7. Arab, . . . 183
 " 8. Phrygian, . . . 180
 " 9, 10. Dacians, . . . 183
 " 11, 12. Dacian women, . . 183
 " 13. Syrian, . . . 180
 " 14. Parthian, . . . 183
 " 15. Celtiberian, . . . 183
 " 16. Iberian woman, . . . 184
 " 17. British woman, . . . 184
 " 18–23. Germans, . . . 184

PLATE 5.

Fig. 1. German dwelling, . . . 186
 " 2. German infant plunged in the
   river, . . . 186
 " 3. German wedding, . . . 186
 " 4–8. Gauls, . . . 184

PLATE 6.

Fig. 1, 2. Egyptian sphinxes, . . 178
 " 3–6. Altars, . . . 179

Fig. 7. Table, ... 179
 " 8–14ab. Pitchers and vases, . . 179
 " 15–19. Cups and other drinking vessels, . . . 179
 " 20. Bowl, . . . 179
 " 21. Dipper (*Simpulum*), . . 179
 " 22ab. Royal necklace, and sceptre, . 179
 " 23, 24. Ethiopian royal headgear, . 182
 " 25. Numidian " " 182
 " 26. Armenian royal headgear (*Kida-
   ris*), . . . 182
 " 27. Dacian headgear, . . . 183
 " 28. Sarmatian headgear, . . 181
 " 29. Scythian royal tiara, . . 181
 " 30, 31. Persian royal tiara, . . 180
 " 32. Assyrian tiara, . . . 180
 " 33–37. Indian caps, . . . 181
 " 38. Assyrian helmet, . . . 180
 " 39. Phrygian cap, . . . 181
 " 40ab. Assyrian headgear, . . 180
 " 41, 45b. Indian necklace and girdle, . 181
 " 42. Chinese imperial cap, . . 181
 " 43–45. Fans and fly-brushes, . . 181
 " 46. Persian covering for the feet, . 180
 " 47. Persian fan, . . . 180
 " 48–50. Persian drinking vessels, . 180
 " 51. The rock-tomb of Midas in Asia
   Minor, . . . 180
 " 52. Rock-tombs at Persepolis, . 180
 " 53. Monument near Tortosa in Syria, 180
 " 54. Absalom's tomb in the valley of
   Josaphat, near Jerusalem, . 180
 " 55–75ab. Carthaginian coins and medals, . . . 182

PLATE 7.

Grecian Costumes.

Figs. 1, 2ab. Maidens, . . . 196
 " 3. Youth, . . . 195
 " 4. Spinner, . . . 196
 " 5. Singer, . . . 196
 " 6. Amazon, . . . 196
 " 7–13. Women, . . . 196
 " 14. Phrygian, . . . 181
 " 15, 16. Greeks from Mount Ida, . 196
 " 17. Philosopher, . . . 195
 " 18. Poet, . . . 195
 " 19. Prefect, . . . 195
 " 20. War-leader, . . . 195

PLATE 8.

Fig. 1. Ceremony at a Greek wedding, . 198
 " 2. Greek dancer, . . . 196
 " 3. Roman funeral ceremony, . . 223
 " 4. Interior of a Greek dwelling, . 197
 " 5. The Areopagus, . . . 192

PLATE 9.

Figs. 1–6. Games of Greek youth, . . 195
 " 7–24. Olympian games, . . 194–196

PLATE 10.

Fig. 1. The philosophers' garden at
   Athens, . . . 195

Figs. 2–34. Various Grecian articles of
   furniture, . . . 197
 " 35–39. Various Grecian tools, . . 197
 " 40–54. Various Grecian articles of
   toilet, . . . 197

PLATE 11.

Fig. 1. The rock-tombs of Tarquinii, . 198
 " 2. Those of Assus, . . . 198
 " 3, 4. Those of Ceræa, and their
   ground plan, . . . 198
 " 5, 6. Tombs of Orcla; elevation, . 198
 " 7, 8. The same; the ground plan, . 198
 " 9, 10. Tombs in Telmessus; elevation and ground plan, . 198
 " 11, 12. Tomb in Falerii; ground plan
   and section, . . . 198
 " 13, 14. Tomb in Agrigentum; elevation and section, . . 198
 " 15. Tomb from an antique vase, . 198
 " 16–20. Urns and vases, . . 198
 " 21–23. Tripods, . . . 198
 " 24–34ab. Greek coins, . . 193

PLATE 12.

Rome.

Figs. 1–3. Emperors, . . . 220
 " 4, 5. Empresses, . . . 220
 " 6, 7. Senators, . . . 216, 220
 " 8. Philosopher, . . . 220
 " 9. Lictor, . . . 217
 " 10. Citizen and his wife, . . 215
 " 11, 12. Youths, . . . 219
 " 13–16. Women, . . . 220
 " 17–29. Female headgear, . . 220
 " 30–32. Male headgear, . . 220

PLATE 13.

Rome.

Fig. 1. Exhibition of captives in the fo-
   rum, . . . 214
 " 2. Gladiators in the theatre, . . 223
 " 3. Gladiators at funerals, . . 224
 " 4. Funeral of emperors, . 223, 224

PLATE 14.

Figs. 1–16. Details from the Circensian
   games, . . . 223

PLATE 15.

Fig. 1. Combat with wild beasts in the
   Coliseum at Rome, under
   Domitian, . . . 223
 " 2–19. Roman consular coins, . 219
 " 20–25. Roman imperial coins, . 219

PLATE 16.

Figs. 1–66. Roman furniture and tools, 216,
   220, 221, 224.

PLATE 17.

Fig. 1. The street of tombs in Pompeii, . 224
 " 2–4. Monuments, . . . 224
 " 5–7. Sarcophagi, . . . 224
 " 8–59. Roman furniture and tools, . 221

PLATE 18.

Fig. 1. Gallic women of the Roman time, ... 221
" 2–6. Bas-reliefs from Gaul, . . 221
" 7, 8ab. Gallic coins, . . . 221
" 9, 10. Gallic sepulchral urns, . . 224
" 11–39. Various Gallic trinkets and utensils, . . . 221
" 40–42. German sepulchral urns, . 224
" 43–56. Coins, medals, and matrices, . . . 219, 221
" 57, 58. Carthaginian monuments, . 224
" 59, 60. Gallic monuments, . . 221
" 61. The Roman column at Cussy, . 221

PLATE 19.

Fig. 1. The Apostles' grotto near Jerusalem, . . . 224
" 2. The catacombs of Syracuse, . 224
" 3–6. The catacombs of Naples; ground plan; vertical section of a part; horizontal section of another part; the chapel, . . 224
" 7–10. The catacombs of San Marcellino near Rome; ground plan, perspective view, and details, . . . 224
" 11. Plan of Platonia, near St. Sebastian, before the walls of Rome, 224
" 12, 13. Tombs of Christian martyrs, 224
" 14. Christian sarcophagus from the catacombs, . . . 224
" 15. Chapel of St. Hermes, . . 224
" 16. Chapel of St. Agnes, . . 224
" 17. Plan of the subterranean church of St. Hermes, . . 224
" 18. External elevation of the subterranean church of St. Prisca, . 224
" 19. Tabernacle of the church of St. Nereus and St. Achilleus, near the baths of Antoninus at Rome, . . . 224

PLATE 20.

The Tribes of the Migration.

Fig. 1. Goth, ... 228
" 2. Sueve, ... 228
" 3. Gepide, ... 229
" 4. Vandal, ... 229
" 5. Marcoman, . . . 230
" 6. Quade, ... 230
" 7. Herulian, ... 231
" 8. Briton, ... 221
" 9. Frank, ... 232
" 10. Hun, ... 232
" 11–14. Picts, ... 233
" 15. Anglo-Saxon chieftain, . . 234
" 16–18. Anglo-Saxons, . . . 234
" 19. Danish king, . . . 234
" 20. Danish warrior, . . . 234
" 21–23. Danes, ... 234

PLATE 21.

Costumes of Central Europe.

Fig. 1. Queen Clotilda (6th century), . 232
" 2. Maid of honor, . . . 232
" 3. Frankish leader, . . . 232
" 4ab. Frankish warriors, . . 232
" 5. King Clovis, . . . 232
" 6. Charlemagne, . . . 237
" 7, 8. Prince and Princess of his house, . . . 237
" 9, 10. Noble and his wife, . . 237
" 11. Leader under Charlemagne, . 237
" 12ab. Warriors, . . . 237
" 13. Bishop, . . . 237
" 14. Common people, . . . 237
" 15–18. Frankish king, queen, prince, and princess, . . 239
" 19, 20. Prebendary and nun, . . 239
" 21. Citizen, ... 239
" 22, 23. Norman king and queen, . 239
" 24–26. Norman nobles, . . . 239
" 27, 28. Norman citizen and peasant, 239

PLATE 22.

Figs. 1. 2. Clovis, king of the Franks, and his queen Clotilda, . 232
" 3. Fredegonda, from her tomb, . 232
" 4. Childebert, king of the Franks, . 232
" 5, 6. Statues of Females from the 8th century, . . 237
" 7. Charlemagne, . . 237
" 8. Charlemagne receiving the submission of Wittekind, . 237
" 9–37. Arms, utensils, and furniture of Charlemagne's time, . 258
" 38. Statue of Wittekind, . 237
" 39–63. Utensils and furniture of Charlemagne's time, . 258

PLATE 23.

Fig. 1. Travelling of Frankish kings in the 8th century, . . 258
" 2. Manner of transporting wounded or sick princes in the 13th century, . . 258
" 3. St. Louis administering justice in the open field, . . 293
" 4. Clerical punishment of French princes in the 13th century, . 288
" 5. Vassals paying homage to their liege lord, . . . 264

PLATE 24.

Fig. 1. Full armor of Emperor Maximilian, . . . 264
" 2. Full armor of King Henry VIII., 264
" 3. English knight, . . . 264
" 4. German knights, . . . 264
" 5. Squires, ... 264
" 6. English knights in tournament, . 264
" 7. German knights before a tournament, . . . 264
" 8. Judge of the tournament, . . 264

PLATE 25.

Fig. 1. Joust with lances in Germany, . 264
" 2. Judicial combat, . . . 264
" 3. Combat with maces in France, . 265
" 4. Judicial combat with shields, . 265
" 5. Combat with swords, . . 265
" 6. Combat with lance points, . . 265
" 7. Carrying the ring in the carrousel, 265
" 8. Squire taking the oath of knighthood on the sword, . . 265

PLATE 26.

Fig. 1. Young knight taking the solemn oath on the altar, . . 265
" 2. The ceremony of dubbing a knight, . . . 265

PLATE 27.

Figs. 1–13. Forms of shields, . . 271
" 14–32. Colors and figures of shields, 270
" 33–43. Divisions of shields, . . 271
" 64–86. Different crowns, . 268–271
" 87–92. Crests of shields, . . 267

PLATE 28.

Figs. 1–21. Coats of arms, . . 271

PLATE 29.

Figs. 1–31. Coats of arms, . . 272

PLATE 30.

The Inquisition, . . 282

Fig. 1. Session of the tribunal, . . 287
" 2. The punishment of the scourge, . 288
" 3. Nailing the hand to the post, . 288
" 4. The punishment of strangling, . 288
" 5. The fire-torture on the wheel, . 288
" 6. Auto-da-fé at Seville, . . 288

PLATE 31.

The Inquisition, . . 282

Fig. 1. The torture of the rope and pulley, ... 285
" 2. The water-torture, . . . 285
" 3. The fire-torture, . . . 286
" 4. Auto-da-fé in Spain, . . 288

PLATE 32.

Fig. 1. St. Augustin, . . . 273
" 2. St. Antony, . . . 273
" 3, 4. Maronite patriarch and monk, . 273
" 5, 6. Armenian patriarch and monk, . 273
" 7. St. Basil, . . . 274
" 8. Greek monk in Poland, . . 274
" 9. Jacobite monk, . . . 274
" 10, 11. Benedictine monk and nun, . 274
" 12. Nun of Fontevrault, . . 275
" 13, 14. Augustine monk and nun, . 275
" 15. Prebendary of the Congregation of the Lateran, . . 275
" 16. Barefoot Carmelite monk, . 276
" 17. Carmelite nun, . . . 276
" 18. Carthusian nun, . . . 275
" 19. Calmalduensian monk, . . 275
" 20. Valombrose monk, . . . 278
" 21. Bernardine nun, . . . 275

Figs. 22, 23. Capuchin monks, . . 276
" 24. Nun of St. Clarissa, . . . 277
" 25. Sylvestrine monk, . . . 275
" 26, 27. Dominican monk and nun, . 276

PLATE 33.

Fig. 1. Monk of the Holy Sepulchre, . 275
" 2. Cœlestine monk, . . . 275
" 3. Franciscan monk, . . . 276
" 4. Ursuline nun, . . . 277
" 5. Theatine nun, . . . 277
" 6. Beguine, ... 277
" 7. Hospitaller of St. Jacques du haut pas, . . . 277
" 8. Alexian monk, . . . 278
" 9. Ambrosian monk, . . . 278
" 10. Religious of the order of Jesus, . 278
" 11. Annunciate nun, . . . 277
" 12. Nun of "the Immaculate Conception," . . . 277
" 13. Nun of "the Visitation of St. Mary," . . . 278
" 14. Nun of "the Word become Flesh," . . . 278
" 15. Franciscan nun, . . . 276
" 16. Hospital nun of Hotel-Dieu in Paris, . . . 277
" 17. Jesuit, ... 277
" 18. Jesuit missionary in China, . 277
" 19. Sister of Charity, . . . 277
" 20. Bethlehemite monk, . . 278
" 21. Priest of the Oratory in France, . 277
" 22. Doctrinary, . . . 276
" 23. Barnabite monk, . . . 277
" 24. Priest of the pious schools of France and Belgium, . . 278
" 25, 26. Feuillantine monk and nun, . 275
" 27. Monk of St. Maurus, . . 275

PLATE 34.

Fig. 1. Visitantine nun in Flanders, . 278
" 2. Nun of " Notre-Dame," . 278
" 3. Nun of " Notre Dame de la Miséricorde," . . . 278
" 4. Priest of the Congregation of Missions, . . . 278
" 5. Sister of Charity of St. Vincent de Paula, . . . 277
" 6. Hospital nun of La Flèche, . 277
" 7a. Trappist monk, . . . 275
" 7b. Poor volunteer monk of Flanders, . . . 278
" 8. Grand master of the Order of Malta, . . . 279
" 9. Grand cross of the same, . . 279
" 10. Knight of Malta, . . . 279
" 11. Lady of the Order of St. John of Jerusalem, . . . 280
" 12. Templar in house dress, . . 280
" 13. Templar in war costume, . . 280
" 14. Templar in full armor mounted, 280
" 15. Grand master of the German Knights, . . . 280
" 16. Knight of St. James of the Sword, 280
" 17. Knight of the Order of Calatrava, 280

Fig. 18. Knight of the Order of Alcantara, 280
" 19. Knight of St. Avis in Portugal, . 280
" 20. Knight of St. Stephen, . 280
" 21. Knight of the Holy Ghost, . 280
" 22. Hospitaller of the Holy Ghost, . 280
" 23. Religious of the Order d'Aubrac, 280

PLATE 35.

Freemasonry.

Fig. 1. Initiation of apprentice, . 281
" 2. Initiation of master, . 281
" 3. Initiation of the 33d degree of the
      Scottish lodge, . 281
" 4. Funeral of a companion, . 281

PLATE 36.

Fig. 1. Hawking in France, . 265
" 2. Departure of crusaders for Pales-
      tine, . 298

PLATE 37.

Fig. 1. Combat between crusaders and
      Saracens, . 298
" 2. Harangue to crusaders before the
      walls of Jerusalem, . 298

PLATE 38.

Fig. 1. Return of crusaders from Pales-
      tine, . 294
" 2. Tournament in Germany, . 264

PLATE 39.

Fig. 1. Ground plan of the church of St.
      Mary of the Manger at Beth-
      lehem, . 294
" 2. Interior of the church of St. Mary
      of the Manger in Bethlehem,
      with the entrance to the cha-
      pel of the Holy Grotto, . 294
" 3. Interior of the chapel with the
      Holy Grotto, . 294
" 4. Ground plan of the church of the
      Holy Sepulchre in Jerusalem, 294
" 5. Portico and entrance to the same, 294
" 6. Interior of the same, with the
      Holy Chapel, . 294

B. ETHNOLOGY OF THE PRESENT DAY (PLATES
      IV. 1–42).

PLATE 1.

The Five Principal Races.

1. Caucasian Race.

Fig. 1. Inhabitants of Central Europe, . 297
" 2. Greek, . 297, 359
" 3. Turk, . 298, 358
" 4. Cossack, . 298, 340
" 5. Persian, . 298, 370
" 6. Hindoo, . 299, 377
" 7. Bedouin, . 298, 374
" 8, 9. Cabyles, . 299

2. Mongolian Race.

Fig. 10. Kalmuck, . 299, 348
" 11. Chinese, . 299, 383
" 12. Samoyede, . 299, 355
" 13. Esquimaux, . 299, 423

3. Ethiopian Race.

Fig. 14. Guinea Negro, . 301, 405
" 15. Boussa Negro, . 301, 405
" 16. Hottentot, . 201, 417
" 23, 24. Papuas (Australia), . 459

4. American Race.

Figs. 17–21. Indians, . 300

5. Malay Race.

Fig. 22. Native of New Zealand, . 299

PLATE 2.

Fig. 1. Peasant girl from Baden, . 305
" 2. Peasant from the Baden highlands, 305
" 3, 4. Inhabitants of the Black Forest, 305
" 5–9. Wirtembergers, . 305, 306
" 10–15. Bavarians, . 306
" 16, 17. Hessians, . 307
" 18, 19. Inhabitants of Rhenish Prussia, 309
" 20. Inhabitants of Brunswick, . 310
" 21, 22. Inhabitants of the District of
      Coblentz (Rhine), . 309
" 23, 24. Inhabitants of Altenburg (Sax-
      ony), . 314

PLATE 3.

Fig. 1. Inhabitants of the District of Er-
      furt (Thuringia), . 314
" 2. Inhabitants of Holstein, . 311
" 3. Inhabitants of the District of Lü-
      neburg (Hanover), . 311
" 4, 5. Inhabitants of the District of
      Hamburg, . 310
" 6–8. Inhabitants of East Friesland
      (Hanover), . 311
" 9–11. Inhabitants of Silesia, . 318
" 12–15. Inhabitants of Tyrol, . 324
" 16–19. Inhabitants of Austria, . 321
" 20–22. Inhabitants of Styria, . 321
" 23. Inhabitants of Bohemia, . 319
" 24. Inhabitants of Illyria, . 322

PLATE 4.

Upper Division.

Figs. 1–12. The German gymnasium, . 326

Lower Division.

Figs. 1–8. Acrobatic feats, . 328

PLATE 5.

Figs. 1–3. Equestrian feats, . 328

PLATE 6.

Figs. 1, 2. Horse races, . 334
" 3. Masked ball at Paris, . 366

PLATE 7.

Fig. 1. Grand promenade in the Elysian
      Fields (Paris), . 366
" 2. Festival at St. Petersburg, . 338
" 3. Public meeting in England, . 335

PLATE 8.

Fig. 1. Naumachy on the Seine in Paris, 366
" 2. Rural ball, . 366
" 3. Illumination in Rome, . 362

PLATE 9.

Fig. 1. Spanish barn, . 364
" 2. Sardinian barn, . 362
" 3. Sardinian wedding, . 362
" 4. The Bolero (Spanish dance), . 364
" 5. Spanish bull-fight, . 364

PLATE 10.

Russian Tribes.

Figs. 1, 2. Strielzi, . 339
" 3. Russo-Polish guard, . 339
" 4–7. Inhabitants of Little Russia, . 336
" 8–10. Fishermen from the Volga, . 336
" 11. Inhabitants of Novgorod, . 336
" 12, 13. Inhabitants of the district of
      Twer, . 336
" 14. Inhabitants of the Ukraine, . 336
" 15. Cossack of the Don, . 340
" 16 Inhabitants of the district of Mos-
      cow, . 336

Caucasian Tribes.

Figs. 17–22. Circassians, . 345
" 23. Turkoman, . 352
" 24. Abasian, . 342
" 25. Mingrelian, . 348
" 26. Imeritian, . 348
" 27. Georgian, . 348

PLATE 11.

Figs. 1, 2. Russian rural games, . 337
" 3. Russian public bath, . 337
" 4, 5. Russian large and small knout, 336

PLATE 12.

Fig. 1. Russian sleighing and gliding hill, 337
" 2. Russian serfs on the Don, . 341
" 3. Russian national dance, . 337
" 4. Festivity at Pergola (Russia), . 339
" 5. Lapland winter cabins, . 330

PLATE 13.

Fig. 1 a–s. Oriental headgear, . 358
" 2. Syrians, . 358
" 3, 4. Smyrnese, . 358
" 5–8. Maronites, . 358
" 9. Girl of Nablous, . 358
" 10. Nazarenes, . 358
" 11–15. Arabs, . 372, 375
" 16, 17. Armenians, . 358
" 18. Turk of Mardin, . 358

PLATE 14.

Fig. 1. Public baths for women in Turkey, 358
" 2. Interior of a harem, . 358
" 3. Supper at the grand vizier's, . 358
" 4. Ceremony in the sultan's presence
      chamber, . 358
" 5. Dance of the dervises, . 358
" 6. Prayer and ablution of the Maho-
      medans, . 358
" 7. Penitent dervise, . 359

PLATE 15.

Figs. 1–9. Persians, . 370
" 10. Beludshis, . 376

Fig. 11. Usbek, . 382
" 12. Afghan, . 376
" 13. Kurd, . 369
" 14. Kirghis, . 350
" 15. Imeritian, . 348
" 16. Georgian, . 348
" 17. Mingrelian, . 348
" 18. Caucasian mountaineer, . 342

PLATE 16.

Figs. 1–3. Bashkirs and Kirghis in
      camp, . 350, 351
" 4–6. Tartars, . 341
" 7, 8. Kurds, . 369
" 9. Persian nobleman, . 370

PLATE 17.

Fig. 1. Wedding in Persia, . 372
" 2. Persian women travelling, . 372
" 3. Persian music, . 372
" 4. Persian meal, . 371
" 5. Persian game, . 371
" 6, 7. Persian punishments, . 371

PLATE 18.

Fig. 1. Rajah of Cutch and his vassals
      (English East Indies), . 382
" 2. Caravan in Kattiavar (English
      East Indies), . 382

PLATE 19.

Fig. 1. Arabian nomades, . 375
" 2. Bedouin camp, . 375
" 3, 4. Arabian music and dance, . 376
" 5, 6. Travelling in Lahore, . 376

PLATE 20.

Figs. 1–3. Indian women and girls, . 378
" 4. Slave of a harem, . 378
" 5. Indian harem, . 378
" 6. Car festival in India, . 380
" 7. Salutation of the Arabians, . 376
" 8. Persian funeral, . 372

PLATE 21.

Fig. 1. Penitent Hindoo fanatic, . 382
" 2. Burning of a Hindoo widow with
      the remains of her husband, . 379
" 3. Wedding ceremony of the Tzin-
      garis (Indian gipsies), . 380
" 4. Nuptial procession of wealthy
      Hindoos, . 380

PLATE 22.

Figs. 1–6. Chinese, . 383
" 7. Corean, . 395
" 8. Loo-Choo islander, . 398
" 9–14. Japanese, . 396

PLATE 23.

Fig. 1. Tea culture in China, . 390
" 2. Silk culture in China, . 392
" 3. Chinese rice-dealer, . 384

PLATE 24.

Fig. 1. Chinese jugglers, . 393

Fig. 2. Chinese theatre, . . . 393
"   3. Chinese punishment, . . . 389

PLATE 25.

Fig. 1. Chinese puppet-show, . . 393
"   2. Chinese mandarin visiting, . 387, 389
"   3. Chinese quack, ... 392

PLATE 26.

Fig. 1. Moorish baths in Algiers, . . 400
"   2,3. Moorish noble and merchant, . 400
"   4. Arabian chief in Algiers, . . 400
"   5. Jewess of Algiers, . . . 399
"   6. Slave, ... 400
"   7. Lady of Cairo, . . . 405
"   8. Girl of Bornou (Senegal), . 413
"   9. Negro king of Boussa, . . 413
"   10, 11. Girls of Timbuktoo and Sokna (Fez), . . . 412
"   12. Idolatry in Central Africa, . 414

PLATE 27.

Fig. 1. Egyptian Fellahs, . . . 405
"   2. Arabian dames and tents, . . 405
"   3. Bedouins, ... 405
"   4,5. Arabian caravan, . . . 405
"   6. Nuptial procession in Cairo, . 405

PLATE 28.

Fig. 1. Abyssinian costumes, . . 402
"   2. Abyssinian travelling, . . 402
"   3. Elephant hunting, . . 414
"   4. Negro chief and suite, . . 416
"   5. Negro funeral south of the Coango River, . . 416
"   6. Christian negro-women of Benguela, . . . 416
"   7. Negro soldier (Portuguese Africa), . . . 416
"   8. Molua negroes guarding their king's dwelling, . . 416
"   9. Human sacrifices of the Cassange negroes, . . 416

PLATE 29.

Figs. 1–7. Sports of Indian tribes, . 429–432

PLATE 30.

Fig. 1. Mexican, ... 438
"   2,3. Inhabitants of La Puebla, . 437
"   4. Woman of Jalapa, . . 437
"   5,6. Costumes of Guatemala, . 439
"   7. Rich mulatto woman, . 438
"   8. Brazilian Mestizo, . . 438
"   9,10. Costumes of Bolivia, . 453
"   11. Girl of Bogota, . . 439
"   12. Girl of Lima, . . . 441
"   13. Squaw of the district of Quito, . 441
"   14. Muleteers of the Cordilleras, . 453
"   15, 16. Costumes of La Conception, . 453
"   17. Costumes of Chili, . . 453
"   18. Gaucho of Buenos Ayres, . 454

PLATE 31.

Fig. 1. Travelling farmer from the Rio Grande in Brazil, 452, 456

Fig. 2. Traveller from the province of Minas, . . . 452
"   3. Brazilian planter's family driving to mass, . . . 452
"   4. Townsmen from the Brazilian Rio Grande travelling, . 452
"   5. Caravan of Brazilian merchants, . 452
"   6. Convoy of diamonds, . 452

PLATE 32.

Fig. 1. Brazil Camacans in the forest, . 449
"   2. Festivity of the Camacans, . 449
"   3. Negroes from Bahia, . . 456
"   4. Free negro bringing up a fugitive slave, . . . 456
"   5. Inhabitants of San Paulo, . 452
"   6,7. Civilized Paraguay Indians, . 447

PLATE 33.

Fig. 1. Brazilian plantation, . . 452
"   2,3. Diamond washing, . . 456
"   4,5. Brazilian sports, . . 452
"   6. Brazilian planter's family walking to mass, . . . 452
"   7. Patagonian camp, . . 446

PLATE 34.

Figs. 1–6. Brazilian slave trade, . . 456

PLATE 35.

Fig. 1. Greenland seal-hunting, . . 425
"   2. Brazilian Indians bird-shooting, . 449
"   3. Attack by Guaycouros horsemen (Brazil), . . 446
"   4. Cattle-hunting on the Pampas (Brazil), . . 452
"   5. Negro dances at San Paulo, . 456
"   6. South Patagonian huts and graves, 446

PLATE 36.

Figs. 1–4. Sports of Brazilian Indians, 448, 456
"   5ab. Duels and combats among the Botocudos, . . 449
"   6. Duel among the Purvis, . 448

PLATE 37.

Fig. 1. Human sacrifice of the ancient Mexicans, . . . 437
"   2. Cannibals of the Paraguay forests, . . . 447
"   3. Cannibals preparing a peculiar beverage, . . . 447
"   4–6. War-dance, execution of captives, and funeral with the Tupinambas, . . 447

PLATE 38.

Figs. 1,2. Funeral of a chief (Sandwich Islands), . . . 463
"   3. Funeral in New Zealand, . 466
"   4. Tahitian girl, carrying presents, . 468
"   5. Dance of the Tahitians, . 468
"   6. Dance of the aborigines of the Caroline Islands, . . 460

PLATE 39.

Fig. 1. Chief from the Tonga islands, . 473
"   2. Combat of Tonga women, . 473
"   3–5. Girlish sports on the Tonga islands, . . . 473
"   6. Dance of Australian aborigines, . 475
"   7–9. Wedding ceremony, funeral, and ball of Australian aborigines, . . . 475
"   10. Ceremony of the Gna-Lung, . 474

PLATE 40.

Fig. 1. War dance of the Booro islanders, 468
"   2. Cock-fight on the Philippine islands, . . . 469
"   3. Making brandy on the Marian islands, . . . 470
"   4. Caroline islander, . . 461
"   5, 6. Aborigines of New Zealand, . 463
"   7. Dance of the same, . . 465

PLATE 41.

Fig. 1. Ceremonial salutation among the aborigines of New Zealand, . 465
"   2. Tattooing of the same, . 466
"   3. Indian and his squaw from the Caroline islands, . . 461
"   4. Dance of the Indians of this tribe, . . . 461
"   5–7. Indians of the island of Hawaï, 462
"   8. Dance of Australian savages, 467

PLATE 42.

Fig. 1. Dance in Samoa, . . . 473
"   2. Dwelling of the Chinooks, . 433
"   3. Meeting on Drummond's island, . 427

ENCYCLOPEDIA OF

Source Illustrations

ICONOGRAPHIC
ENCYCLOPÆDIA

OF

SCIENCE, LITERATURE, AND ART.

BY

J. G. HECK.

THE TEXT TRANSLATED AND EDITED

BY

SPENCER F. BAIRD, A.M., M.D.,

PROFESSOR OF NATURAL SCIENCES IN DICKINSON COLLEGE, CARLISLE, PA.

PLATES.

VOL. I.

CONTAINING THE ILLUSTRATIONS TO DIVISIONS I.—IV.

I.—MATHEMATICS AND ASTRONOMY.   III.—GEOGRAPHY.

II.—NATURAL SCIENCES.   IV.—HISTORY AND ETHNOLOGY.

NEW YORK: 1851.

PUBLISHED BY RUDOLPH GARRIGUE,

2 BARCLAY STREET (ASTOR HOUSE).

ICONOGRAPHIC

ENCYCLOPÆDIA.

DIVISION I.

MATHEMATICS AND ASTRONOMY.

FOURTEEN PLATES.

[THE LIST OF THE FIGURES ON THE PLATES WILL BE FOUND IN THE TABLES OF CONTENTS OF THE TEXT.]

THE PLATES ARE NUMBERED I. 1—15.

———————

NEW YORK: 1851.

PUBLISHED BY RUDOLPH GARRIGUE,

2 BARCLAY STREET (ASTOR HOUSE).

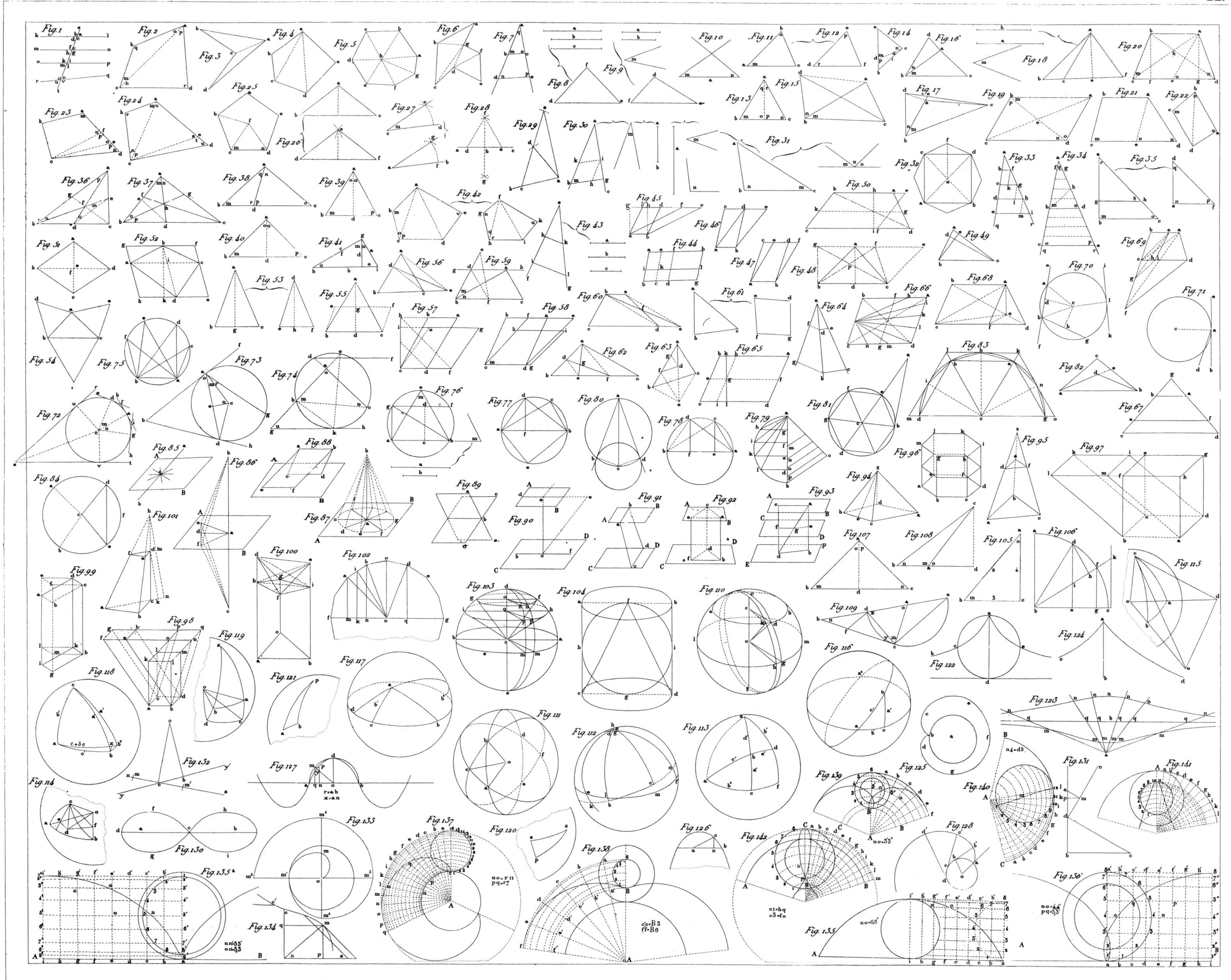

G. Heck dir.t

Henry Winkles sculp.t

G. Heck dir.t

Henry Winkles sculp.t

Taf. 5.

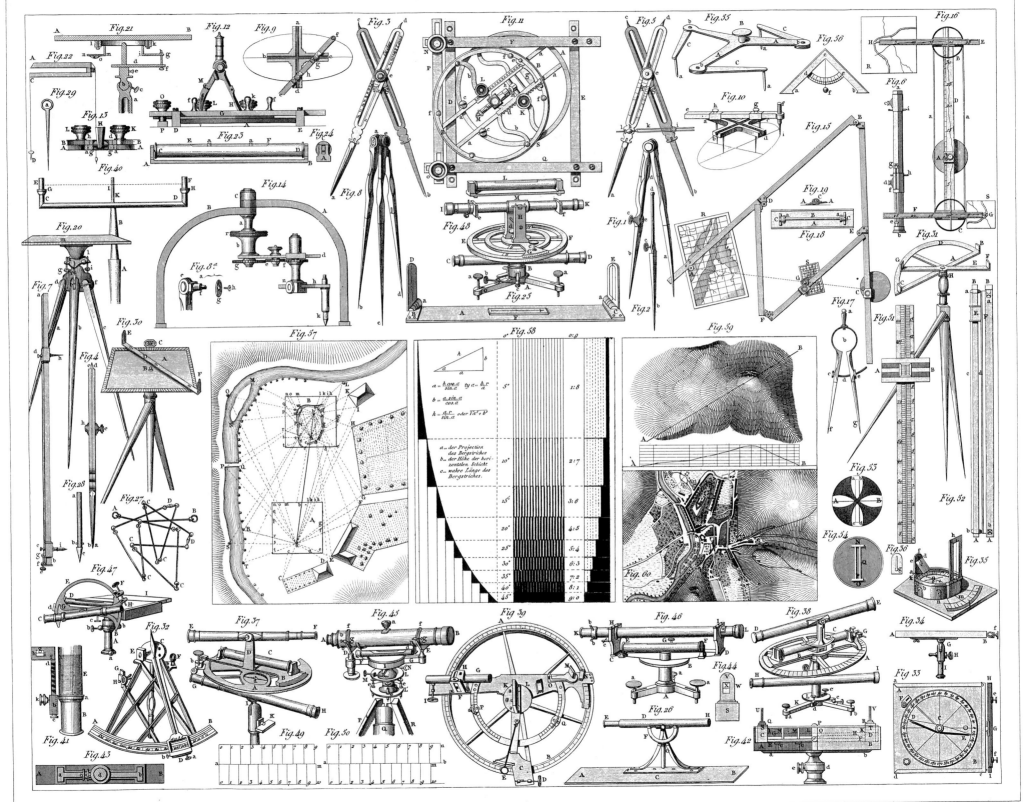

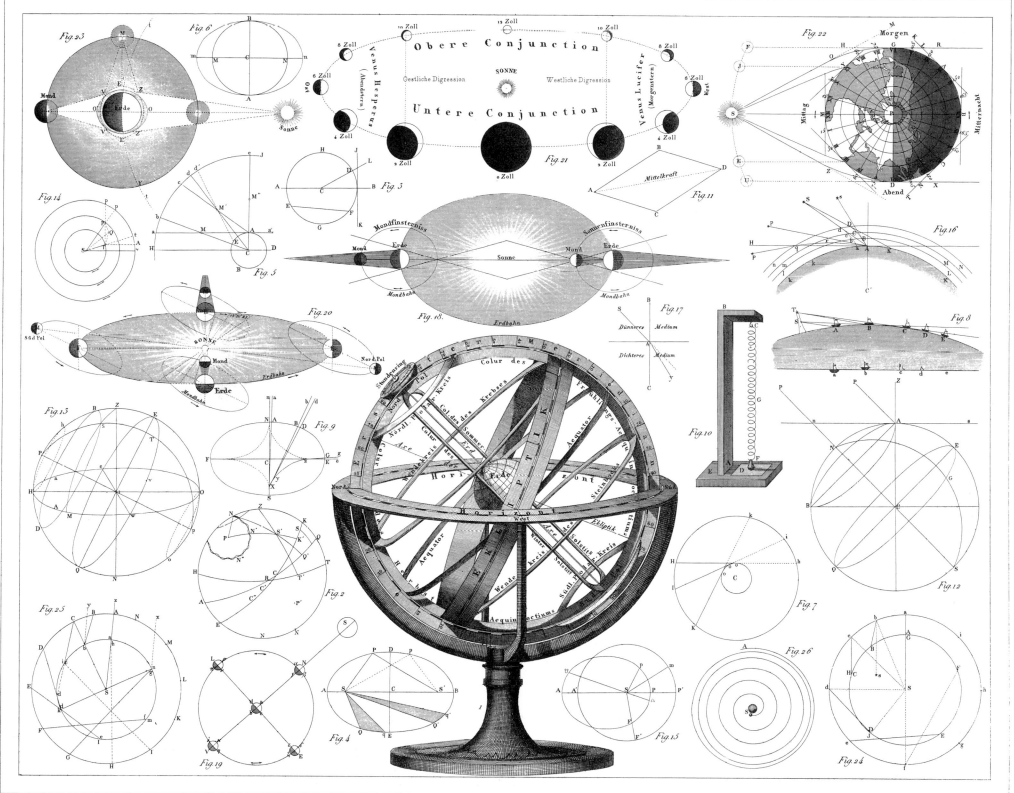

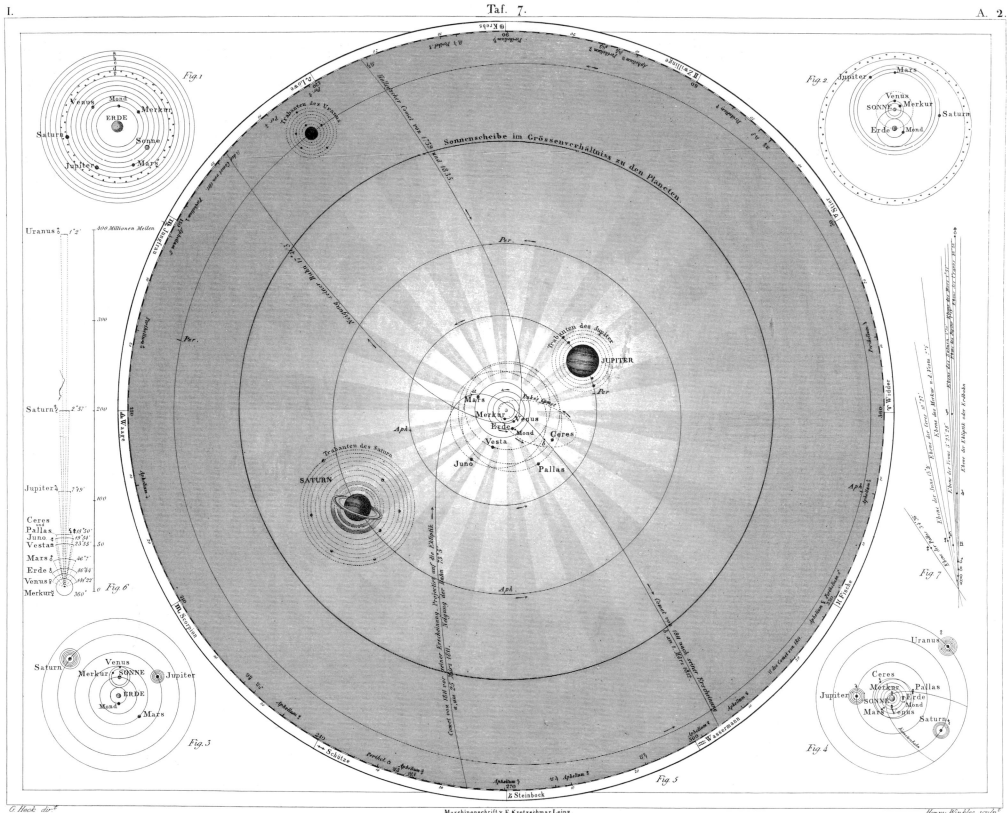

Fig. 1
ERDE · Sonne · Venus · Mond · Merkur · Saturn · Jupiter · Mars

Fig. 2
Jupiter · Mars · Venus · Merkur · SONNE · Erde · Mond · Saturn

Fig. 3
Saturn · Venus · Merkur · SONNE · Jupiter · ERDE · Mond · Mars

Fig. 4
Uranus · Jupiter · Ceres · Merkur · Pallas · SONNE · Erde · Mond · Mars · Venus · Saturn

Fig. 5

Fig. 6
Uranus ♅   1°2'
Saturn ♄   2°57'
Jupiter ♃   7°19'
Ceres und Pallas   18°30'
Juno   19°54'
Vesta   23°55'
Mars ♂   46°7'
Erde ♁   86°44'
Venus ♀   161°22'
Merkur ☿   360°

400 Millionen Meilen
300
200
100
50

Fig. 7

Sonnenscheibe im Grössenverhältniss zu den Planeten.

Trabanten des Uranus
Trabanten des Jupiter
Trabanten des Saturn

JUPITER
SATURN

Mars · Merkur · Venus · Erde · Mond · Ceres · Vesta · Juno · Pallas

♋ Krebs
♌ Löwe
♍ Jungfrau
♎ Waage
♏ Scorpion
♐ Schütze
♑ Steinbock
♒ Wassermann
♓ Fische
♈ Widder

G. Heck dir.t   Maschinenschrift v. E. Kretzschmar Leipz.   Henry Winkles sculp.t

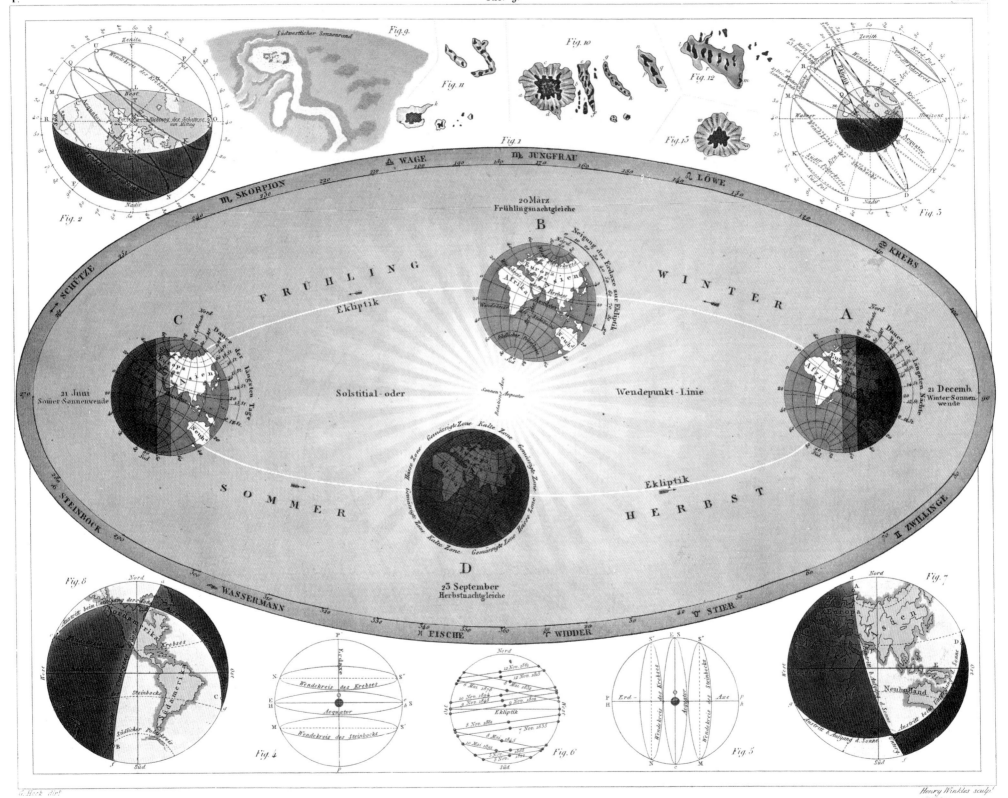

Fig. 9.
Südwestlicher Sonnenrand

Fig. 10

Fig. 11

Fig. 12

Fig. 2

Fig. 5

Fig. 15

Fig. 1

WAGE
JUNGFRAU
SKORPION
LÖWE
SCHÜTZE
KREBS
FRÜHLING
WINTER

20 März
Frühlingsnachtgleiche
B
Neigung der Ekliptik zur Ekliptik

Ekliptik

C
21 Juni
Sommer-Sonnenwende
Dauer der längsten Tage

A
21 Decemb.
Winter-Sonnenwende
Dauer der längsten Nächte

Solstitial- oder
Sonnen-Axe
Wendepunkt-Linie

Gemässigte Zone   Kalte Zone
Heisse Zone   Gemässigte Zone
Gemässigte Zone   Kalte Zone

Ekliptik

SOMMER
HERBST

STEINBOCK
ZWILLINGE

WASSERMANN
D
23 September
Herbstnachtgleiche
STIER

FISCHE
WIDDER

Fig. 8
Fig. 4
Fig. 6
Fig. 5
Fig. 7

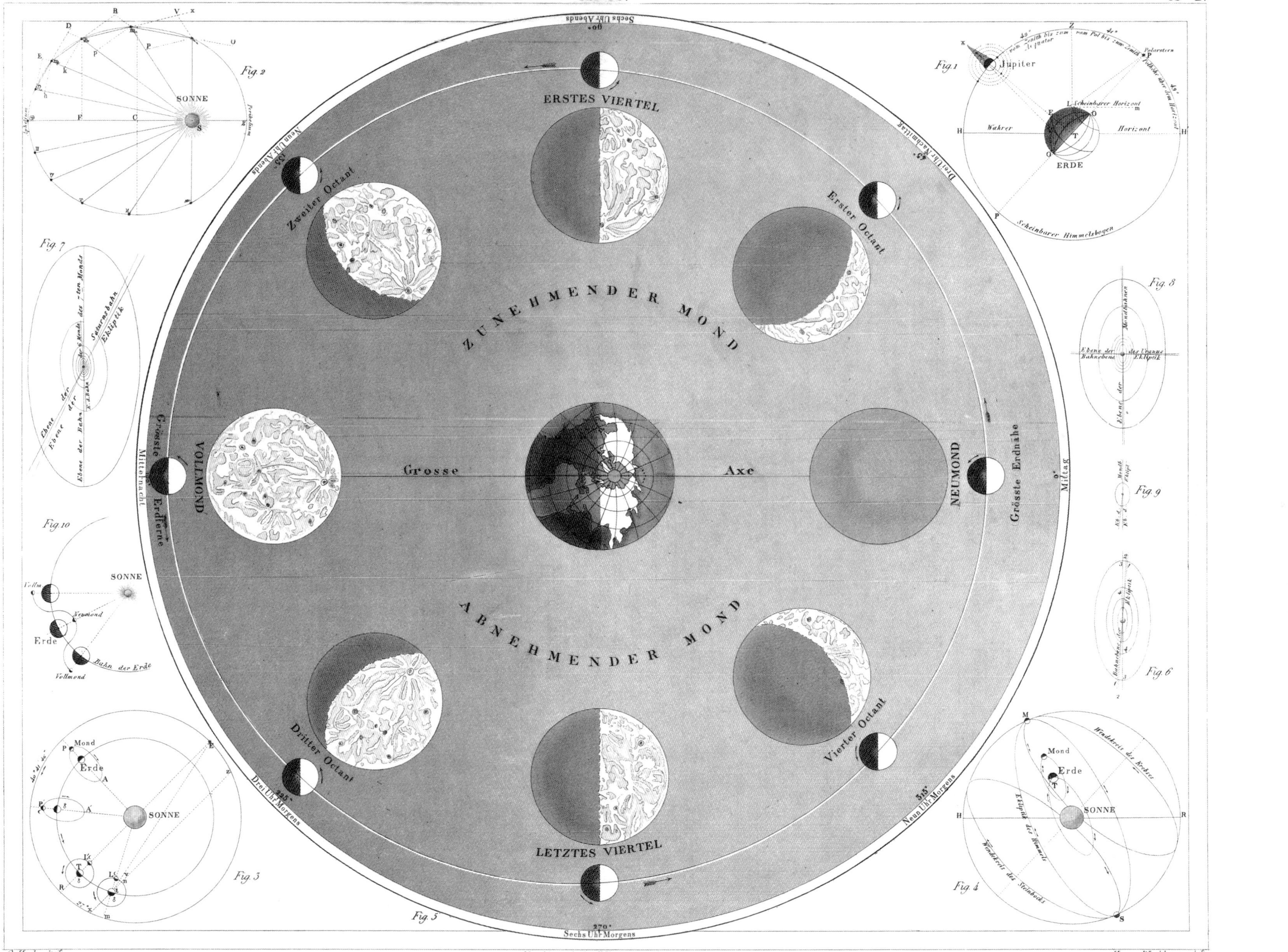

Fig 1
Fig. 2
SONNE
Jupiter
ERDE

Sechs Uhr Abends

ERSTES VIERTEL

Zweiter Octant
Erster Octant

Fig. 7
ZUNEHMENDER MOND
Fig. 8

VOLLMOND
Grosse   Axe
NEUMOND
Grösste Erdnähe

Fig. 9

ABNEHMENDER MOND
Fig. 6

Fig. 10
SONNE
Erde

Dritter Octant
Vierter Octant

LETZTES VIERTEL
SONNE

Fig. 3
Fig. 4

Sechs Uhr Morgens

Maschinenschrift v. E. Kretzschmar Leipz.

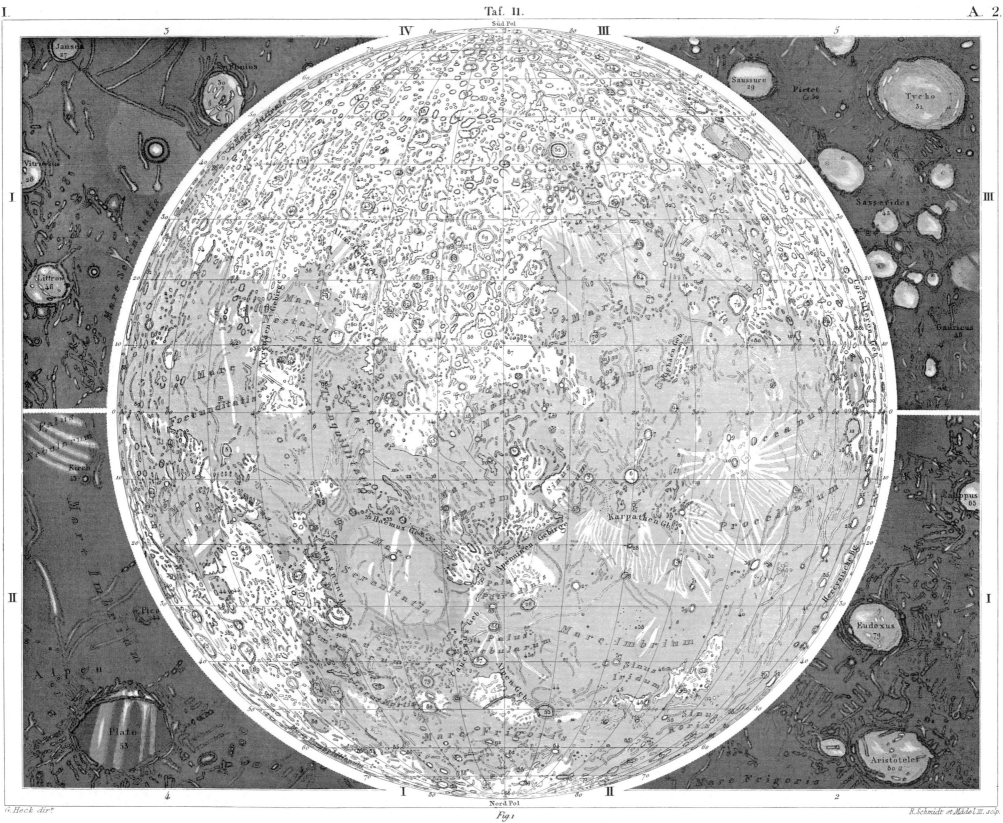

Süd Pol

Nord Pol

Fig. 1

G. Heck dir.

R. Schmidt et Mädel III. sculp.

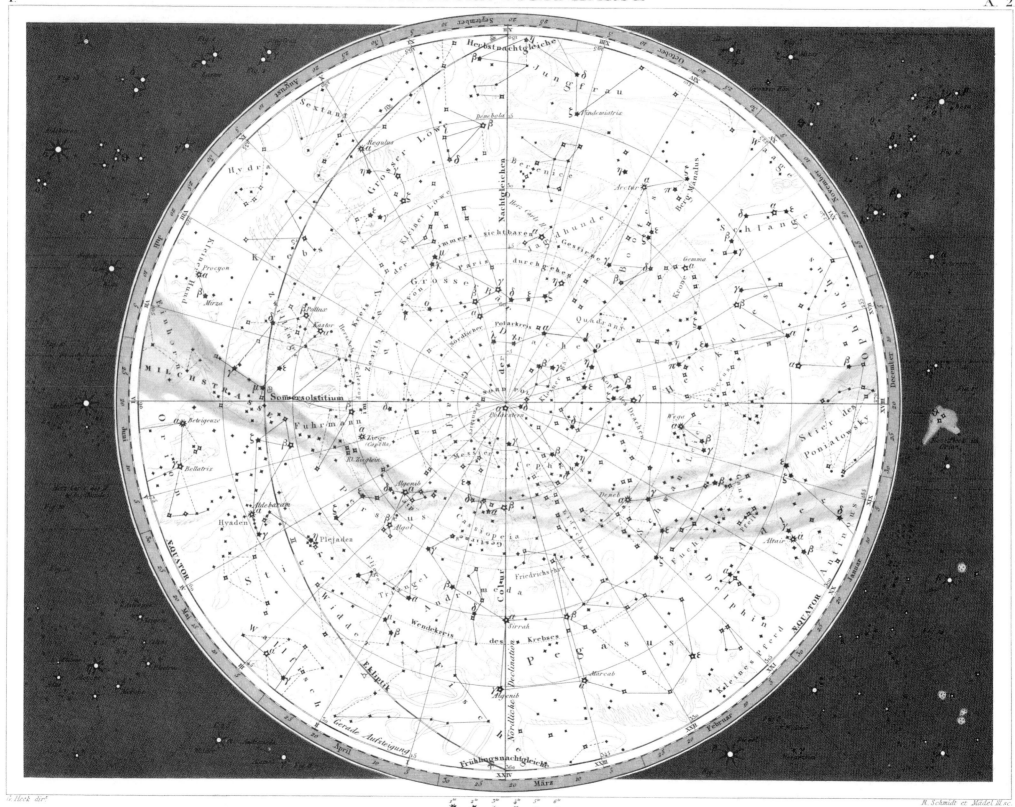

G. Heck dir.t

R. Schmidt et Mädel lith. sc.

Sterngrösse

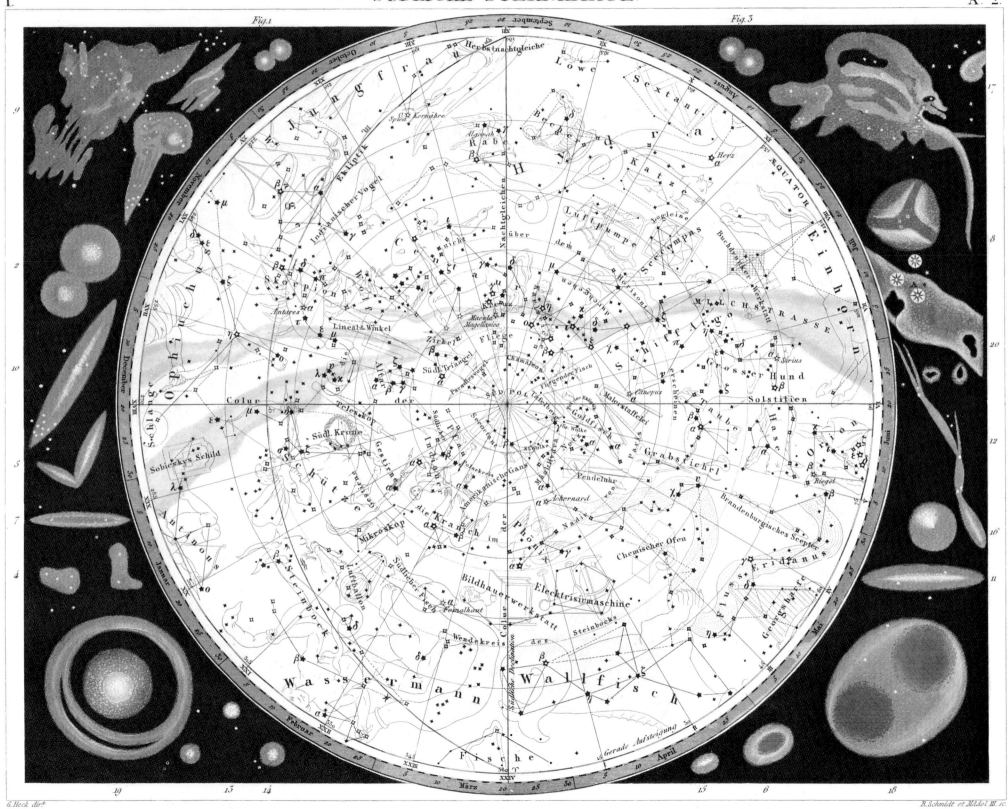

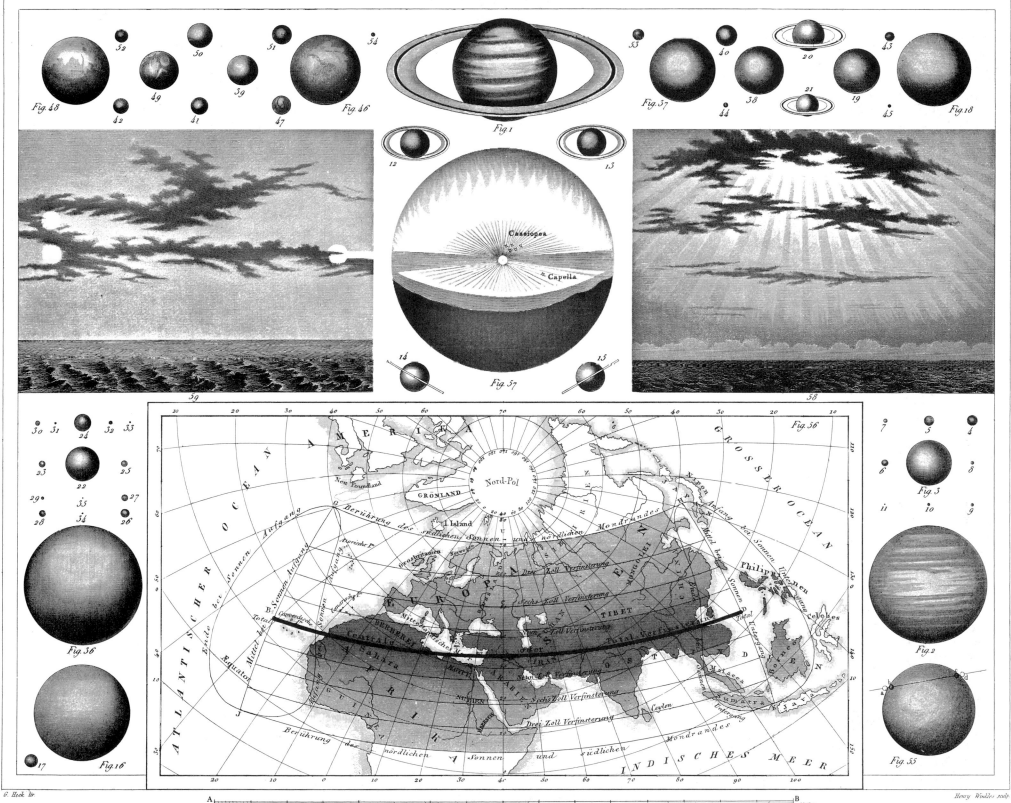

Fig. 48   52   50   51   54   53   40   20   43
           49   39   38   19   Fig. 18
42   41   47   Fig. 46   44   21   45

Fig. 37
Fig. 1

12   13

Cassiopea

☆ Capella

14   15

Fig. 57

59   58

30 31   24   32 33   7   5   4
23   22   25   6   8
29   35   27   Fig. 3
28   34   26   11   10   9

Fig. 36   Fig. 56   Fig. 2

AMERIKA   Nord-Pol   GROSSER OCEAN

Neu Foundland

GRÖNLAND

I Island

ATLANTISCHER OCEAN   EUROPA

17   Fig. 16   Fig. 55

INDISCHES MEER

A   B   Meilen

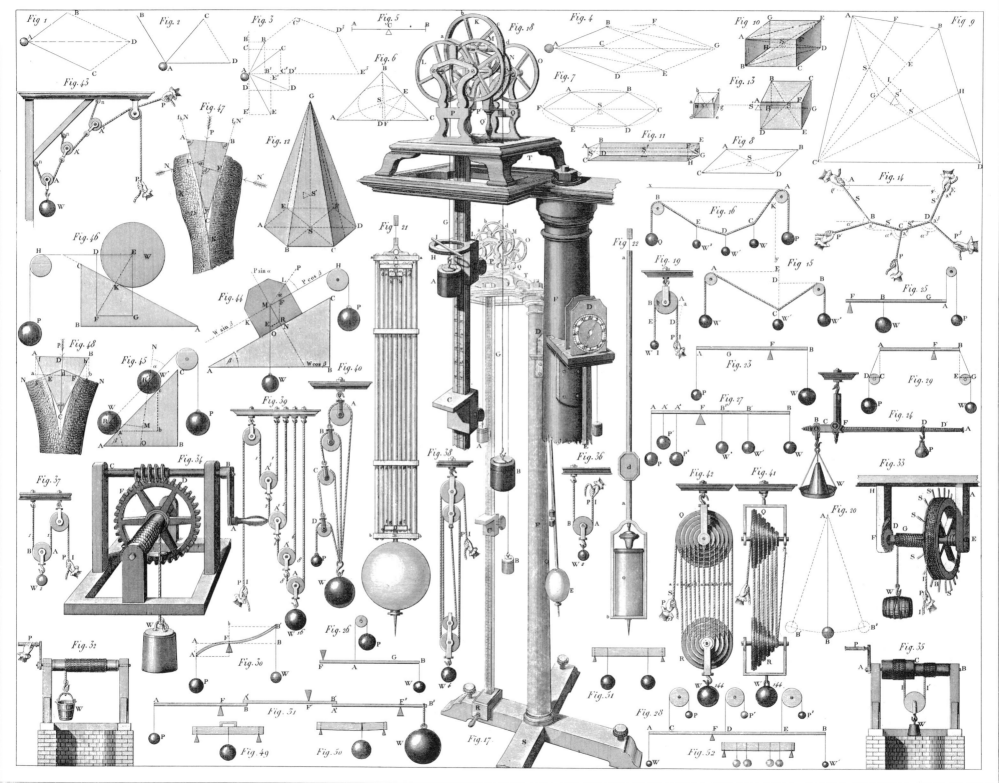

Fig. 1. *Fig. 2.* *Fig. 3.* *Fig. 5.* *Fig. 4.* *Fig. 10.* *Fig 9.*
Fig. 43. *Fig. 6.* *Fig. 7.* *Fig. 13.* *Fig. 18.*
Fig. 47. *Fig. 12.* *Fig. 11.* *Fig. 8.*
Fig. 46. *Fig. 14.*
Fig. 44. *Fig. 16.* *Fig. 15.* *Fig. 25.*
Fig. 48. *Fig. 19.*
Fig. 45. *Fig. 40.* *Fig. 23.* *Fig. 29.*
Fig. 37. *Fig. 39.* *Fig. 21.* *Fig. 27.* *Fig. 24.*
Fig. 34. *Fig. 38.* *Fig. 36.* *Fig. 33.*
Fig. 42. *Fig. 41.* *Fig. 20.*
Fig. 32. *Fig. 26.* *Fig. 35.*
Fig. 30. *Fig. 31.* *Fig. 28.*
Fig. 51. *Fig. 17.* *Fig. 52.*
Fig. 49. *Fig. 50.*

$P \sin \alpha$ $P \cos \beta$ $W \sin \beta$ $W \cos \beta$

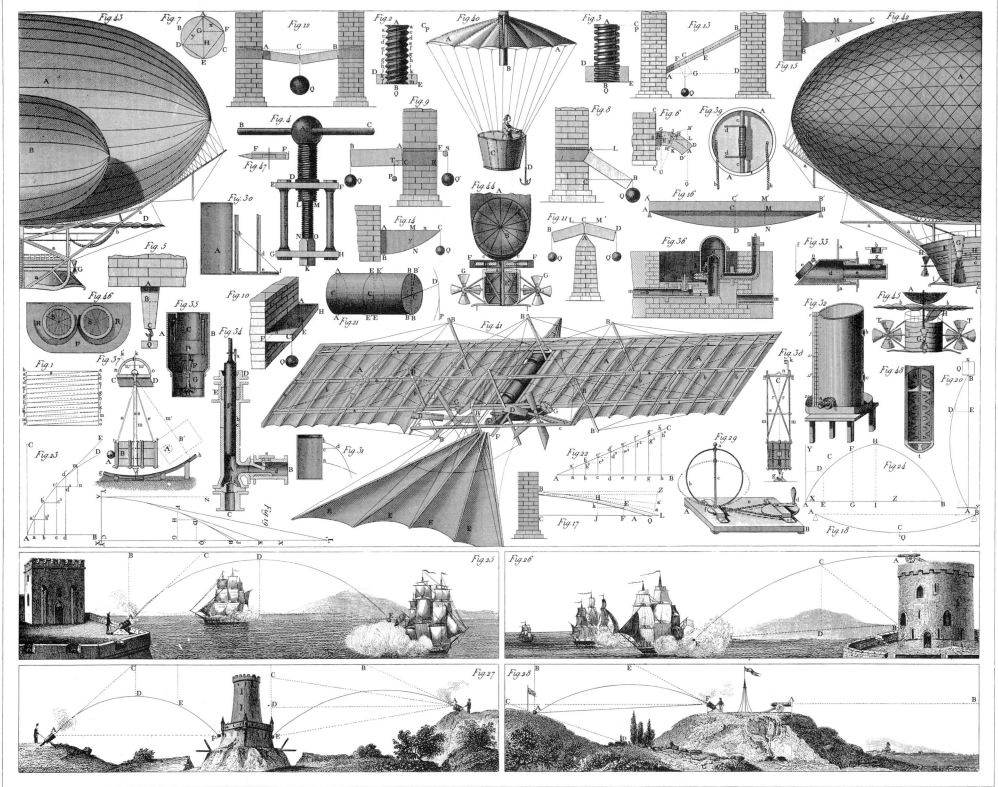

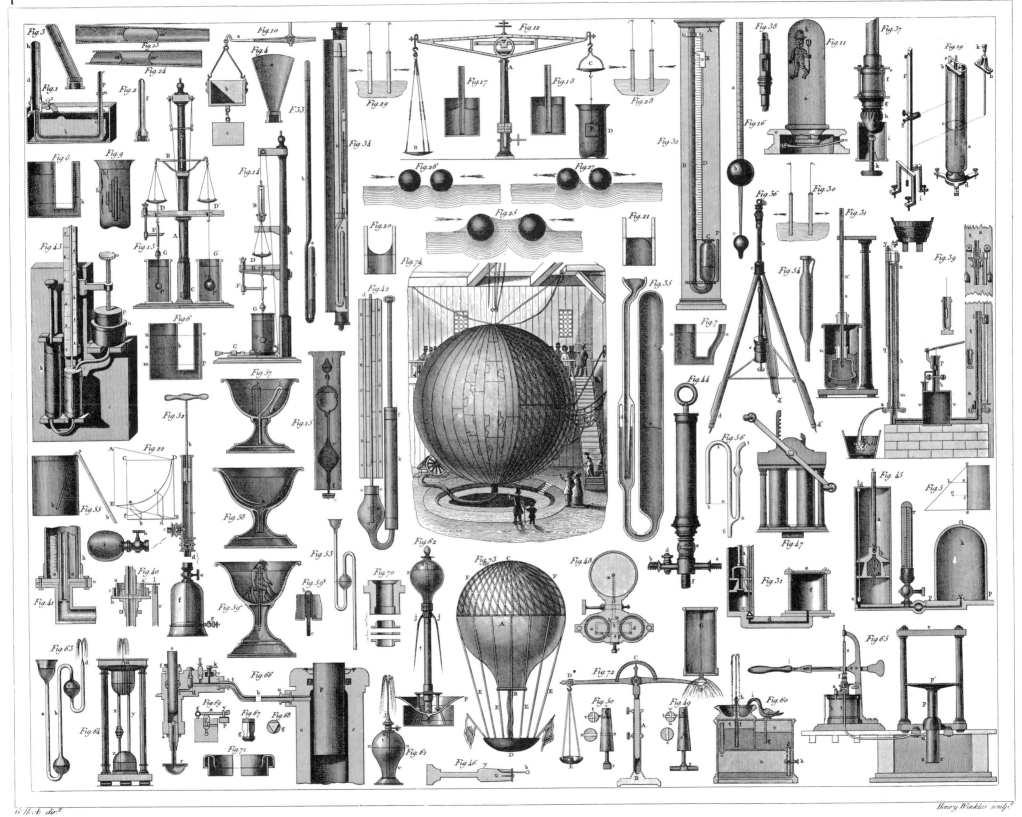

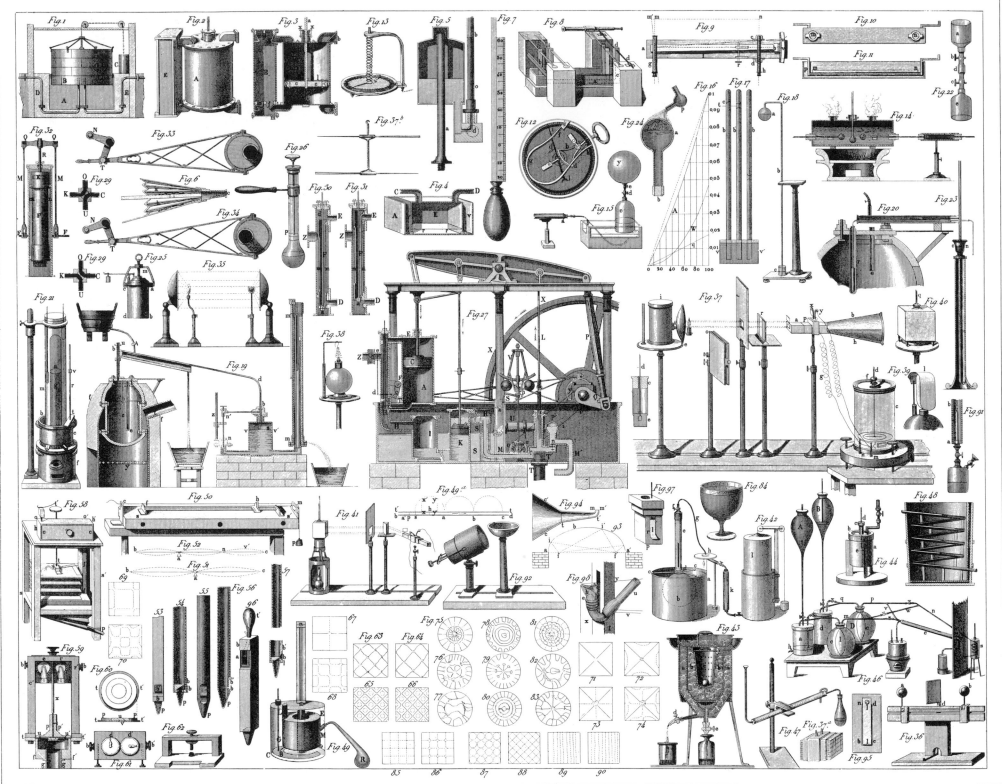

G. Heck dir.t

Henry Winkles sculp.t

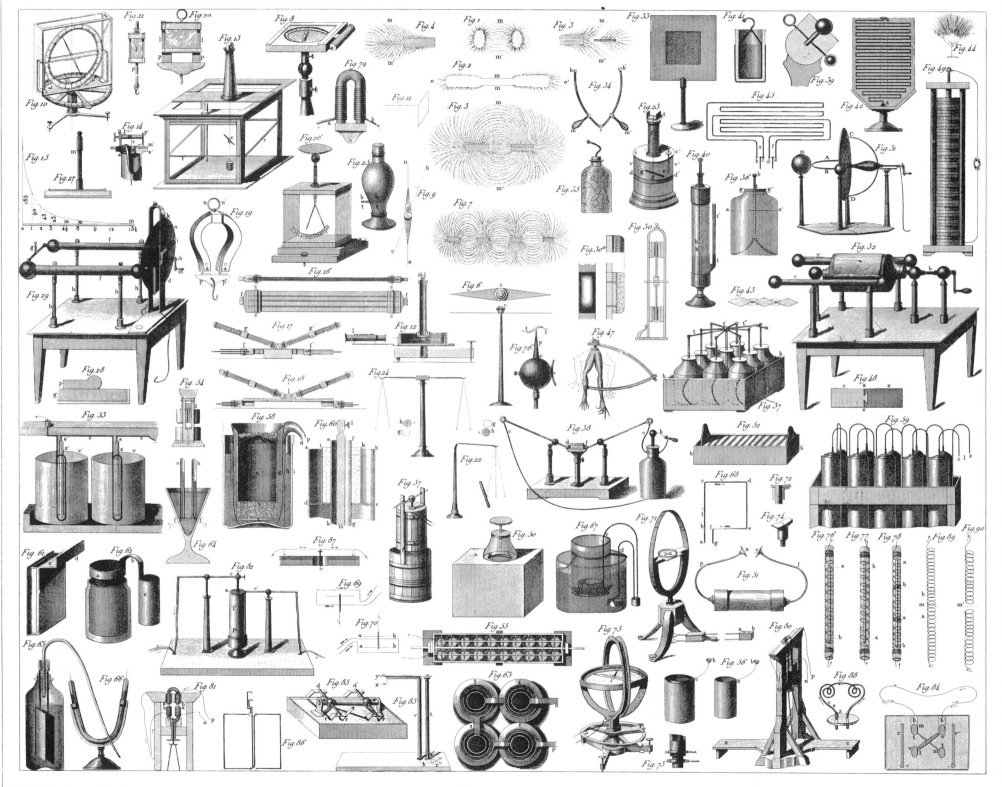

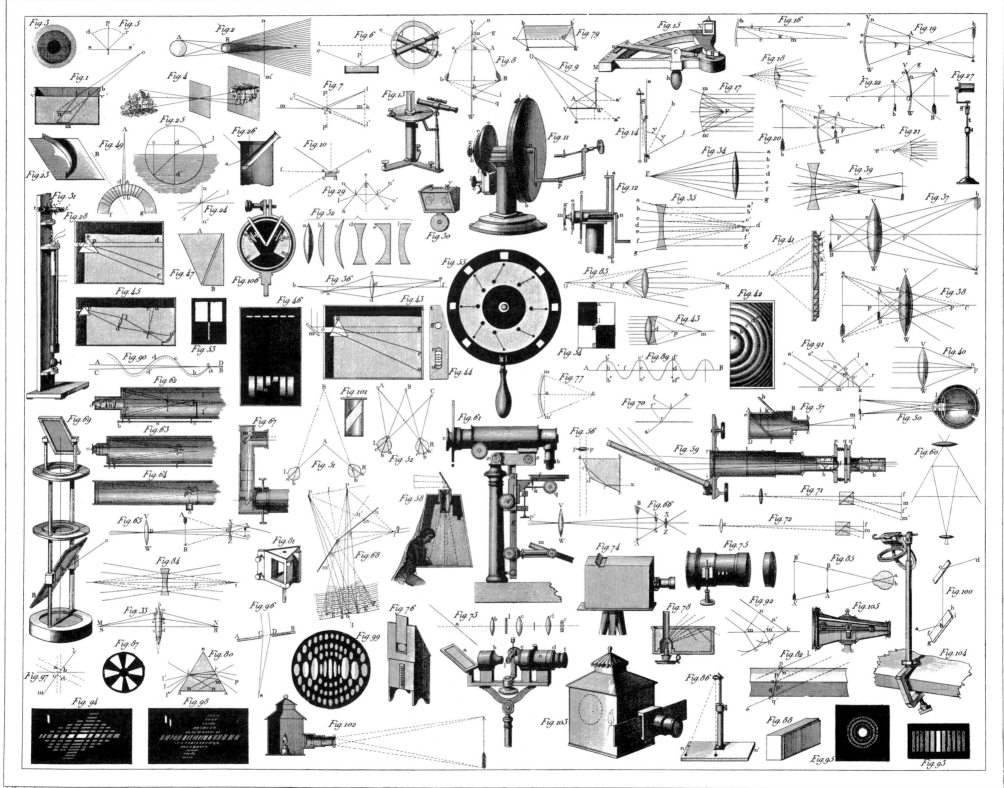

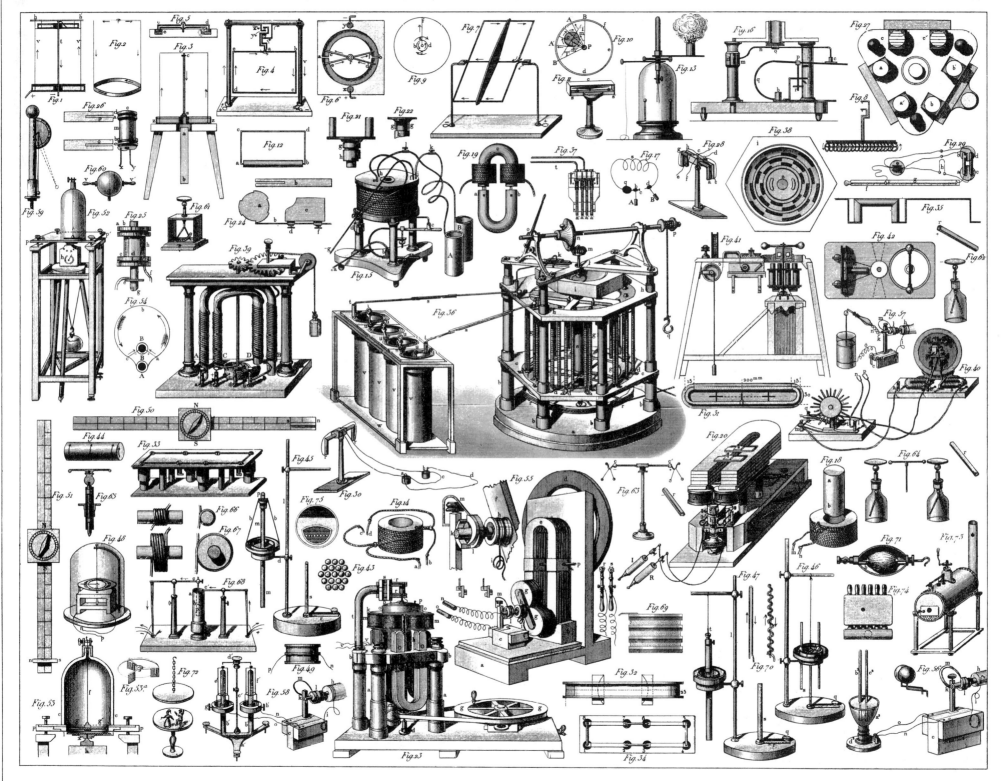

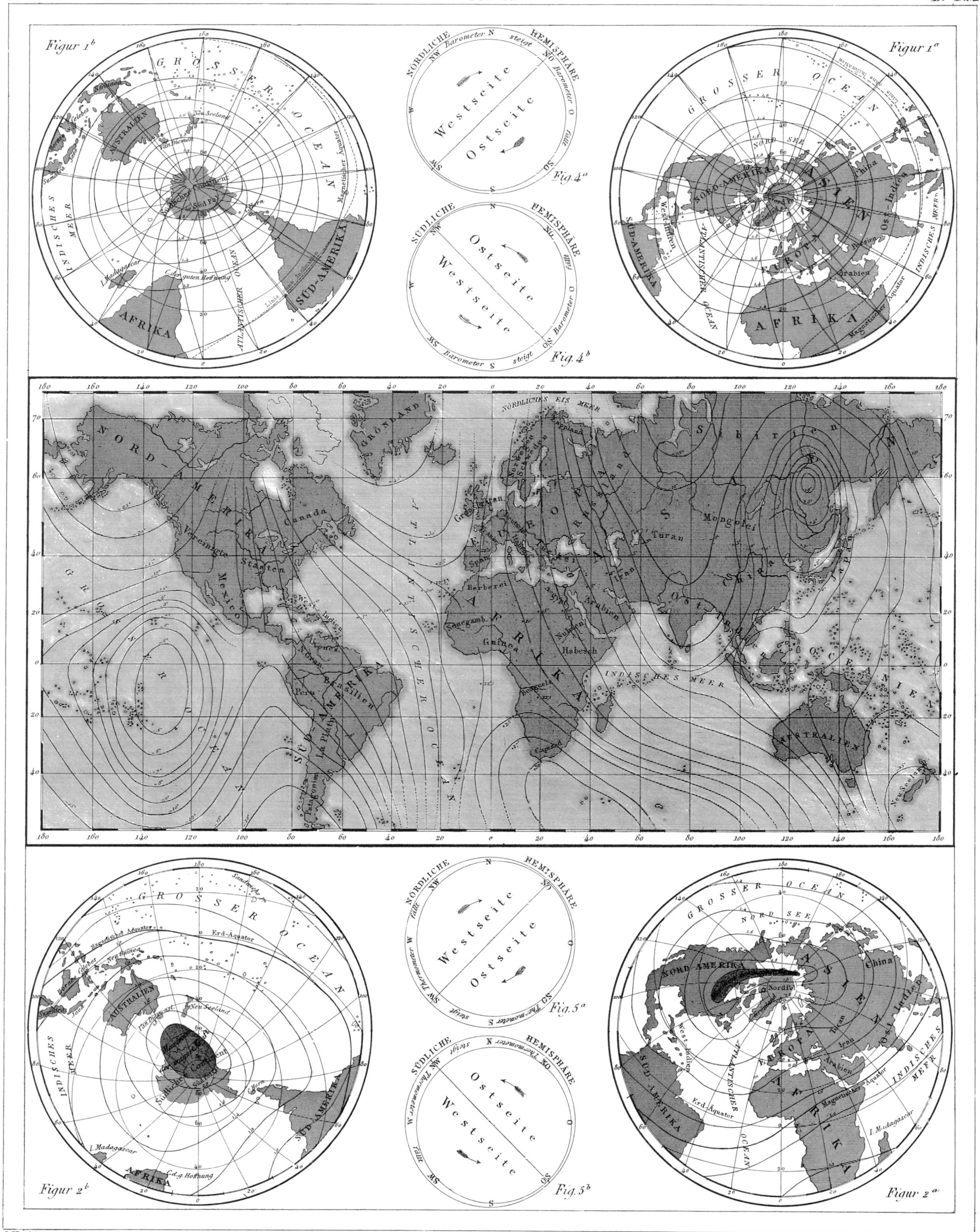

Figur 1ª

Figur 1ᵇ

Figur 2ª

Figur 2ᵇ

NÖRDLICHE HEMISPHÄRE

SÜDLICHE HEMISPHÄRE

Ostseite

Westseite

Fig. 4ª

Fig. 4ᵇ

NÖRDLICHE HEMISPHÄRE

SÜDLICHE HEMISPHÄRE

Ostseite

Westseite

Fig. 5ª

Fig. 5ᵇ

R. Schmidt et. Medel III sculp⁵

G. Heck dir⁴

I.

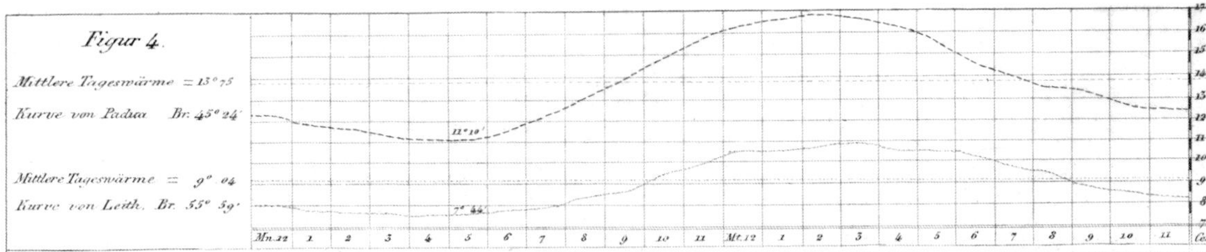

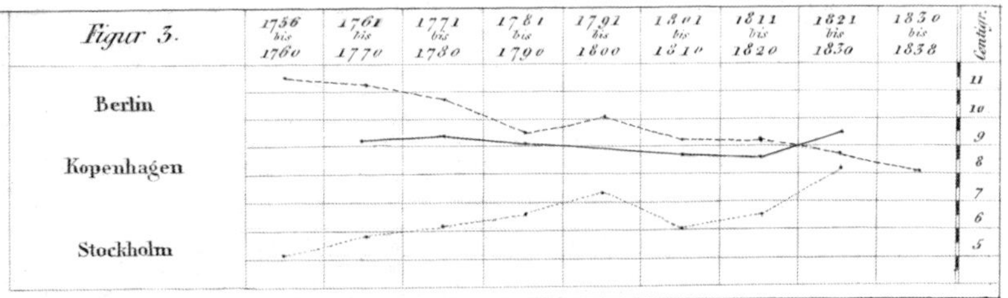

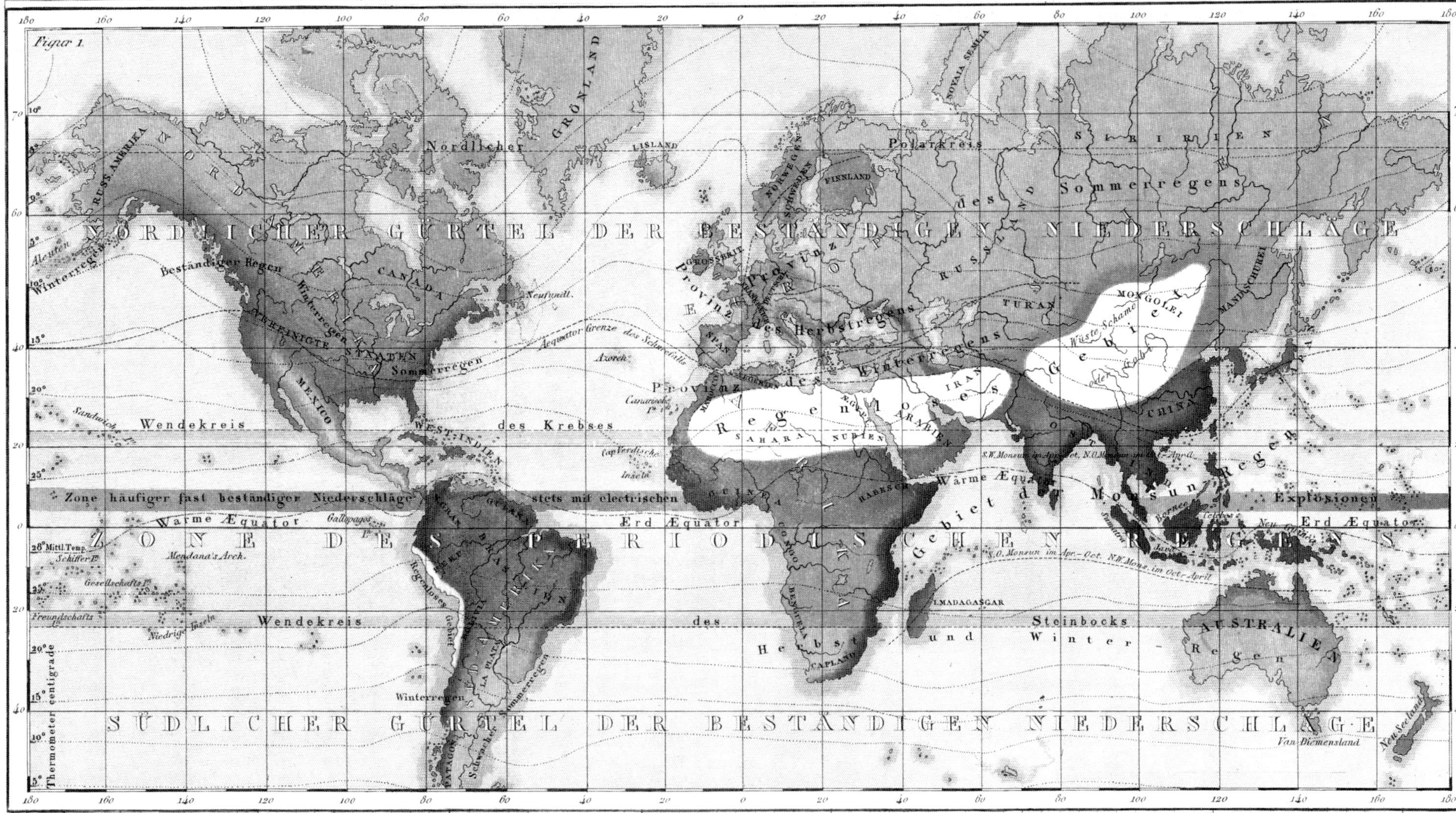

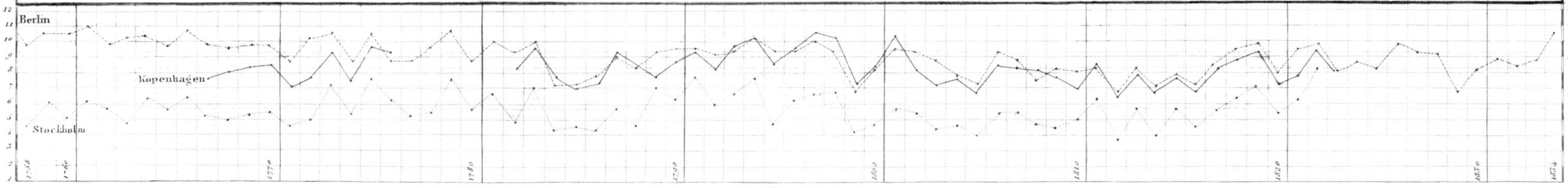

Figur 4.

Mittlere Tageswärme = 13°75
Kurve von Padua   Br. 45° 24

Mittlere Tageswärme = 9° 04
Kurve von Leith   Br. 55° 59

Figur 3.	1756 bis 1760	1761 bis 1770	1771 bis 1780	1781 bis 1790	1791 bis 1800	1801 bis 1810	1811 bis 1820	1821 bis 1830	1830 bis 1838	
Berlin										
Kopenhagen										
Stockholm										

Figur 1.

NORDLICHER GÜRTEL DER BESTÄNDIGEN NIEDERSCHLÄGE

ZONE DES PERIODISCHEN REGENS

SÜDLICHER GÜRTEL DER BESTÄNDIGEN NIEDERSCHLÄGE

Figur 2.

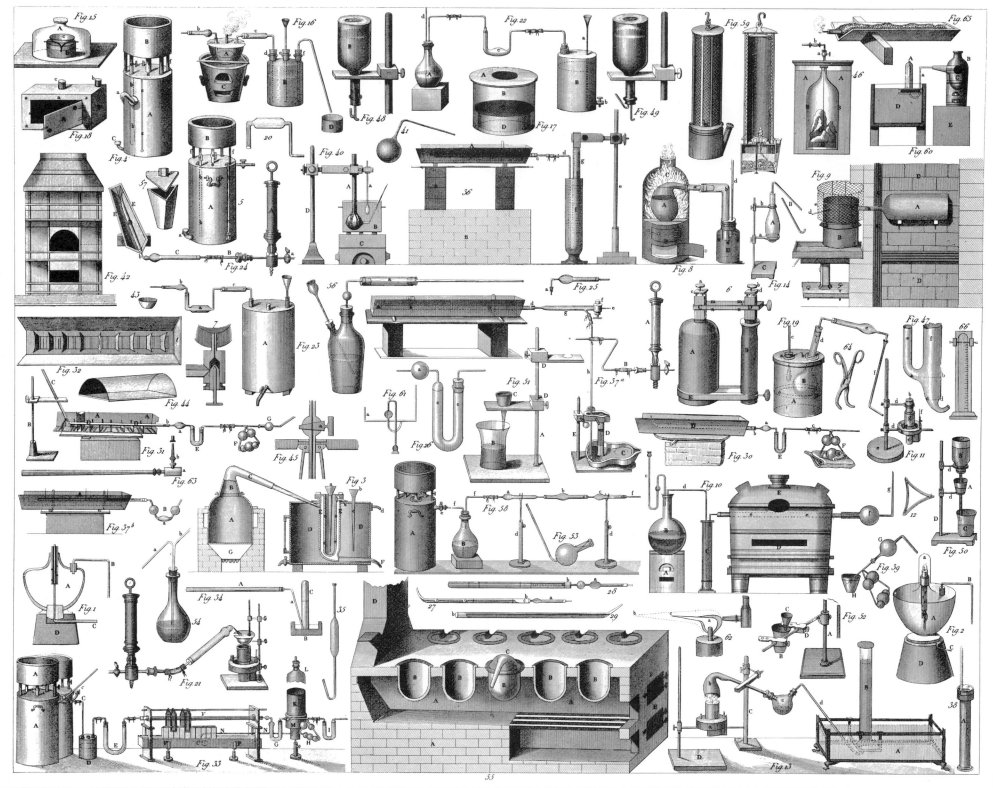

Fig. 15. Fig. 16. Fig. 22. Fig. 59. Fig. 65. Fig. 46. Fig. 48. Fig. 17. Fig. 49. Fig. 60. Fig. 18. Fig. 4. Fig. 40. Fig. 41. Fig. 9. Fig. 57. Fig. 5. Fig. 36. Fig. 8. Fig. 14. Fig. 42. Fig. 24. Fig. 43. Fig. 56. Fig. 25. Fig. 6. Fig. 23. Fig. 19. Fig. 47. Fig. 66. Fig. 52. Fig. 61. Fig. 51. Fig. 37ᵃ. Fig. 44. Fig. 31. Fig. 45. Fig. 26. Fig. 30. Fig. 11. Fig. 63. Fig. 3. Fig. 10. Fig. 50. Fig. 37ᵇ. Fig. 58. Fig. 53. Fig. 39. Fig. 1. Fig. 34. Fig. 35. Fig. 54. Fig. 21. Fig. 52. Fig. 2. Fig. 33. Fig. 13. Fig. 38. Fig. 55.

G. Heck. dir.ᵗ   Henry Winkles sculp.ᵗ

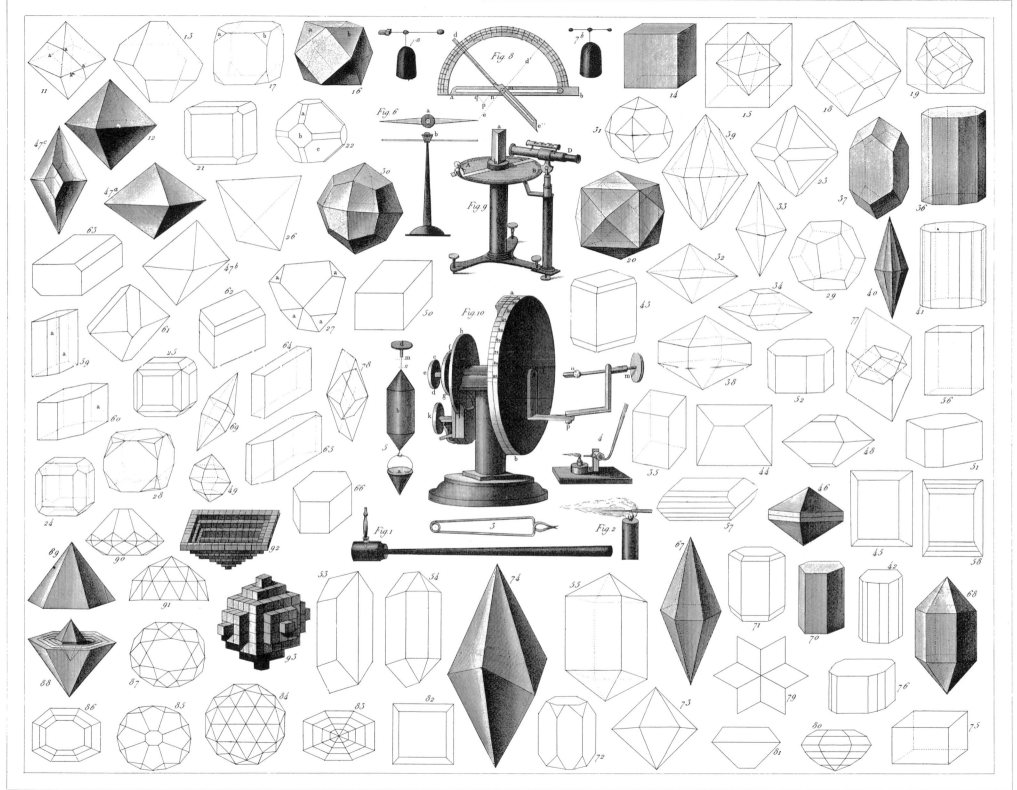

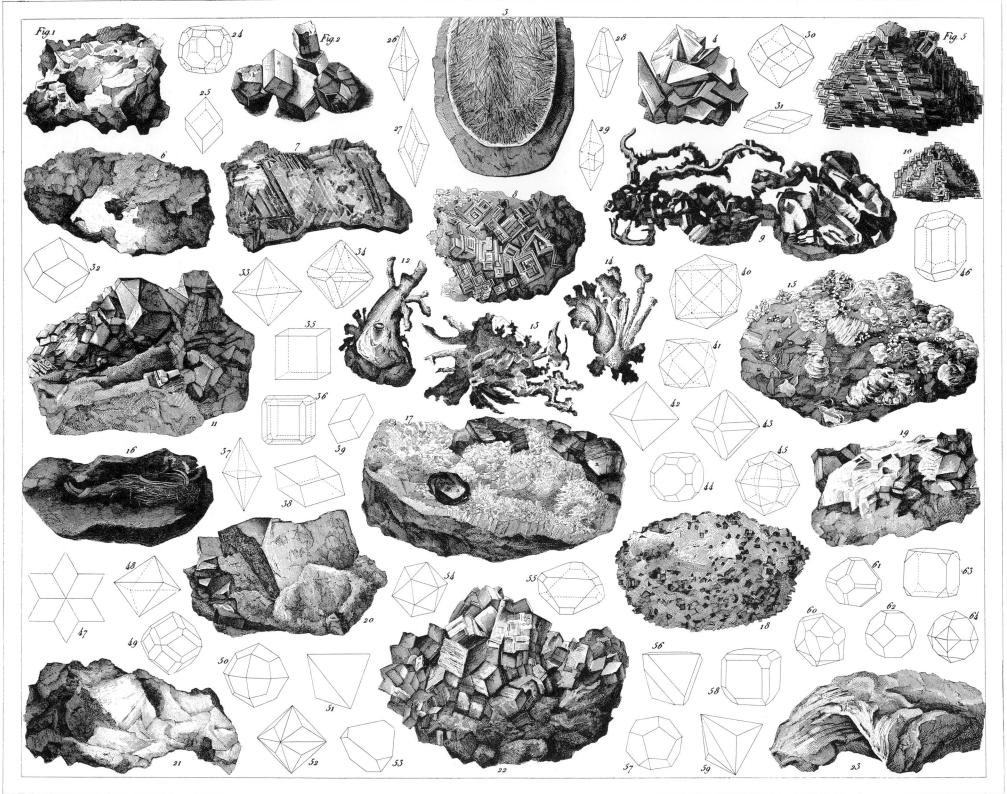

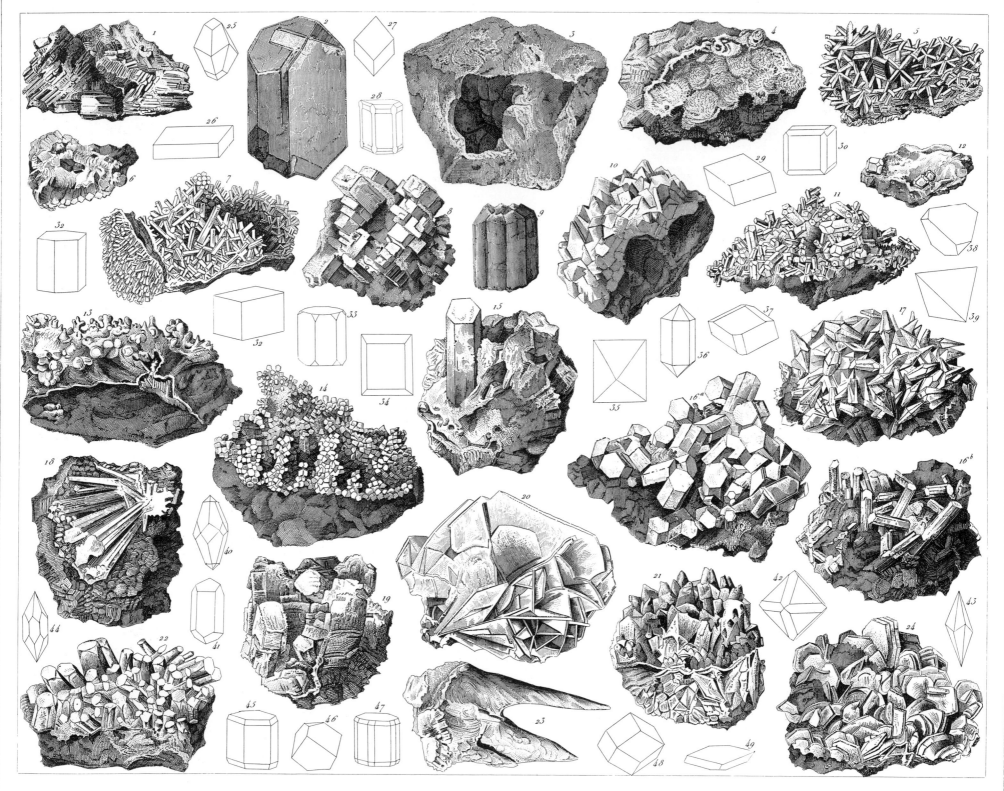

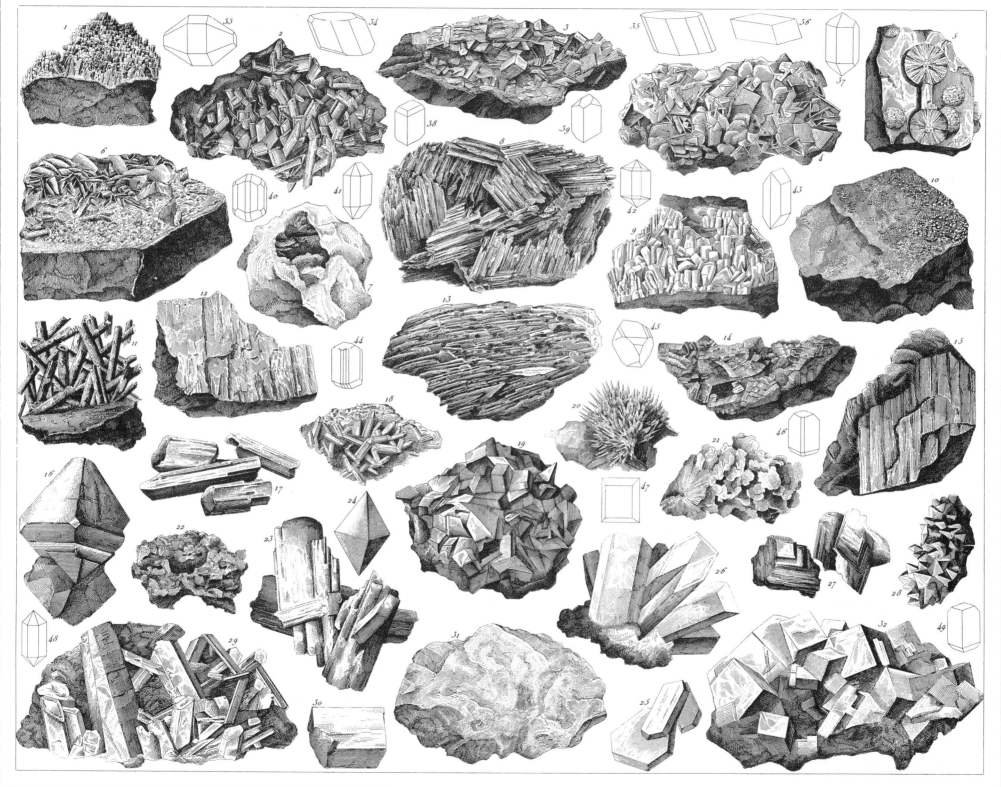

G. Heck dir.t

Henry Winkles sculp.t

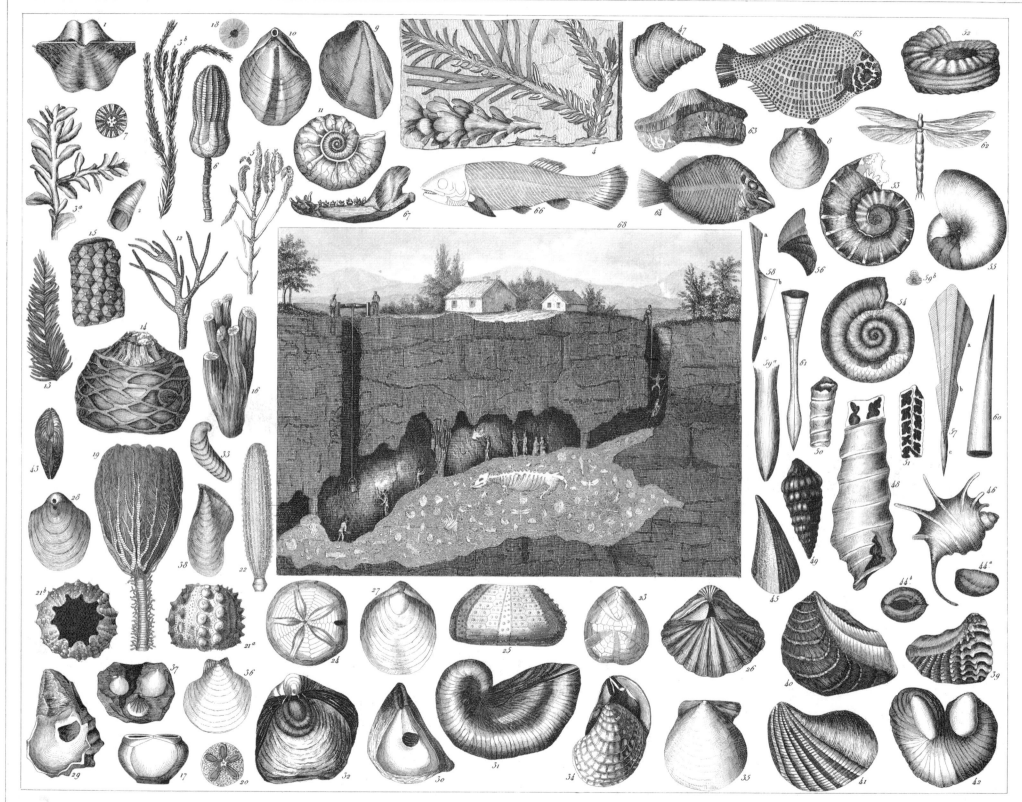

G. Heck dir.t

Henry Winkles sculp.t

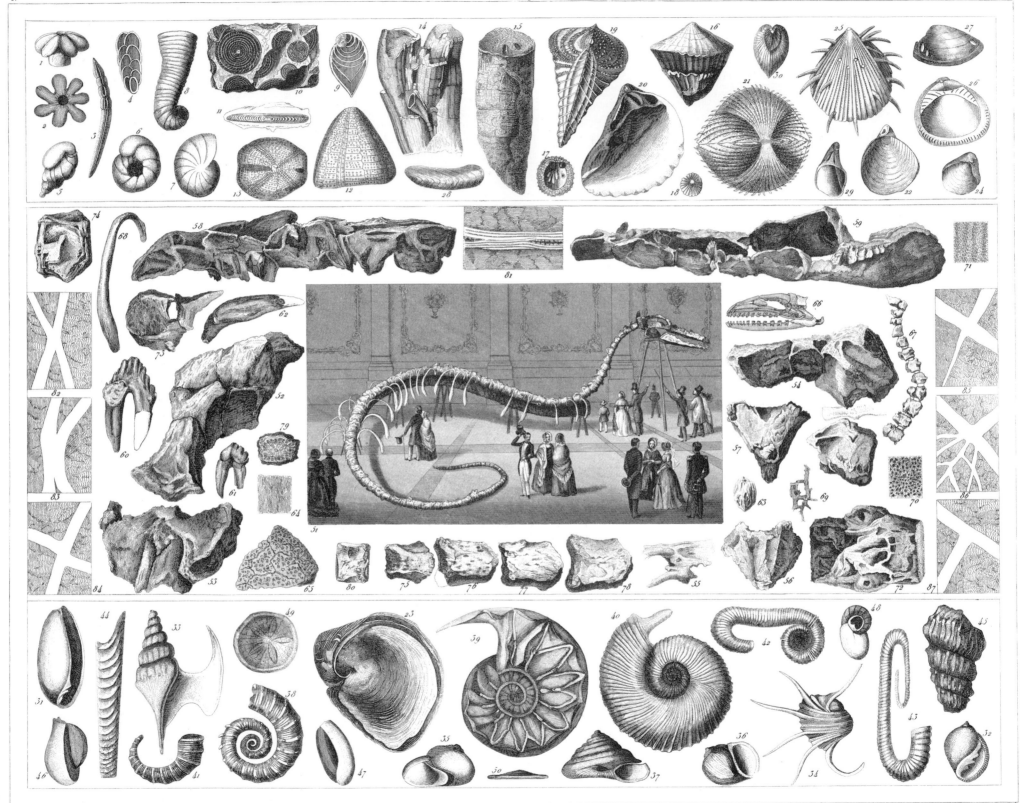

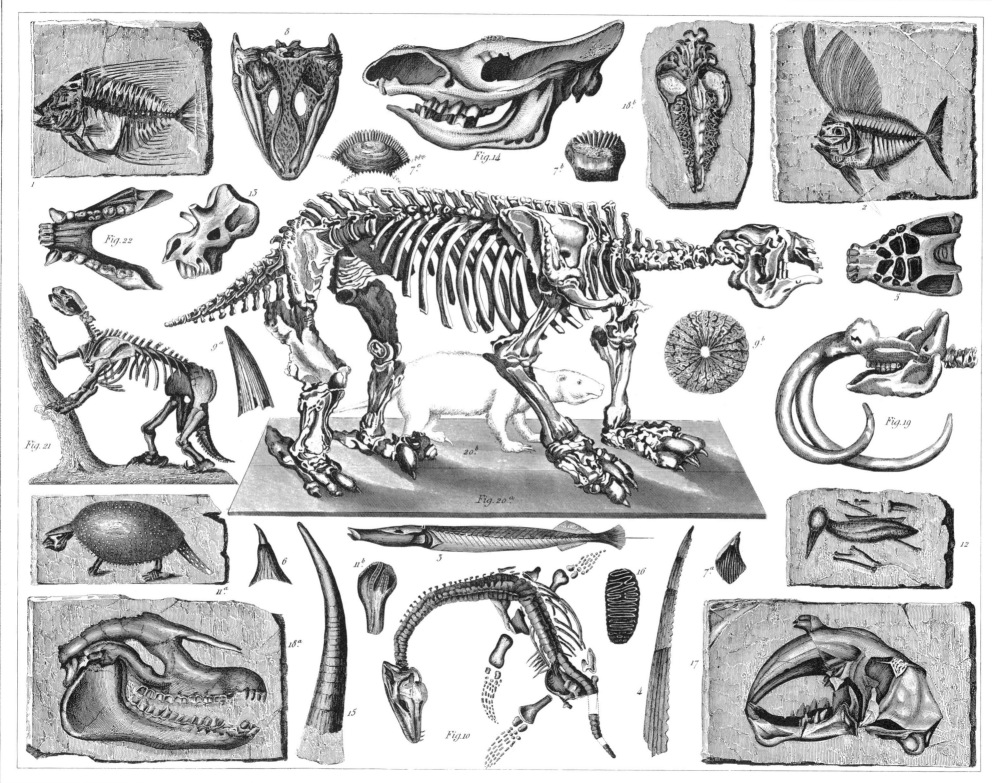

8

1

7.ᶜ

Fig.14

7.ᵇ

18.ᵇ

2

Fig.22

13

5

9.ᵃ

9.ᵇ

Fig. 19

Fig. 21

20.ᵇ

Fig. 20.ᵃ

12

11.ᵃ

6

5

11.ᵇ

7.ᵃ

18.ᵃ

16.ᶜ

17

15

Fig.10

4

G.Heck dir.ᵗ

Henry Winkles sculp.ᵗ

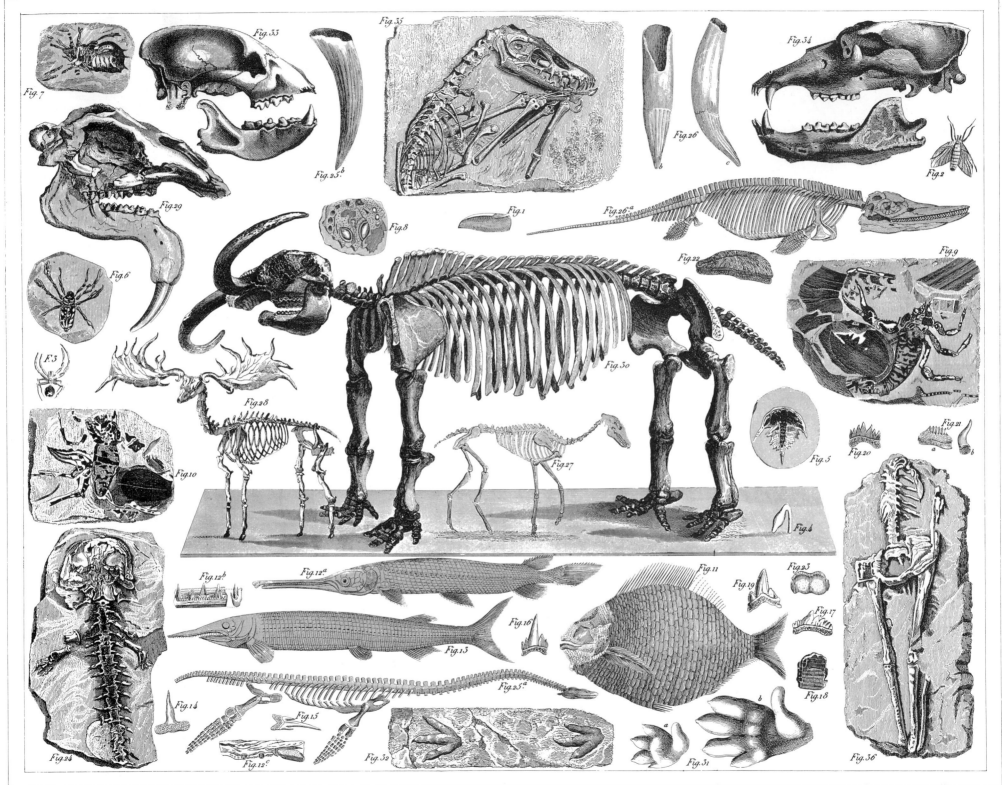

G. Heck dir.t Henry Winkles sculp.t

Karte des Pariser Tertiarbeckens

Tertiärgebilde.   Kreide.   Juraformat.n   Trias.   Uebergangsgeb.n   Primit:Gesteine.   Steinkohle.

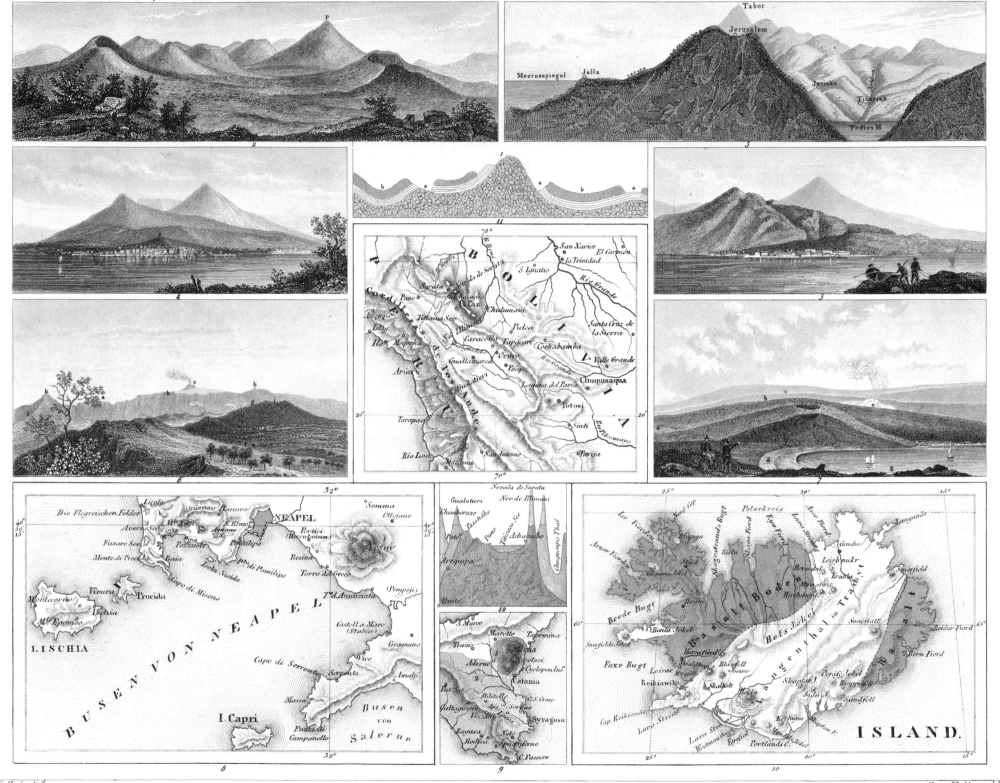

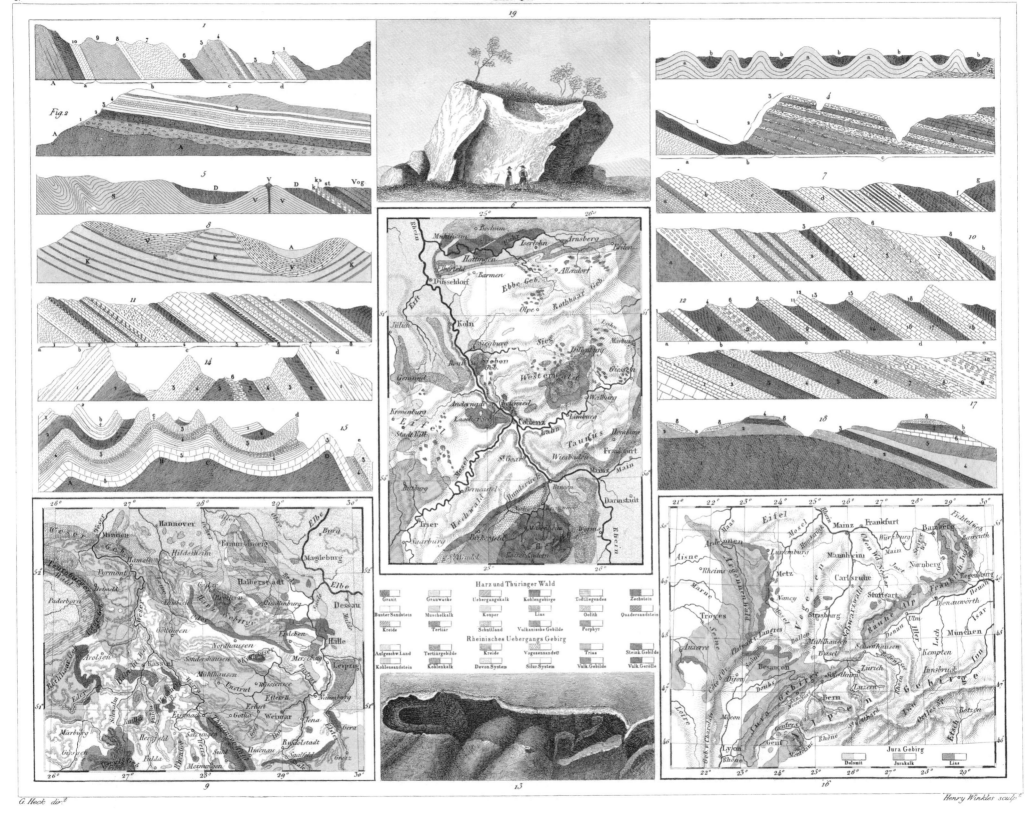

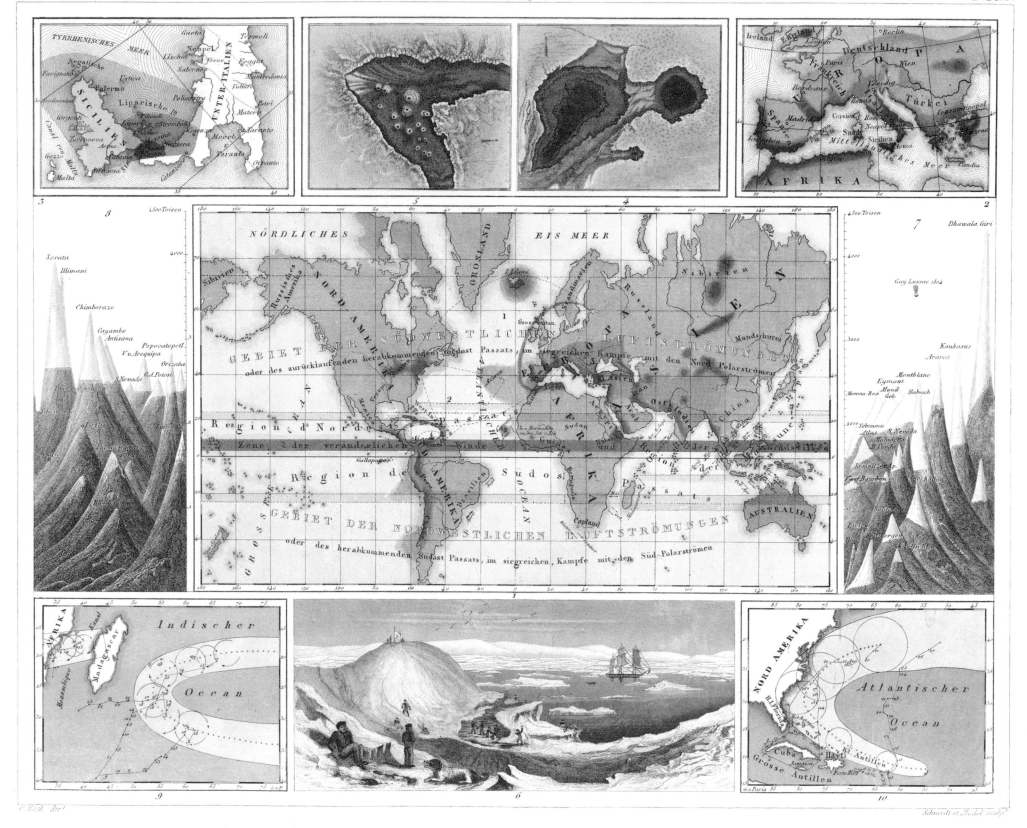

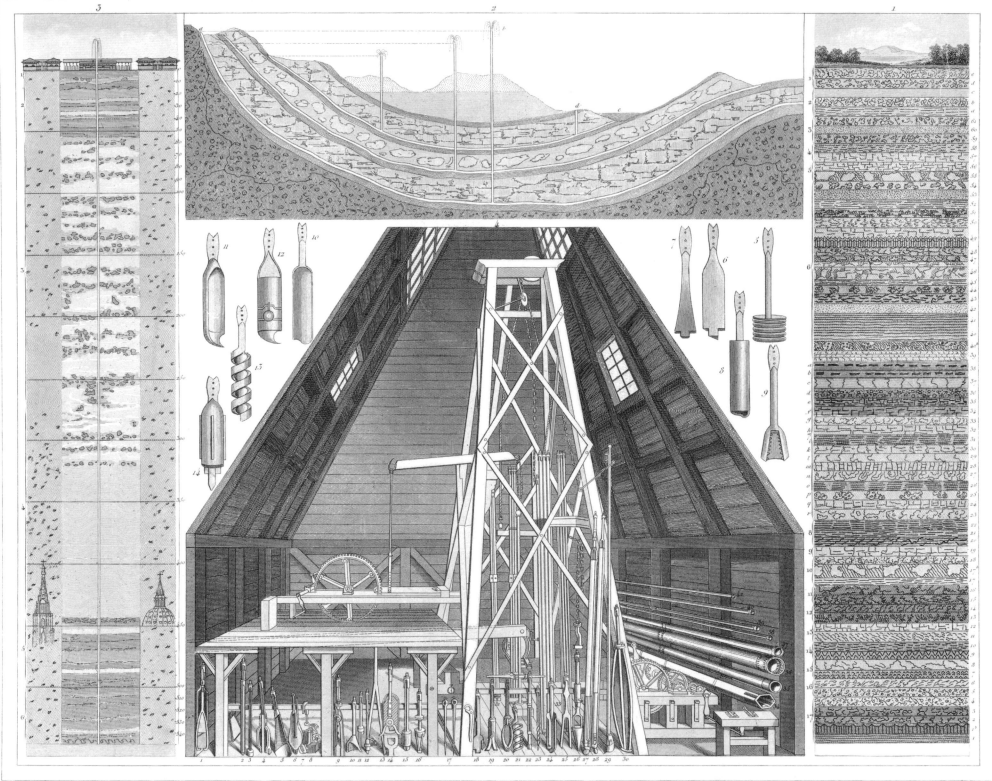

G. Heck dir!. Henry Winkles sculp!.

G.Heck dirt. Henry Winkles sculp.

G. Heck dir.t　　　　　　　　　　　　　　　　　　　　　Henry Winkles sculp.t

Felsen von Gibraltar — Ceuta

Tarifa — Alcazar

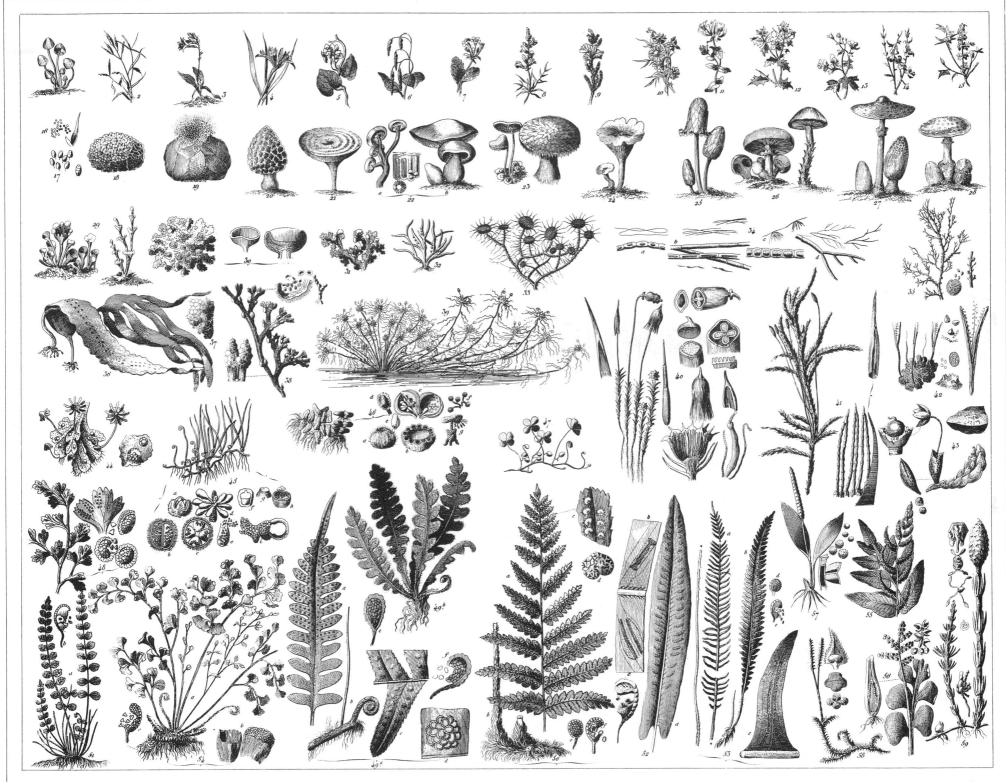

Feigen oder Bananen Baum.

G. Heck dir.t

Henry Winkles sculp.t

Fig. 1.
Fig. 2.
Fig. 5.
Fig. 6.
Fig. 7.
Fig. 8.
Fig. 9.
Fig. 10.
Fig. 11.
Fig. 12.
Fig. 13.
Fig. 14.
Fig. 15.

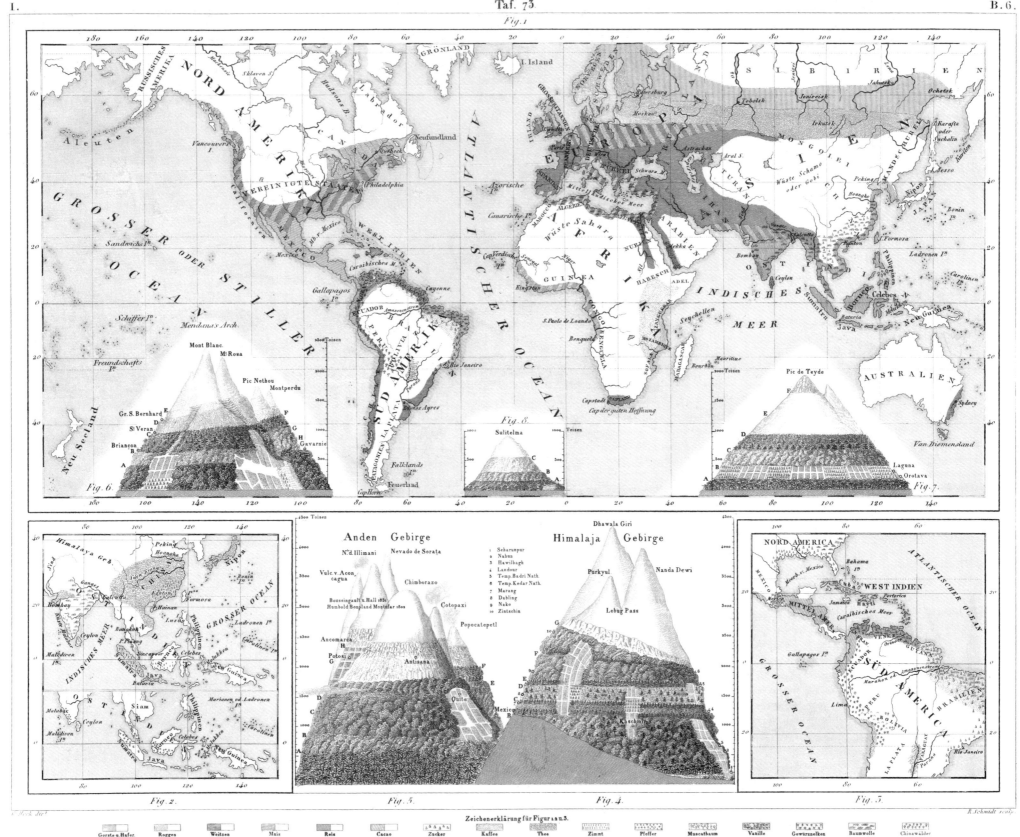

Fig. 6.
Fig. 8.
Fig. 7.

Anden Gebirge   Himalaja Gebirge

Fig. 2.
Fig. 5.
Fig. 4.
Fig. 5.

Zeichenerklärung für Figur 1.u.5.

Gerste u.Hafer. | Roggen | Weitzen | Mais | Reis | Cacao | Zucker | Kaffee | Thee | Zimmt | Pfeffer | Muscatbaum | Vanille | Gewürznelken | Baumwolle | Chinawälder

G. Heck dir!

Henry Winkles sculp!

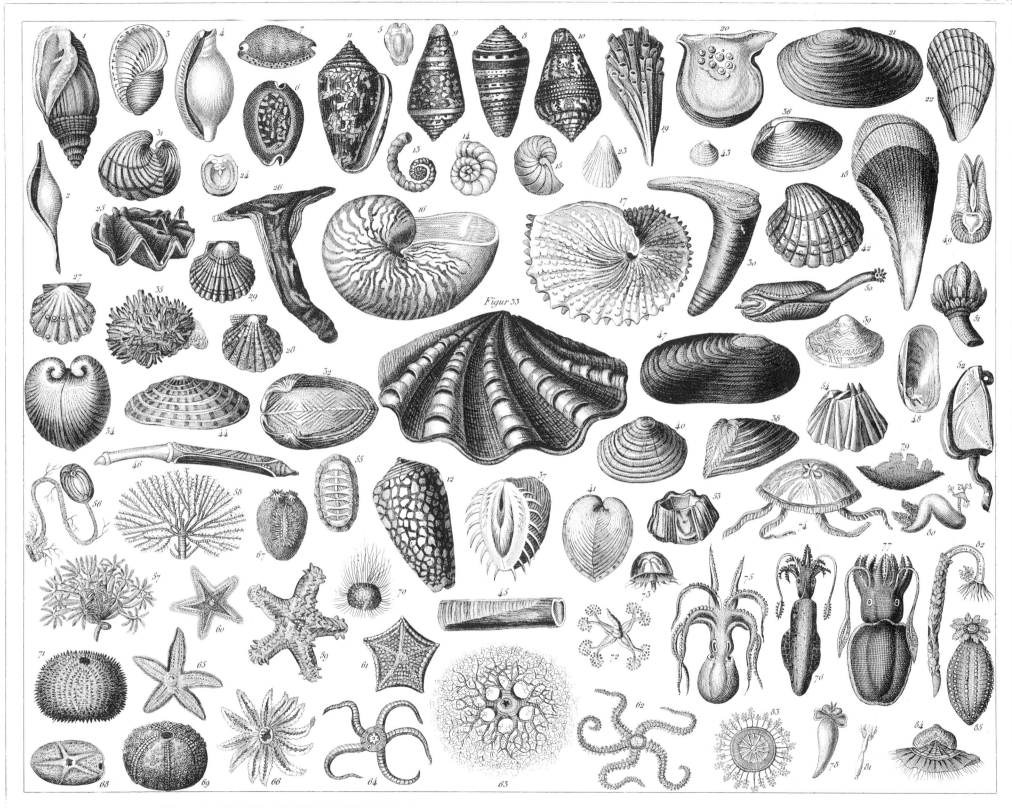

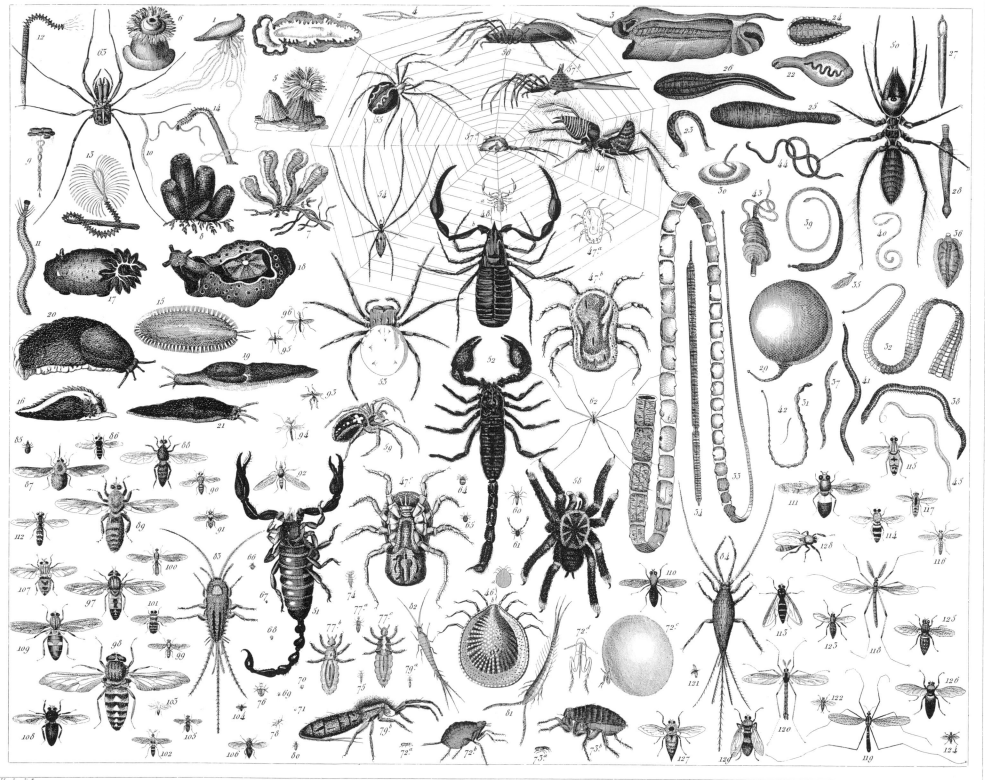

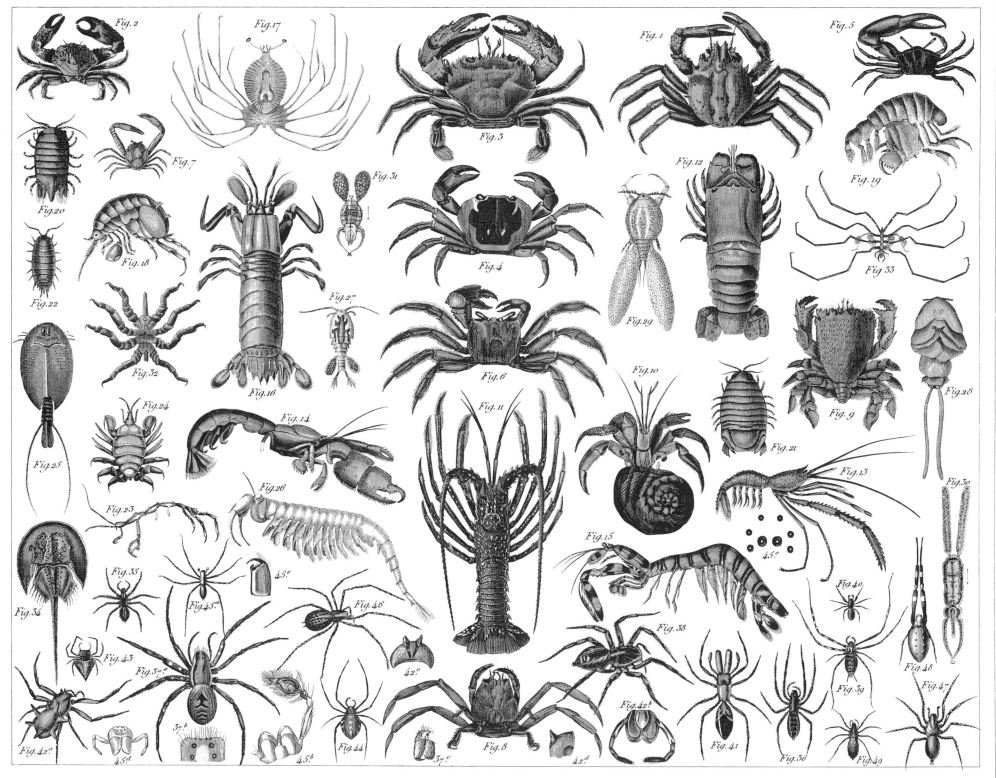

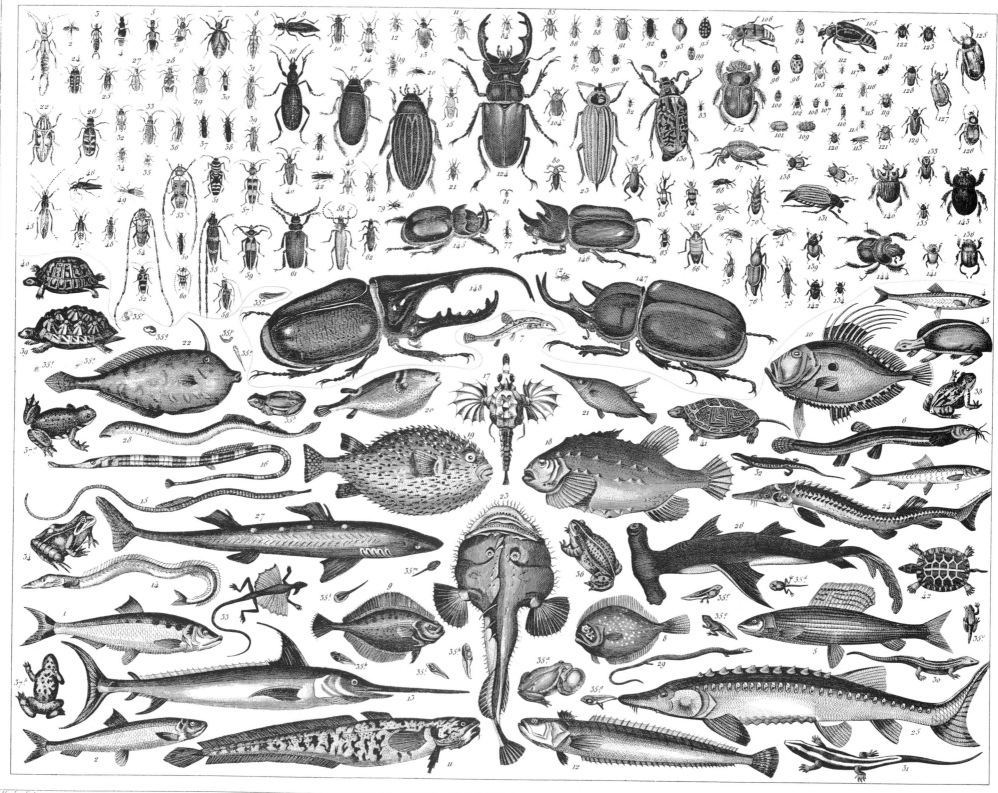

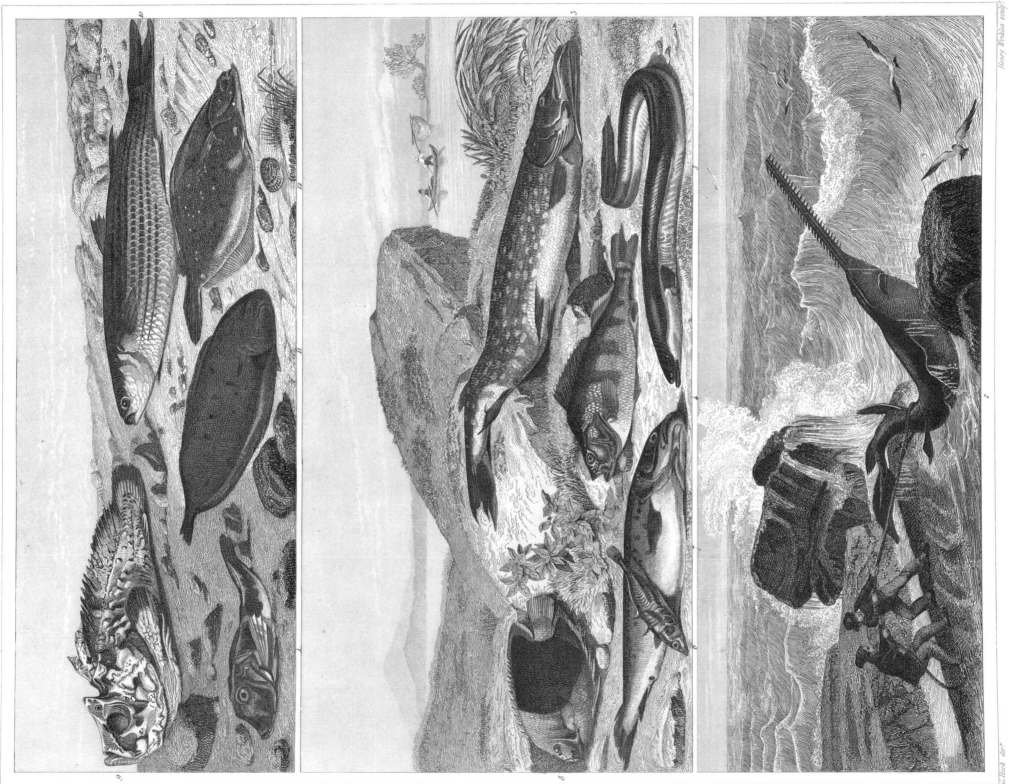

Henry Winkles sculp.

G. Heck del.

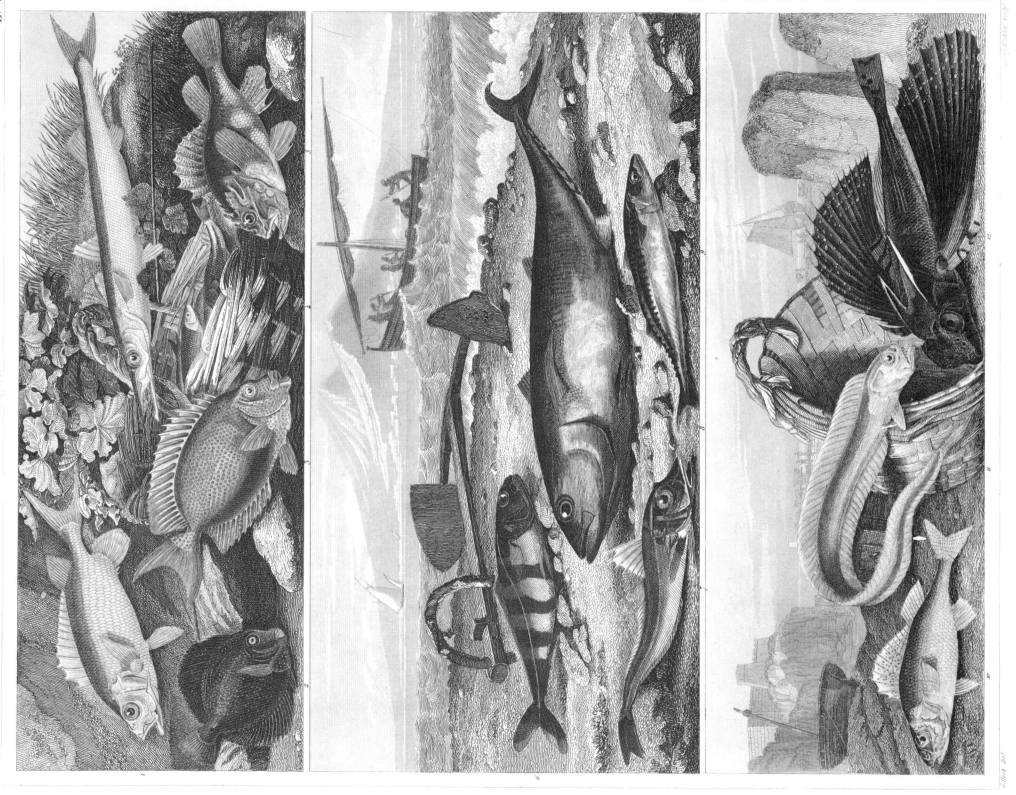

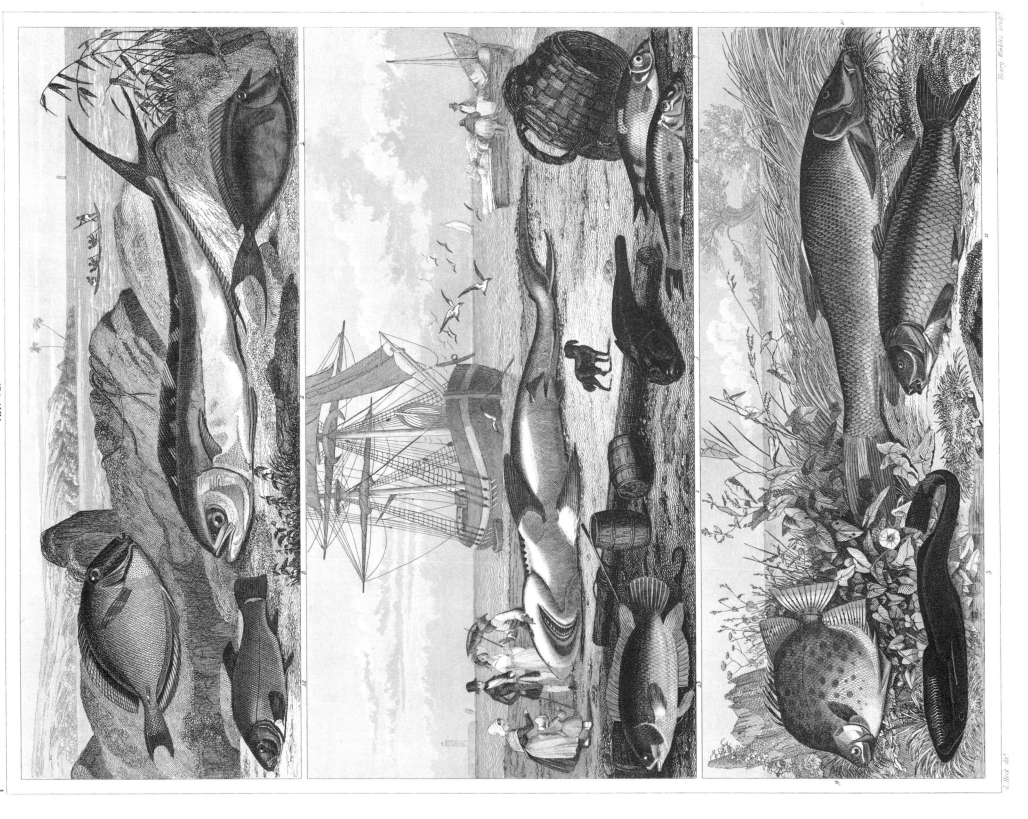

G. Heck del.   Henry Winkles sculp.

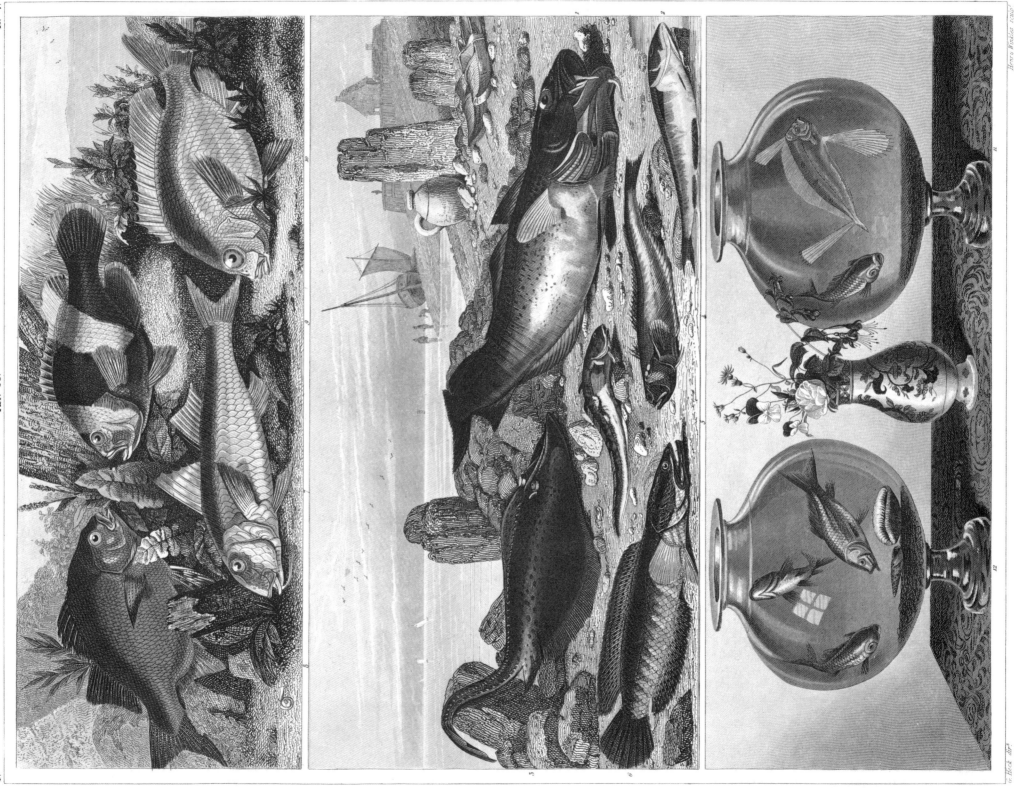

Henry Winkles sculp.

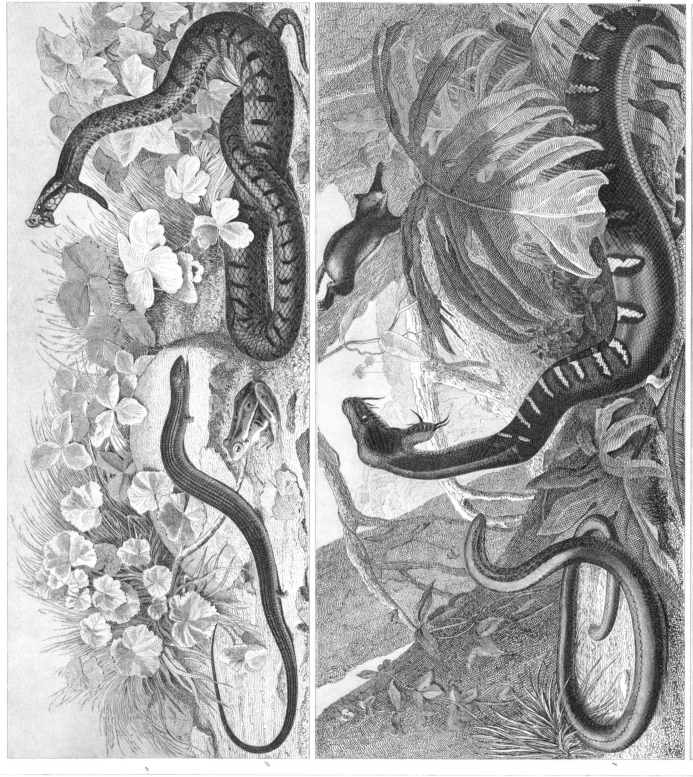

Henry Winkles sculp.

G. Heck dir.t

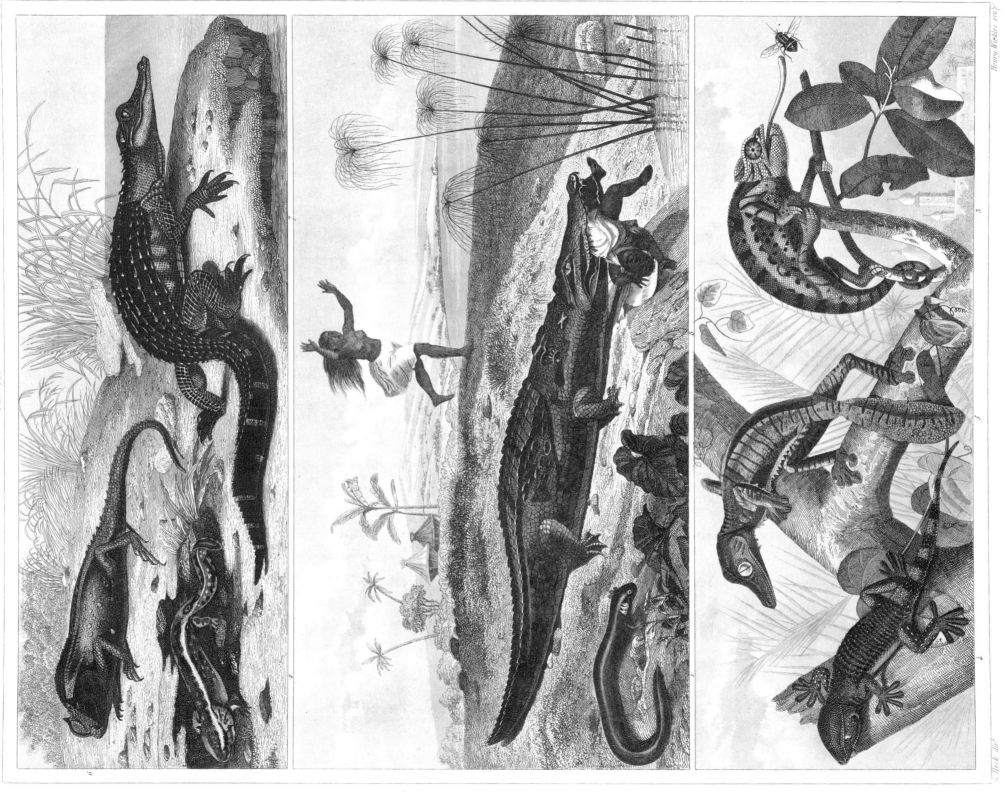

n. Heck dir.

Henry Winkles sculp.

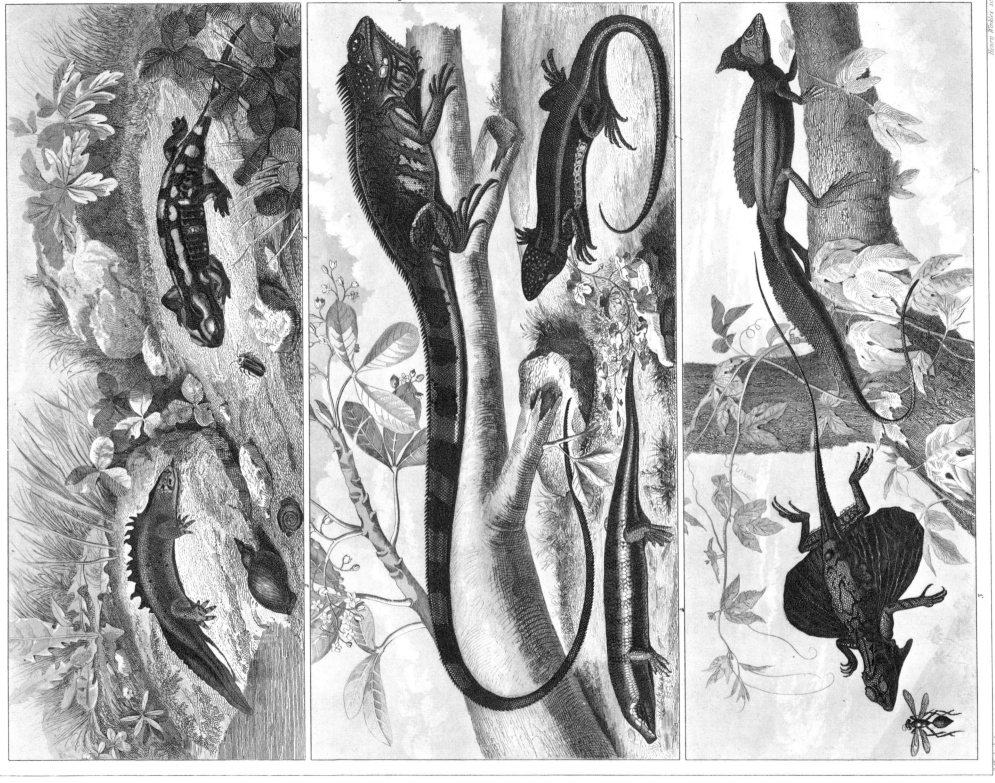

Henry Winkles sculp.

G. Heck del.

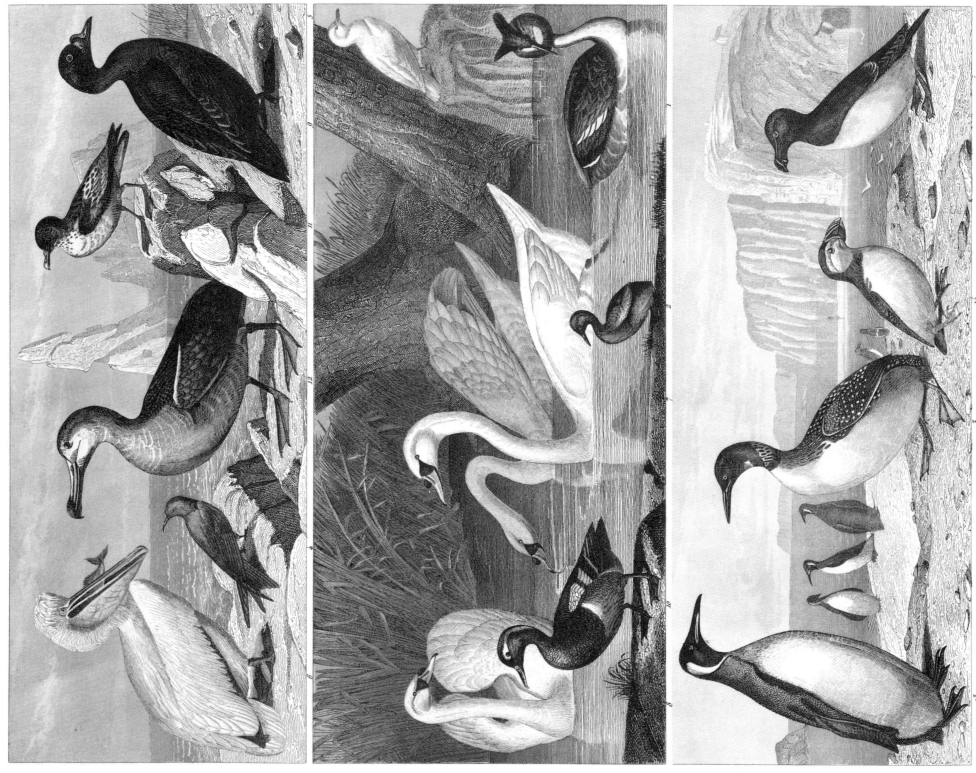

Henry Winkles sculpt.

C. Heck dir.

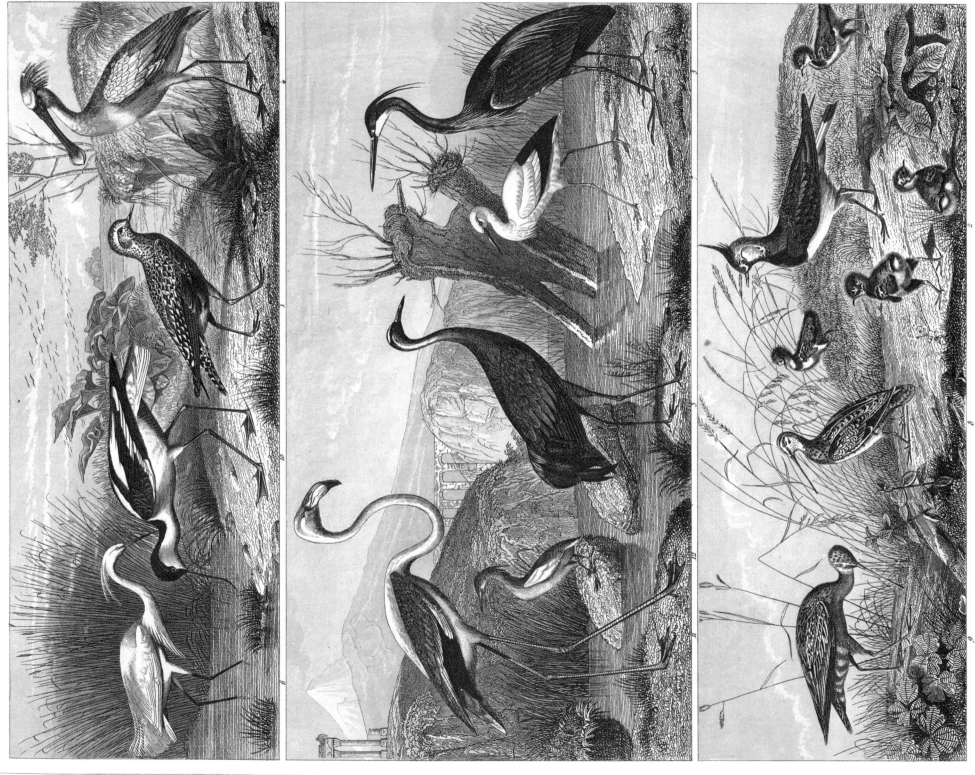

G. Heck dir.

Henry Winkles sculp.

Taf. 94.

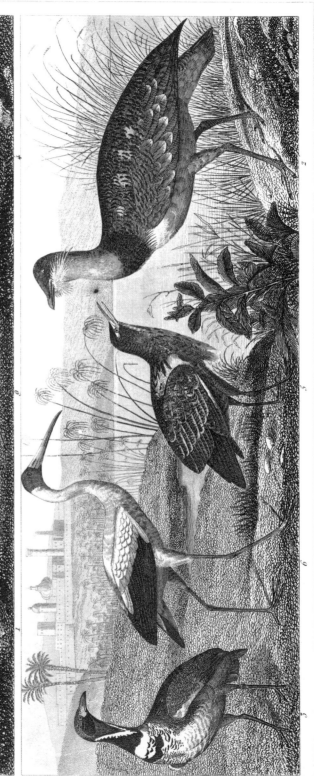

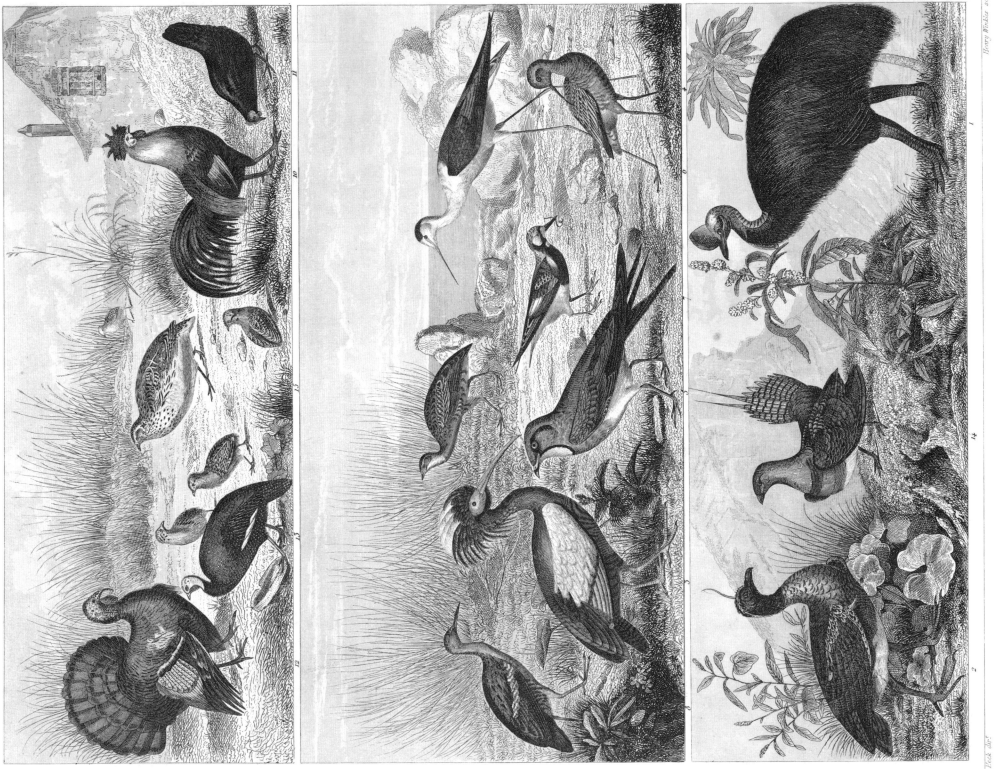

Henry Winkles sculp.

G. Heck del.

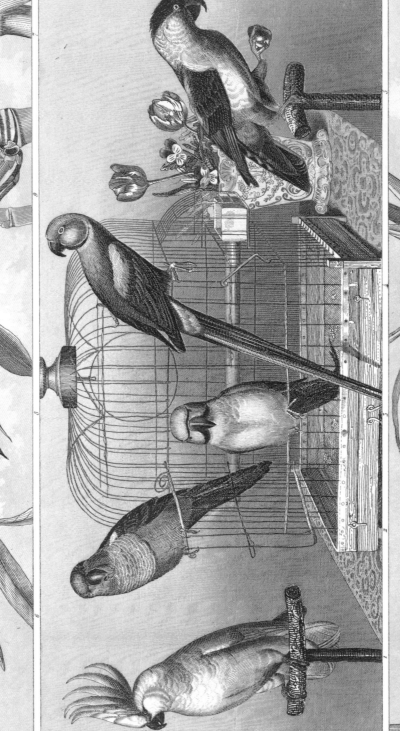

G. Heck dir.

Henry Winkler sculp.

Taf. 101.

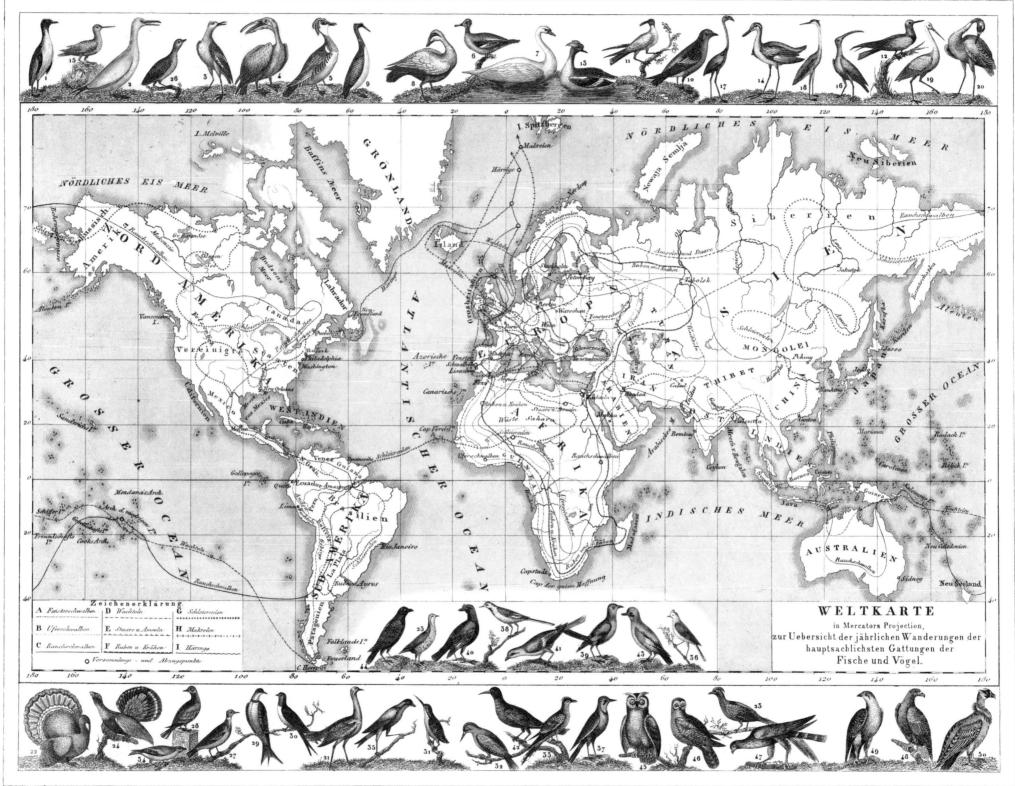

WELTKARTE

in Mercators Projection,

zur Uebersicht der jährlichen Wanderungen der
hauptsächlichsten Gattungen der
Fische und Vögel.

Zeichenerklärung.

A	Fensterschwalben.	D	Wachteln.	G	Schleiereulen.
B	Uferschwalben.	E	Staare u. Amseln.	H	Makrelen.
C	Rauchschwalben.	F	Raben u. Krähen.	I	Häringe.

○ Versammlungs- und Abzugspunkte.

G. Heck dirᵗ.   Henry Winkles sculp.

1

2

3

4

G. Heck dir.ᵗ

Henry Winkles sculp.ᵗ

Gust.Heck. direx.

Henry Winkles sculp!

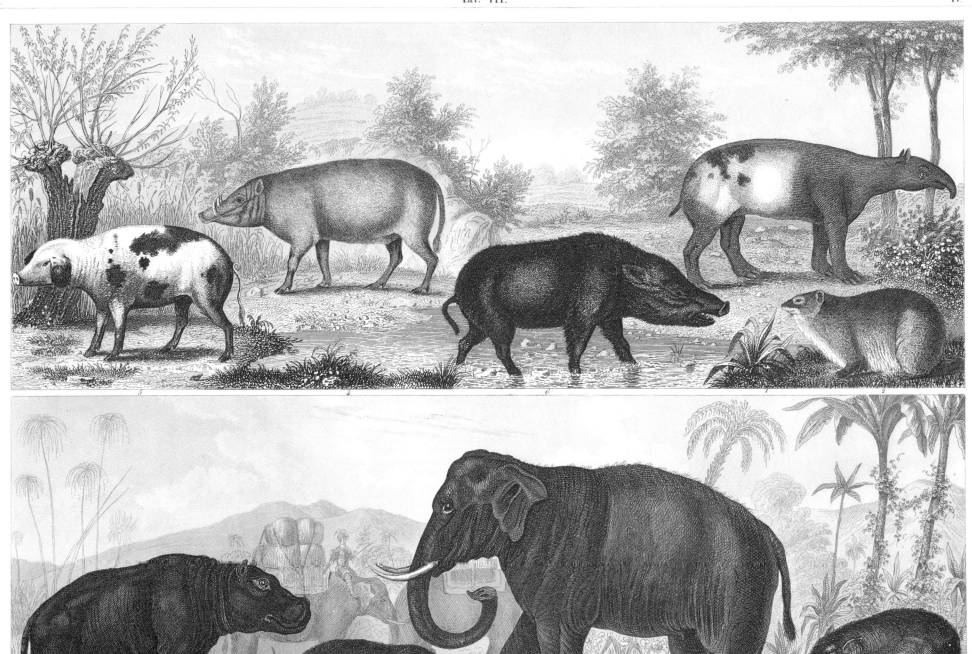

G. Heck dir.t   Henry Winkles sculp.t

Henry Winkles sculp.

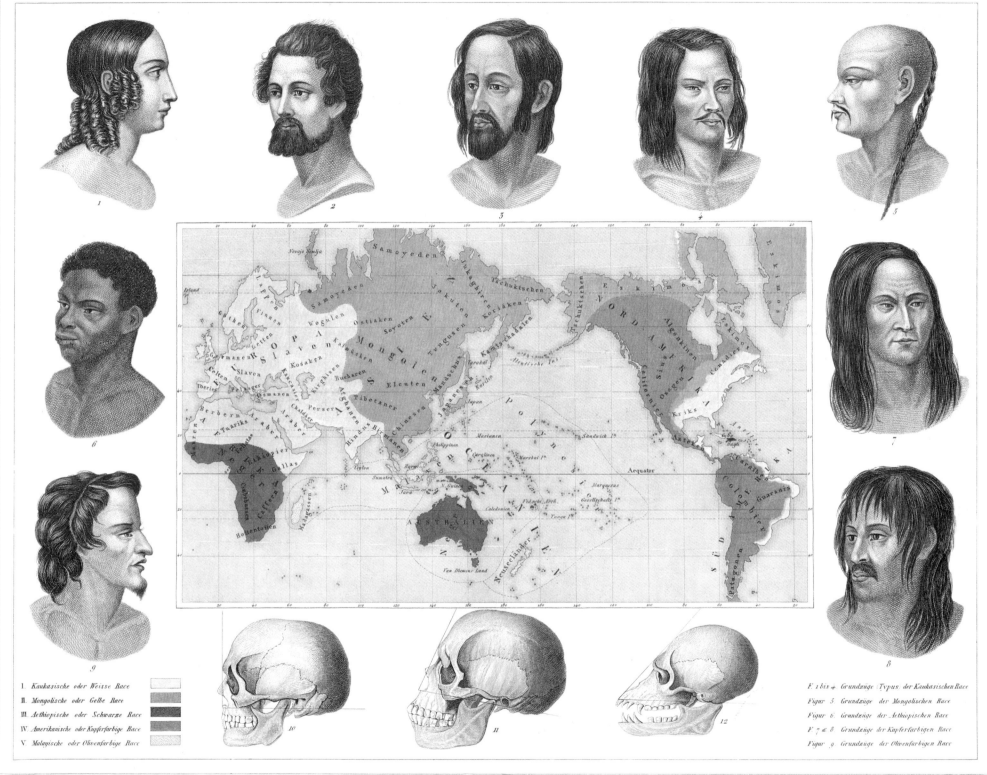

I. Kaukasische oder Weisse Race
II. Mongolische oder Gelbe Race
III. Aethiopische oder Schwarze Race
IV. Amerikanische oder Kupferfarbige Race
V. Malayische oder Olivenfarbige Race

F. 1 bis 4. Grundzüge (Typus) der Kaukasischen Race
Figur 5. Grundzüge der Mongolischen Race
Figur 6. Grundzüge der Aethiopischen Race
F. 7 & 8. Grundzüge der Kupferfarbigen Race
Figur 9. Grundzüge der Olivenfarbigen Race

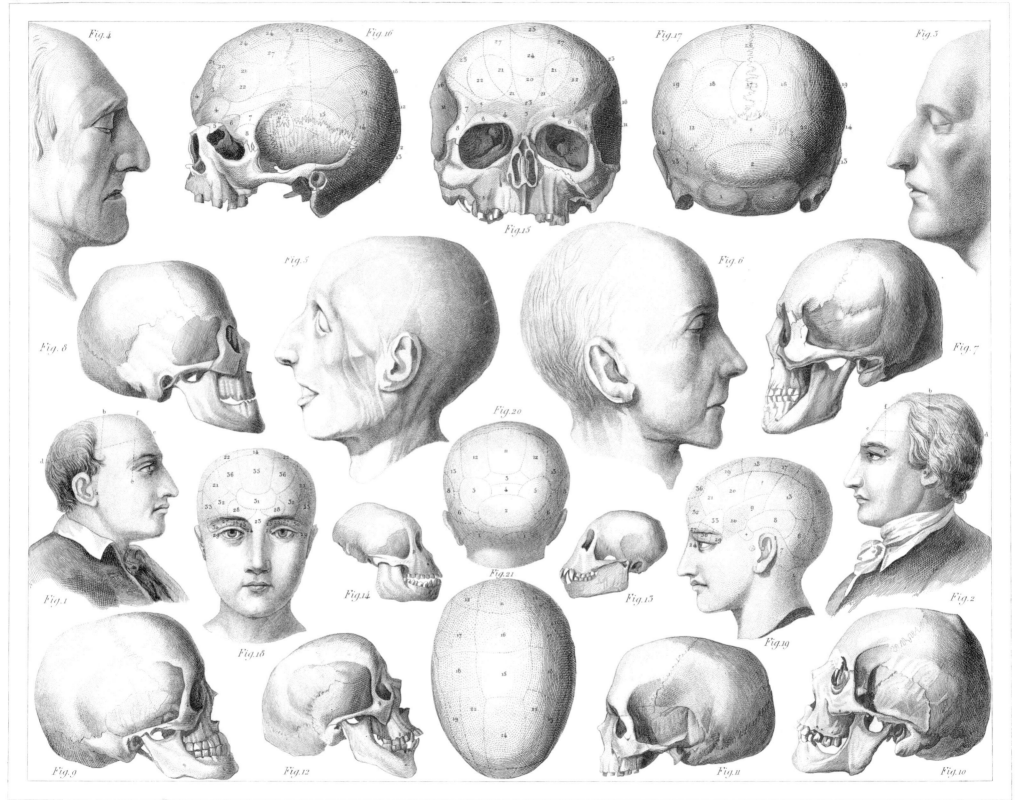

Fig. 4.
Fig. 16.
Fig. 17.
Fig. 3.
Fig. 15.
Fig. 8.
Fig. 5.
Fig. 6.
Fig. 7.
Fig. 20.
Fig. 1.
Fig. 18.
Fig. 14.
Fig. 21.
Fig. 13.
Fig. 19.
Fig. 2.
Fig. 9.
Fig. 12.
Fig. 11.
Fig. 10.

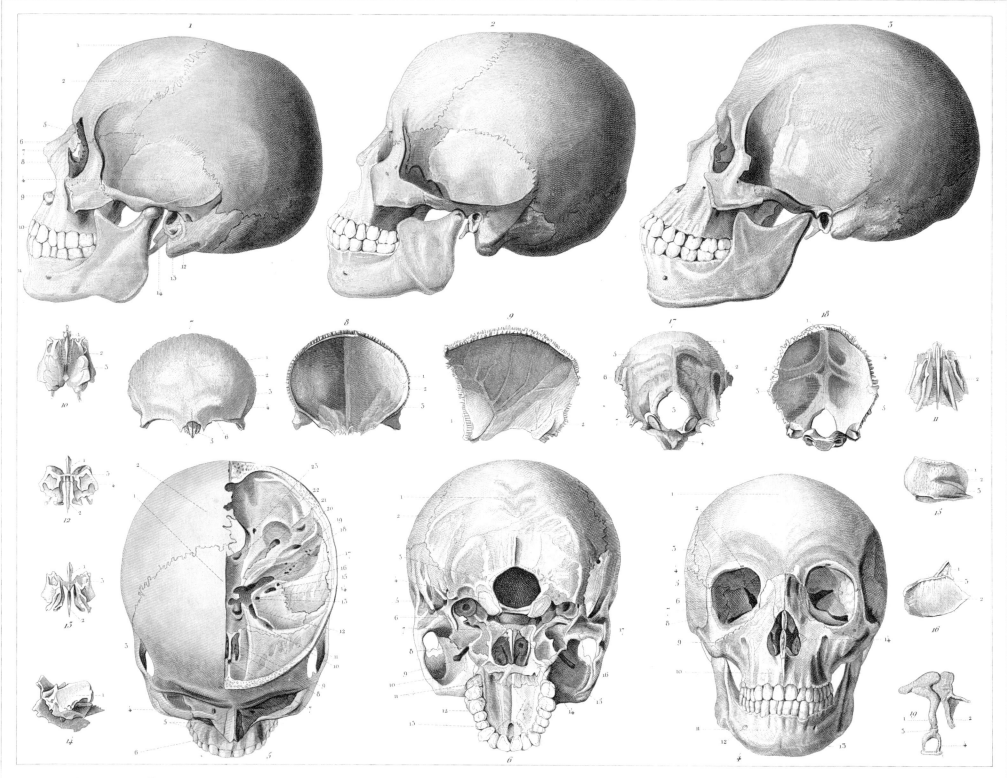

G. Heck dir.t Henry Winkles sculp.t

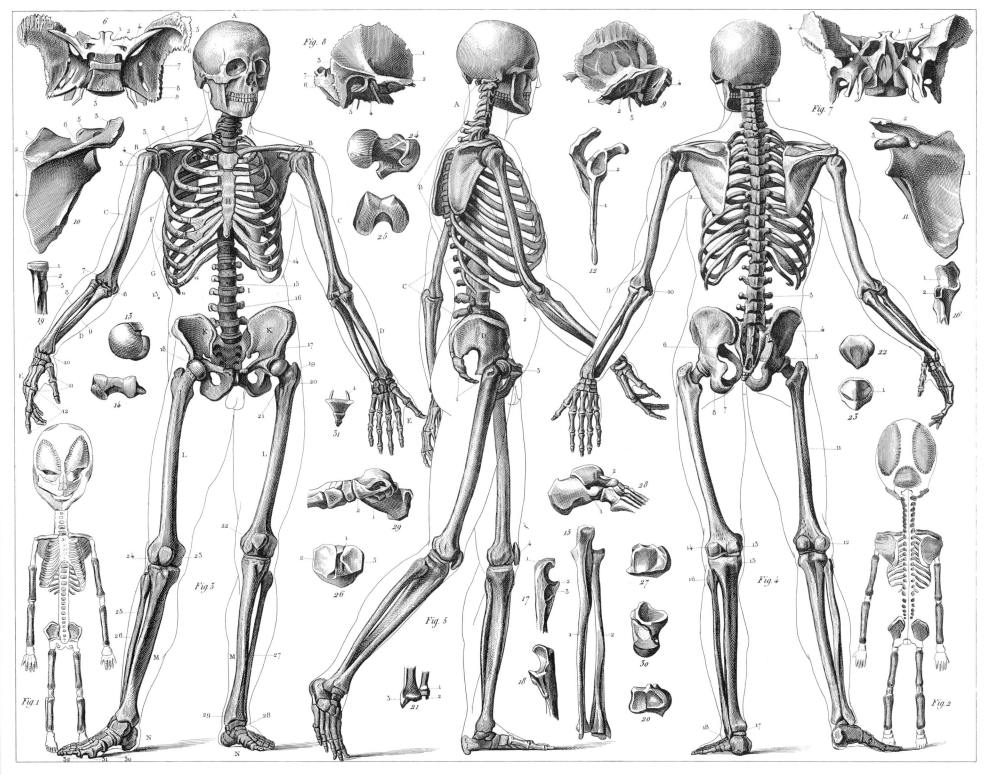

Fig. 8

Fig. 7

Fig. 1

Fig. 3

Fig. 5

Fig. 4

Fig. 2

G. Heck dir.t

Henry Winkles sculp.t

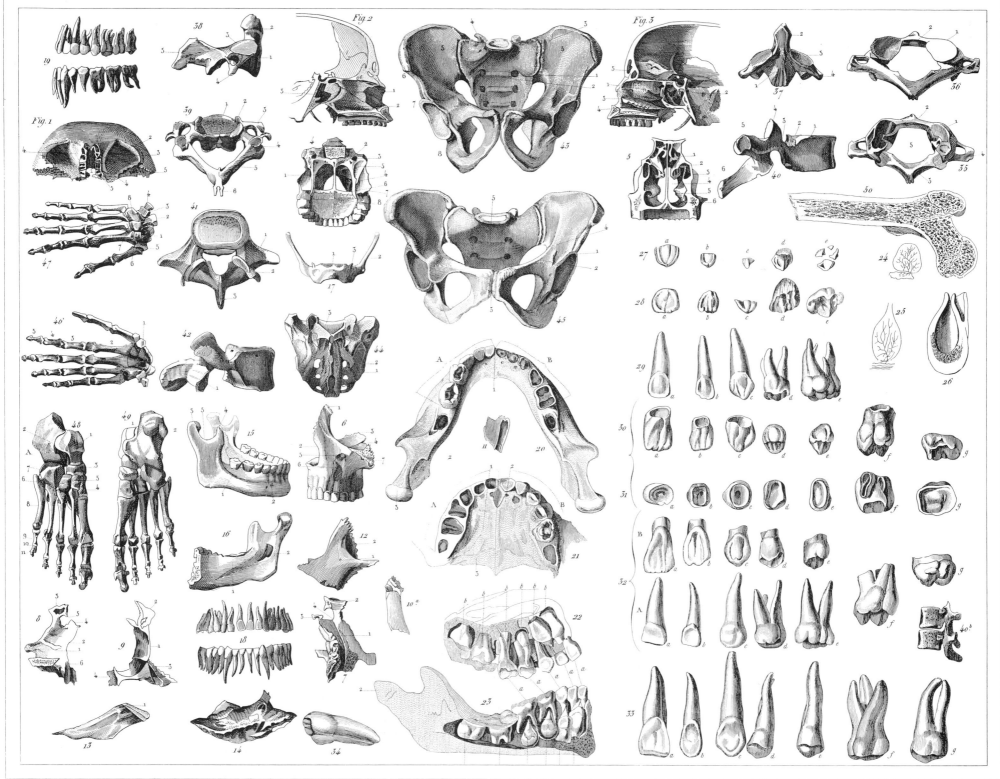

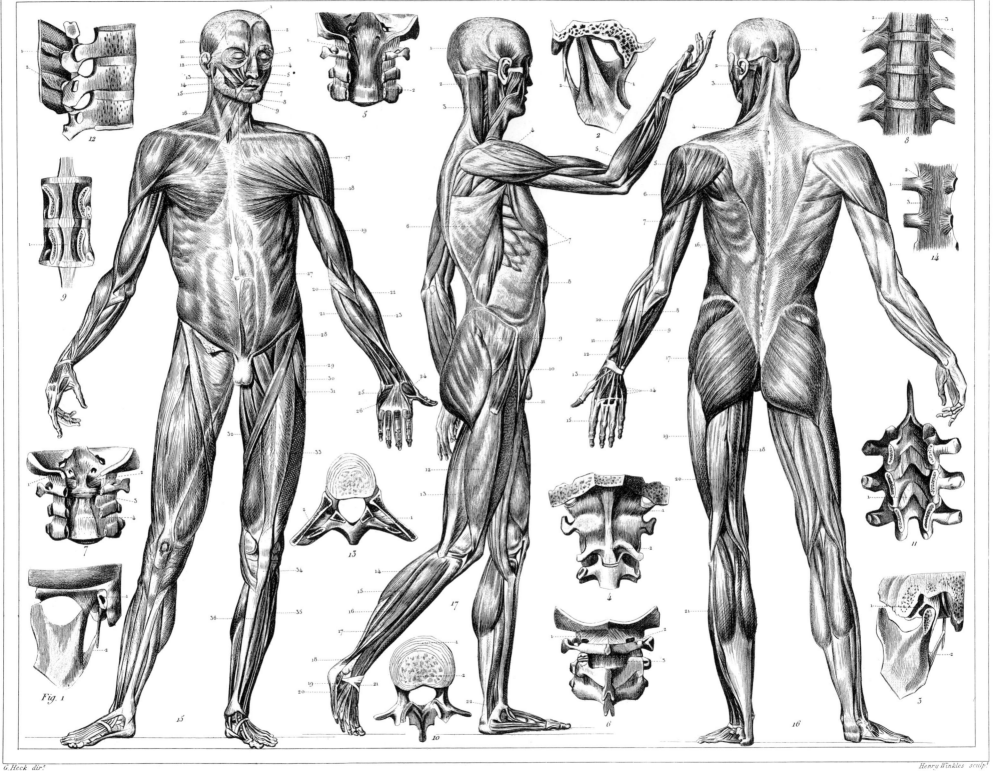

Fig. 1.

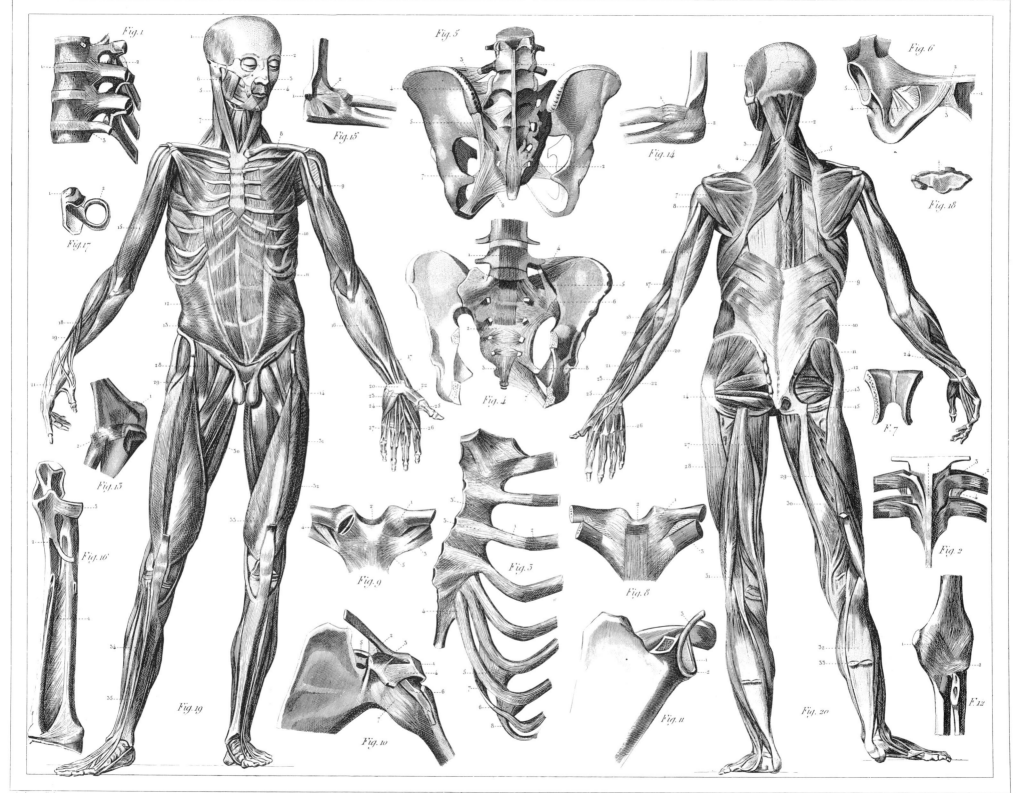

Fig. 1
Fig. 5
Fig. 6
Fig. 15
Fig. 14
Fig. 17
Fig. 18
Fig. 4
Fig. 13
Fig. 7
Fig. 16
Fig. 2
Fig. 9
Fig. 3
Fig. 8
Fig. 19
Fig. 10
Fig. 11
Fig. 20
Fig. 12

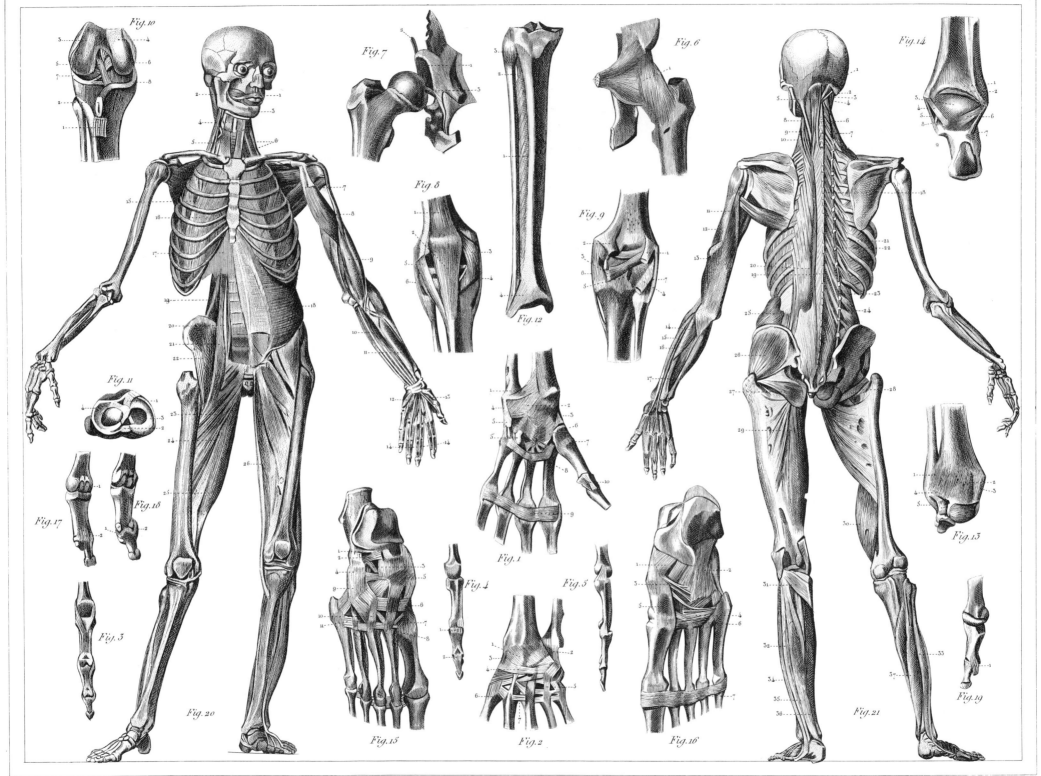

Fig.10
Fig.7
Fig.6
Fig.14
Fig.8
Fig.9
Fig.12
Fig.11
Fig.17
Fig.18
Fig.1
Fig.13
Fig.3
Fig.15
Fig.4
Fig.5
Fig.16
Fig.19
Fig.2
Fig.20
Fig.21

G. Heck dir.t

Henry Winkles sculp.t

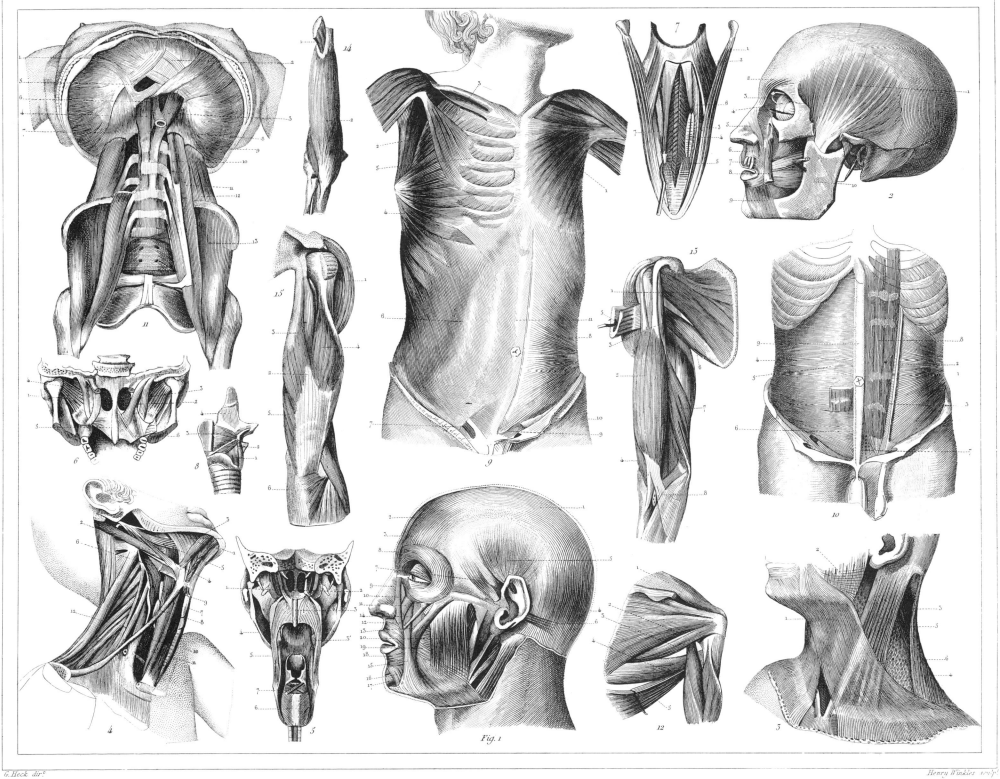

Fig. 1

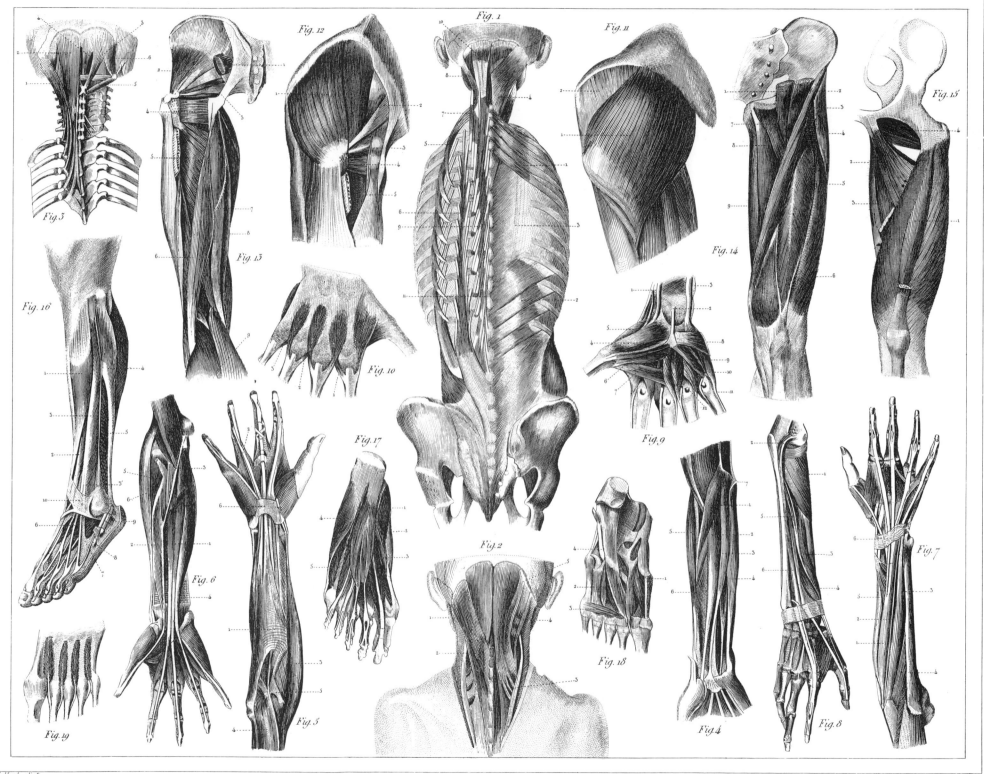

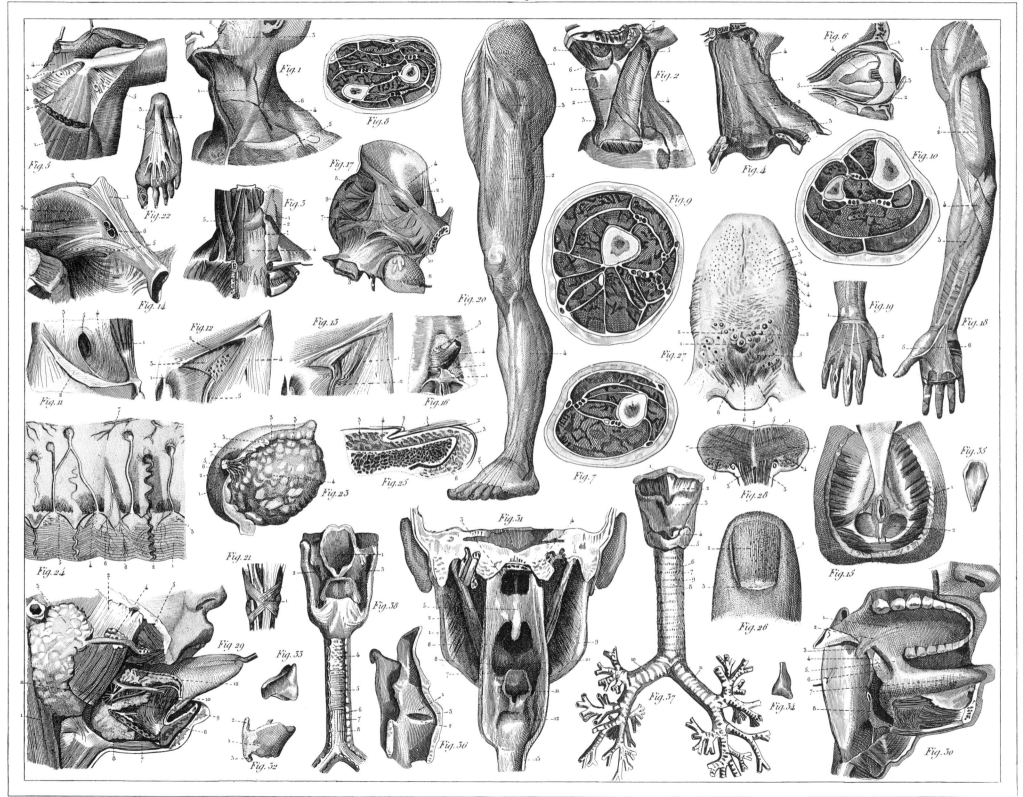

Fig. 5
Fig. 22
Fig. 1
Fig. 8
Fig. 2
Fig. 4
Fig. 6
Fig. 14
Fig. 3
Fig. 17
Fig. 20
Fig. 9
Fig. 10
Fig. 19
Fig. 18
Fig. 11
Fig. 12
Fig. 13
Fig. 16
Fig. 27
Fig. 28
Fig. 35
Fig. 24
Fig. 21
Fig. 23
Fig. 25
Fig. 7
Fig. 15
Fig. 31
Fig. 26
Fig. 29
Fig. 38
Fig. 33
Fig. 37
Fig. 34
Fig. 36
Fig. 32
Fig. 30

G. Heck dir.t

Henry Winkles sculp.t

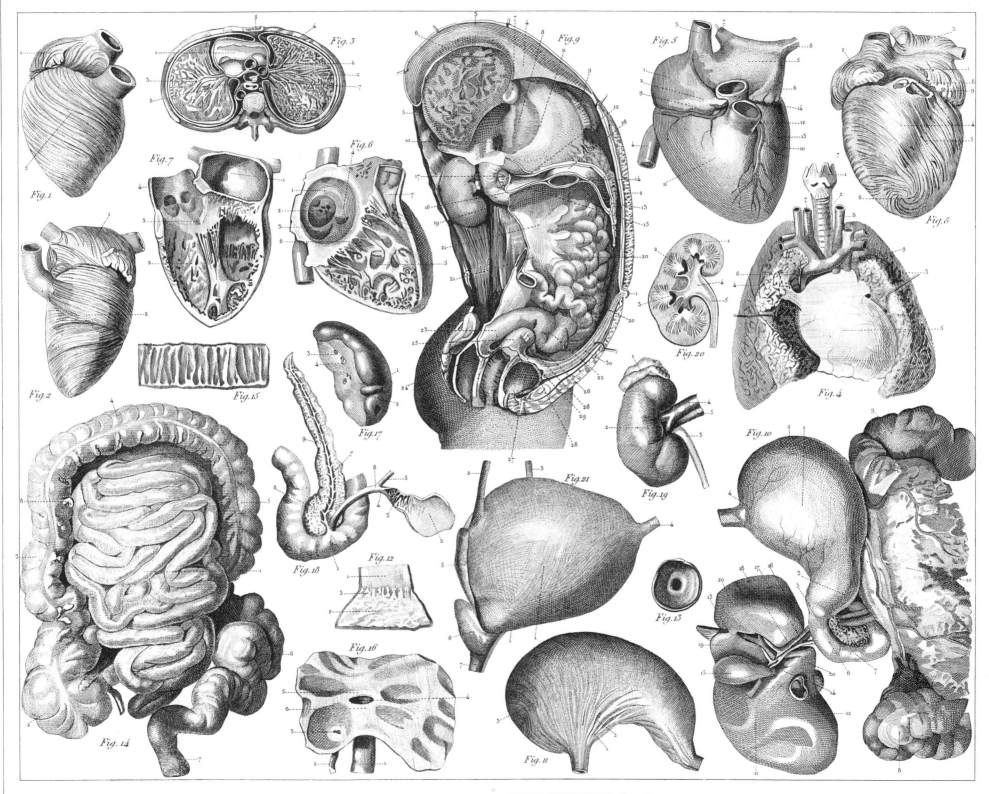

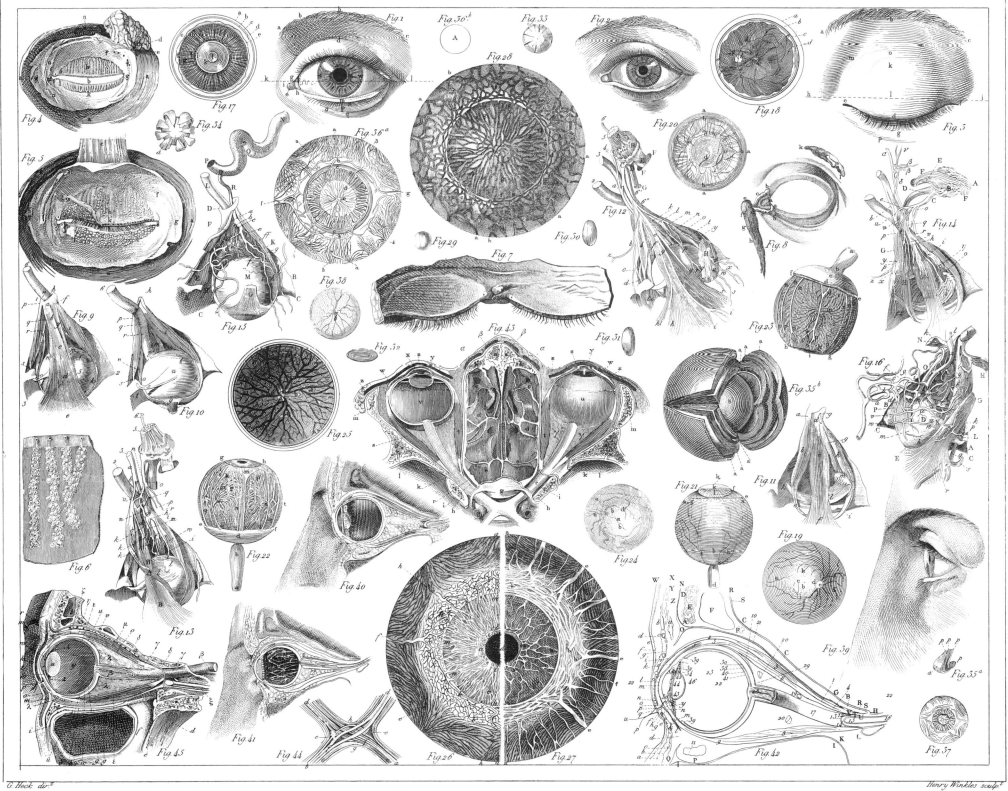

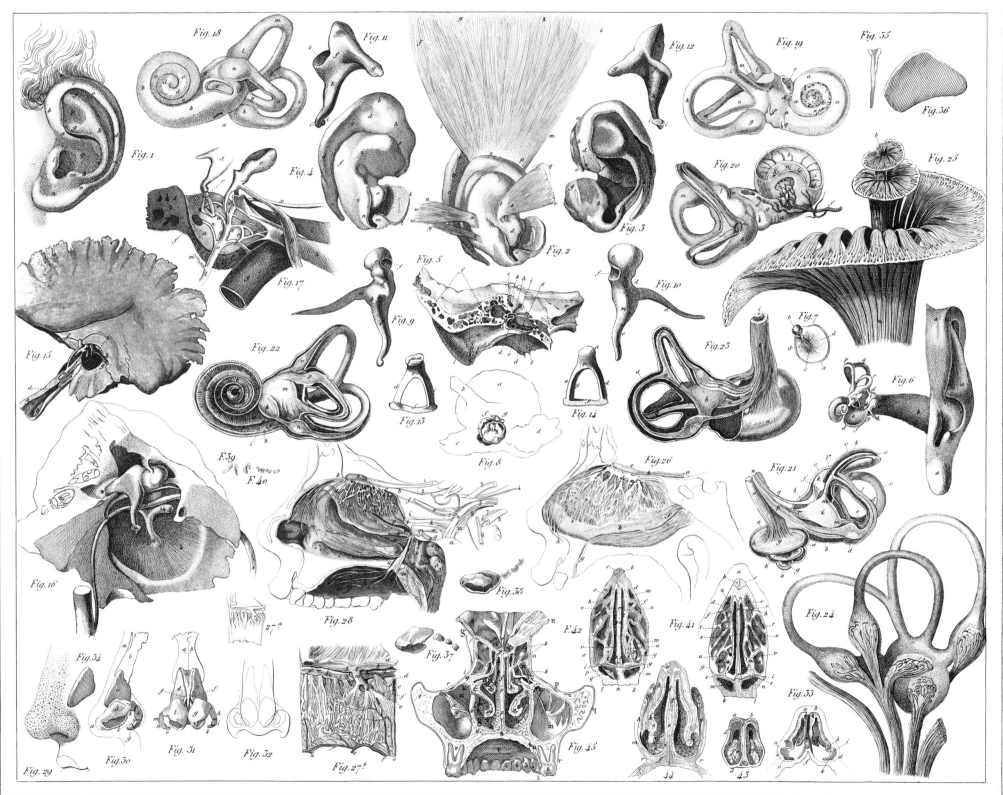

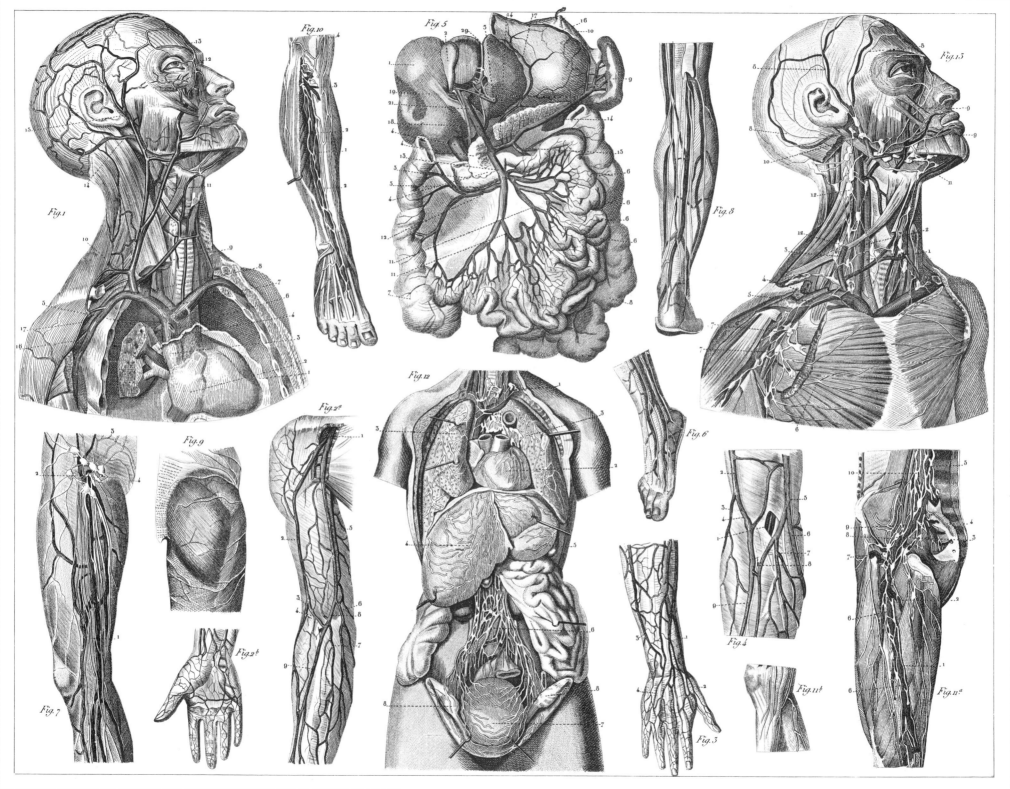

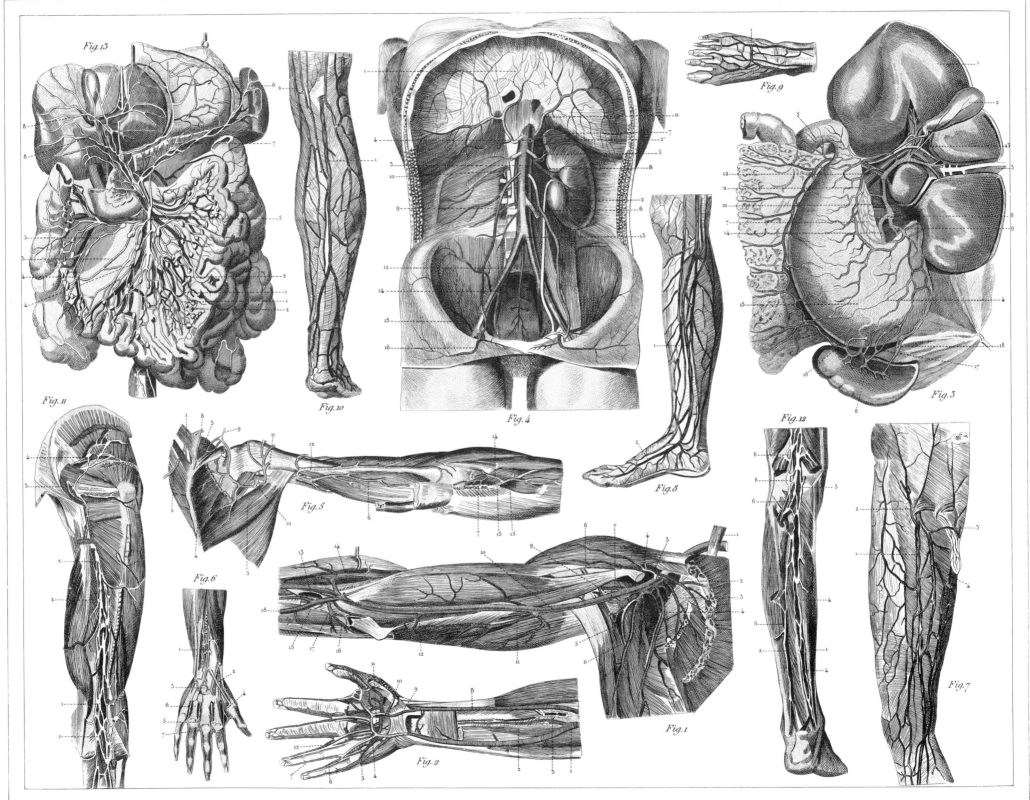

Fig. 13

Fig. 10

Fig. 9

Fig. 4

Fig. 3

Fig. 11

Fig. 5

Fig. 6

Fig. 8

Fig. 12

Fig. 1

Fig. 2

Fig. 7

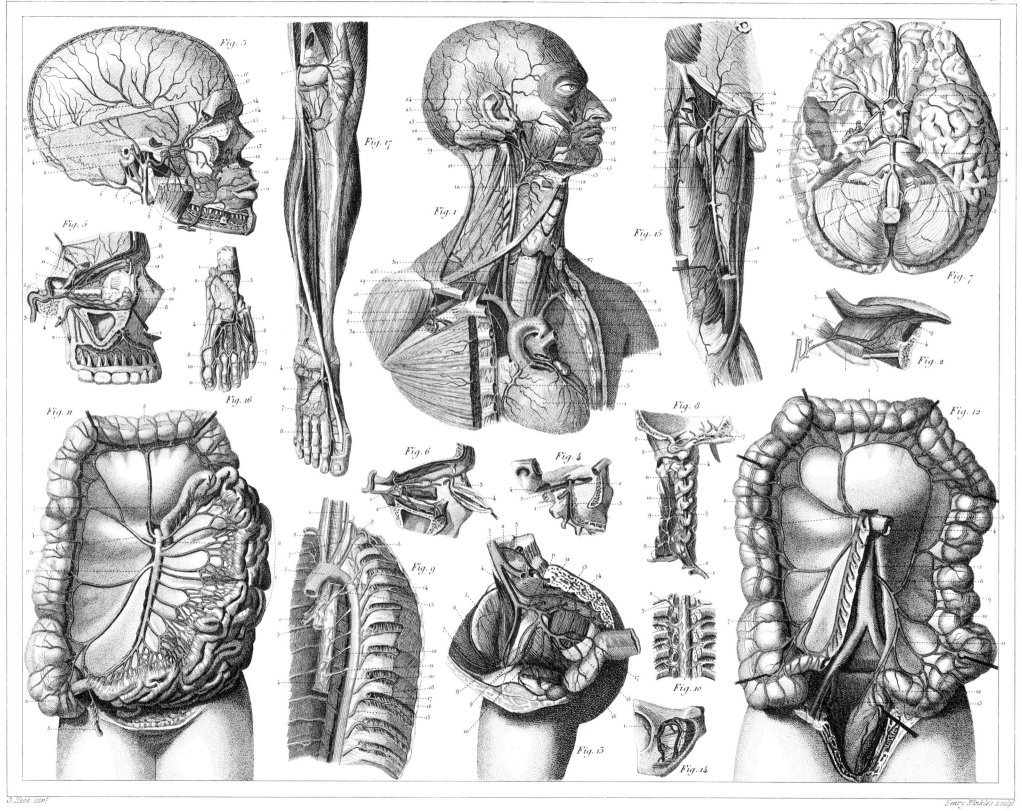

Fig. 5

Fig. 5

Fig. 16

Fig. 11

Fig. 17

Fig. 1

Fig. 6

Fig. 9

Fig. 4

Fig. 13

Fig. 15

Fig. 8

Fig. 10

Fig. 14

Fig. 7

Fig. 2

Fig. 12

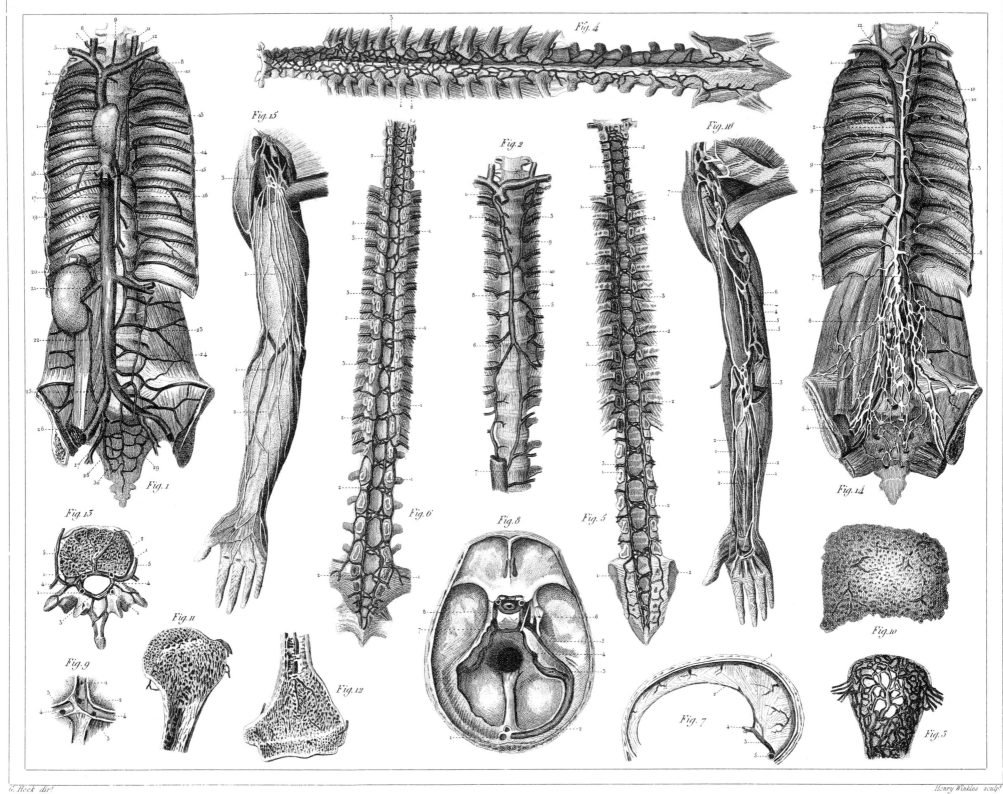

Fig. 4

Fig. 15

Fig. 13

Fig. 2

Fig. 10

Fig. 1

Fig. 6

Fig. 8

Fig. 5

Fig. 14

Fig. 13

Fig. 11

Fig. 9

Fig. 12

Fig. 10

Fig. 7

Fig. 3

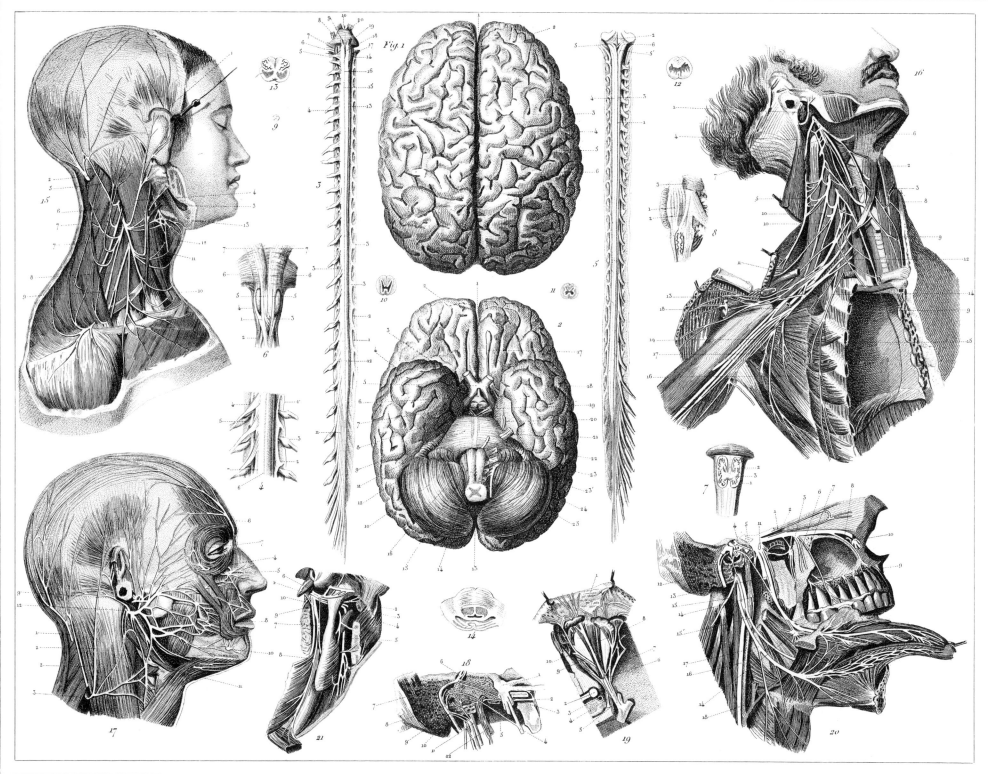

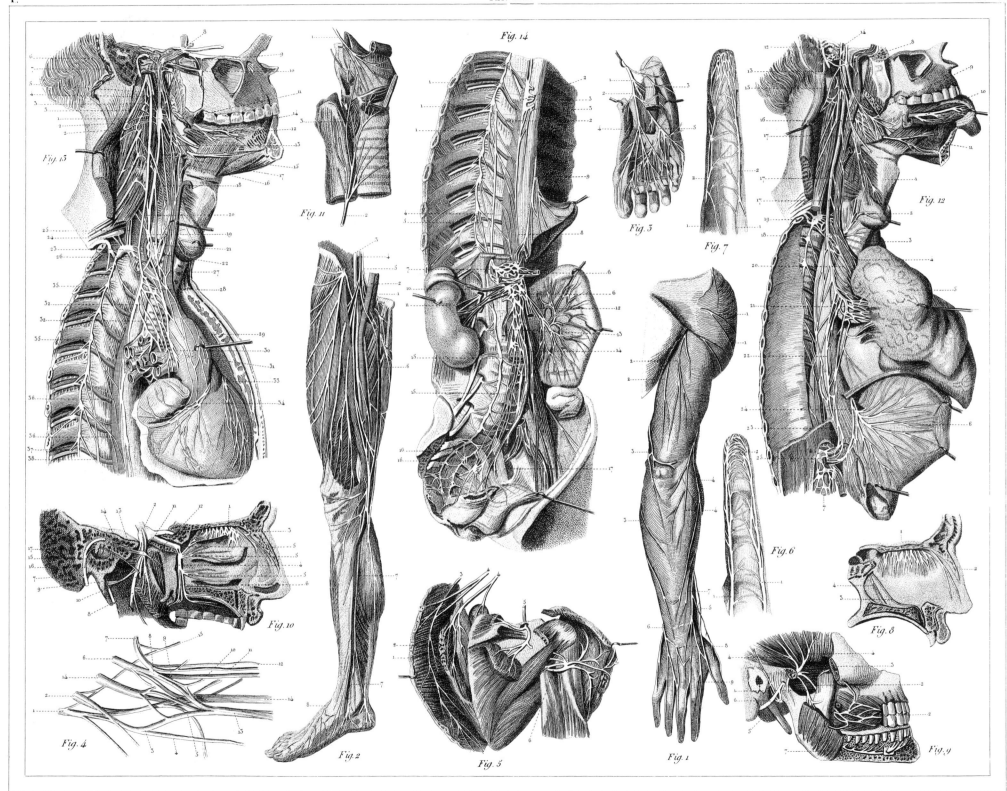

Fig. 15   Fig. 11   Fig. 14   Fig. 3   Fig. 7   Fig. 12

Fig. 10   Fig. 2   Fig. 5   Fig. 6   Fig. 8

Fig. 4   Fig. 1   Fig. 9

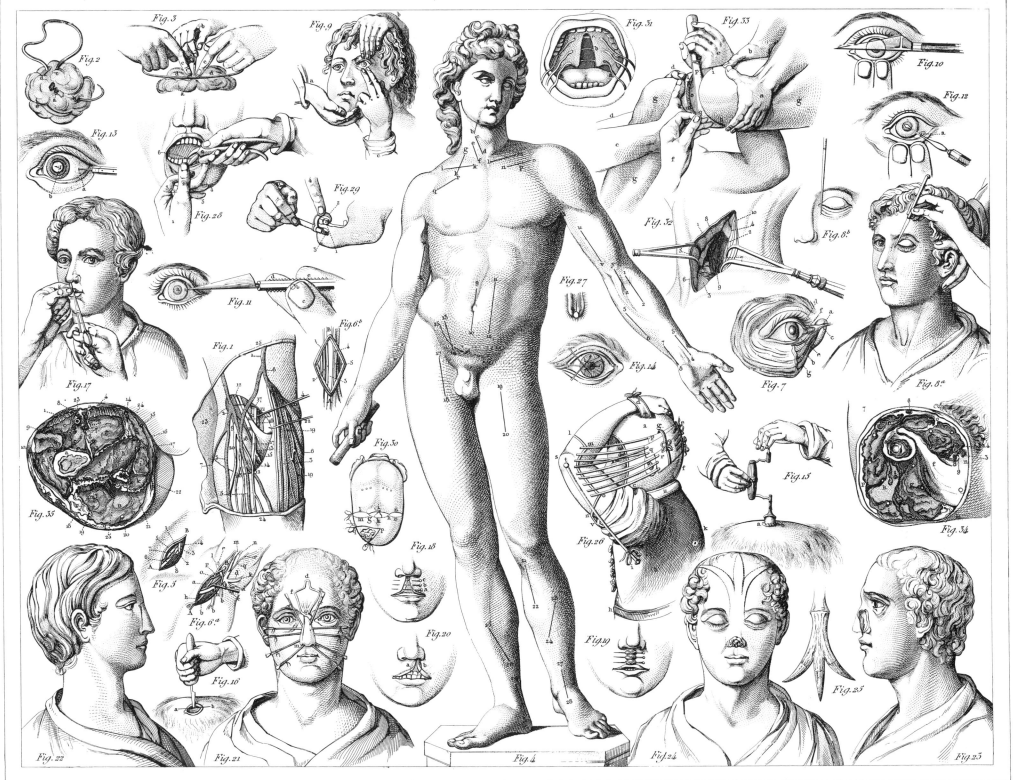

Fig. 2
Fig. 3
Fig. 9
Fig. 31
Fig. 33
Fig. 10
Fig. 12
Fig. 13
Fig. 28
Fig. 29
Fig. 32
Fig. 8.b
Fig. 11
Fig. 6.b
Fig. 27
Fig. 7
Fig. 8.a
Fig. 17
Fig. 1
Fig. 14
Fig. 35
Fig. 30
Fig. 15
Fig. 34
Fig. 5
Fig. 6.a
Fig. 18
Fig. 26
Fig. 10
Fig. 21
Fig. 20
Fig. 19
Fig. 25
Fig. 22
Fig. 4
Fig. 24
Fig. 23

G. Heck dir.t
Henry Winkles sculp.t

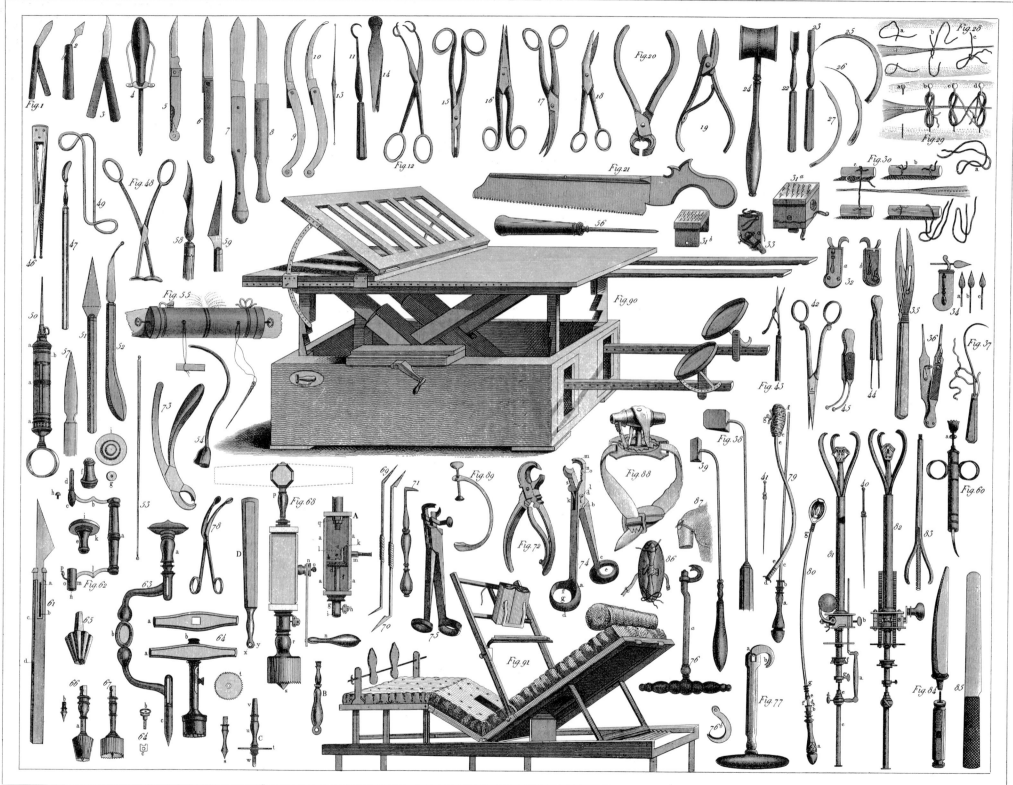

G. Heck dir.t

Henry Winkles sculp.t

ICONOGRAPHIC
ENCYCLOPÆDIA.

DIVISION II.

NATURAL SCIENCES,

COMPRISING

PHYSICS AND METEOROLOGY, CHEMISTRY, GEOGNOSY AND GEOLOGY, BOTANY,
ZOOLOGY, AND ANTHROPOLOGY.

ONE HUNDRED AND TWENTY-FOUR PLATES.

[THE LIST OF THE FIGURES ON THE PLATES WILL BE FOUND IN THE TABLES OF CONTENTS OF VOLS. I. AND II. OF THE TEXT.]

THE PLATES ARE NUMBERED I. 16—105, 105^b—140.

———————

NEW YORK: 1851.

PUBLISHED BY RUDOLPH GARRIGUE,

2 BARCLAY STREET (ASTOR HOUSE).

Physikalische Karte
von
EUROPA.

Strom und Gebirgs-System
von
MITTELEUROPA.

NORDSEE

OSTSEE

MITTELLÄNDISCHES MEER

ADRIATISCHES MEER

SCHWARZES MEER

Berlin

London

Wien

Prag

Thames

Donau

Oder

Elbe

Weichsel

Karpathisches Waldgebirge

Nieder Ungarische Eben.

Wallachische Tiefland

Plateau v. Orleans

Apenninen

Buzen v. Genua

Bus. v. Venedig

ATLANTISCHER OCEAN

NOERDL. EIS MEER

Polarkreis

EUROPA

RUSSISCHES REICH

SIBIRIEN

NORD SEE

Schwarzes Meer

Donau

Don

MONGOLEI

HOHE TATAREI

TURAN

PERSIEN

AFGANISTAN

TAFELLAND von IRAN

BILUDSCHISTAN

ARABIEN

NUBIEN

HABESCH

G. v. Aden

I. Socotora

C. Guardafui

PERSISCHES MEER

ARABISCHES ODER

AFRIKA

Aequator

INDISCHER OCEAN

Madagascar

Comoro I.

BUSEN VON BENGALEN

Ceylon

Maledwen

Andamanen

Nicobaren

Atschin

BIRMA

SIAM

Bangkok

Tonkin

Hainan

Formosa

Japanisches Meer

Kurilen

Ochotsk. Meer

Behrings Meer

Die Aleutischen Inseln

GROSSER OCEAN

STILLER OCEAN

Die Philippinen

Mindoro

Palawan

Borneo

Celebes See

Sunda See

SUNDA INS.

Java

Madura

Flores

Timor

NEU HOLLAND

NEU GUINEA

Karolinen

Marianen

Pelew

Wendekreis des Krebses

Warme Aequator

Physikalische Karte
von
ASIEN.

Entworfen u. gezeichnet v. Ph. Weber in Carlsruhe   Gestochen v. J.L.v. Baehr in Halle

Maasstab 1:51,300,000

Deutsche Meilen   Lieues

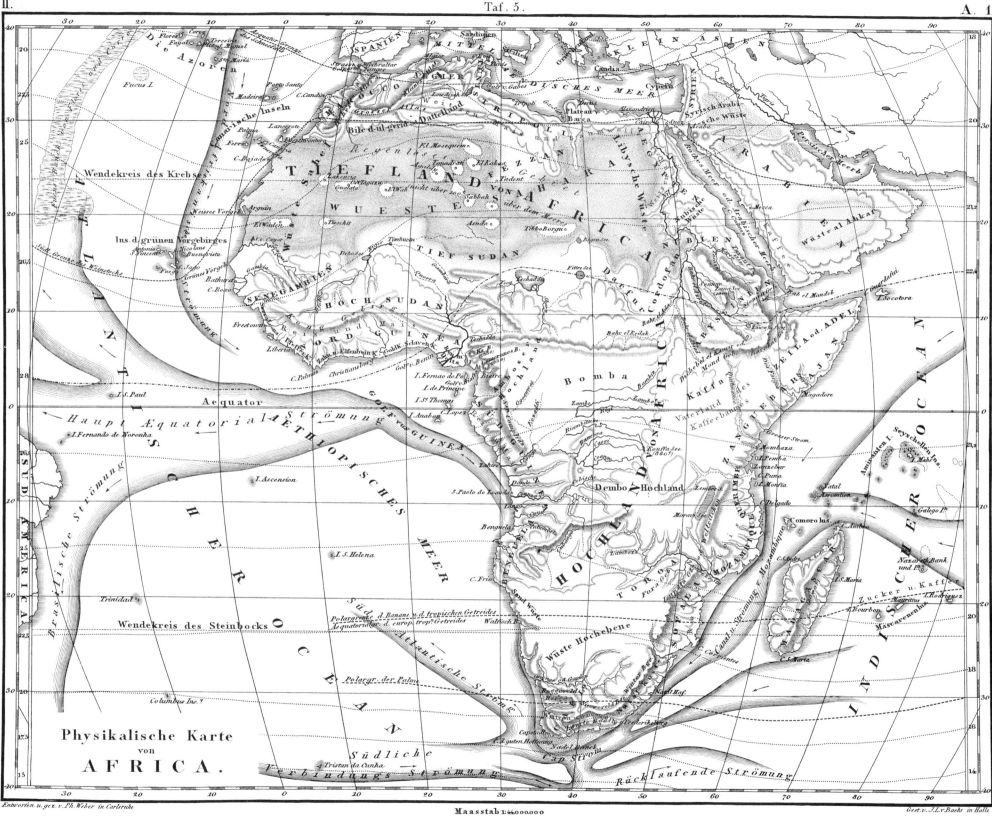

Physikalische Karte
von
AFRICA.

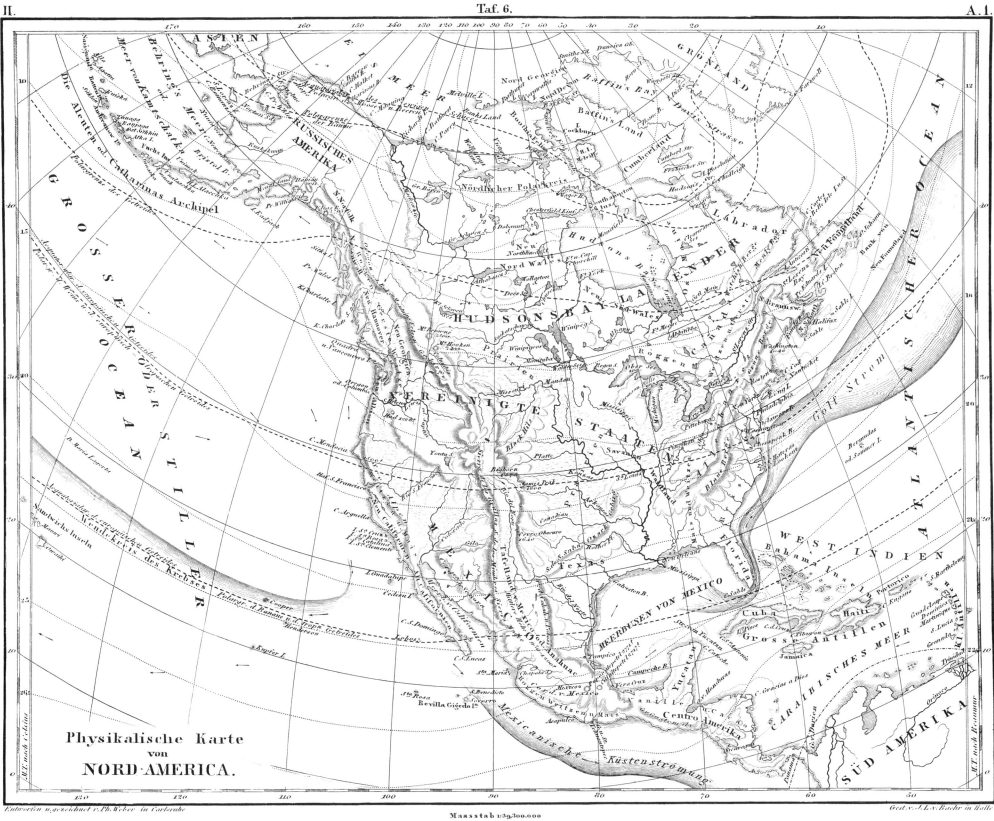

Physikalische Karte
von
NORD-AMERICA.

Entworfen u. gezeichnet v. Ph. Weber in Carlsruhe.   Maasstab 1:39,300.000   Gest. v. J. L. v. Baehr in Halle.

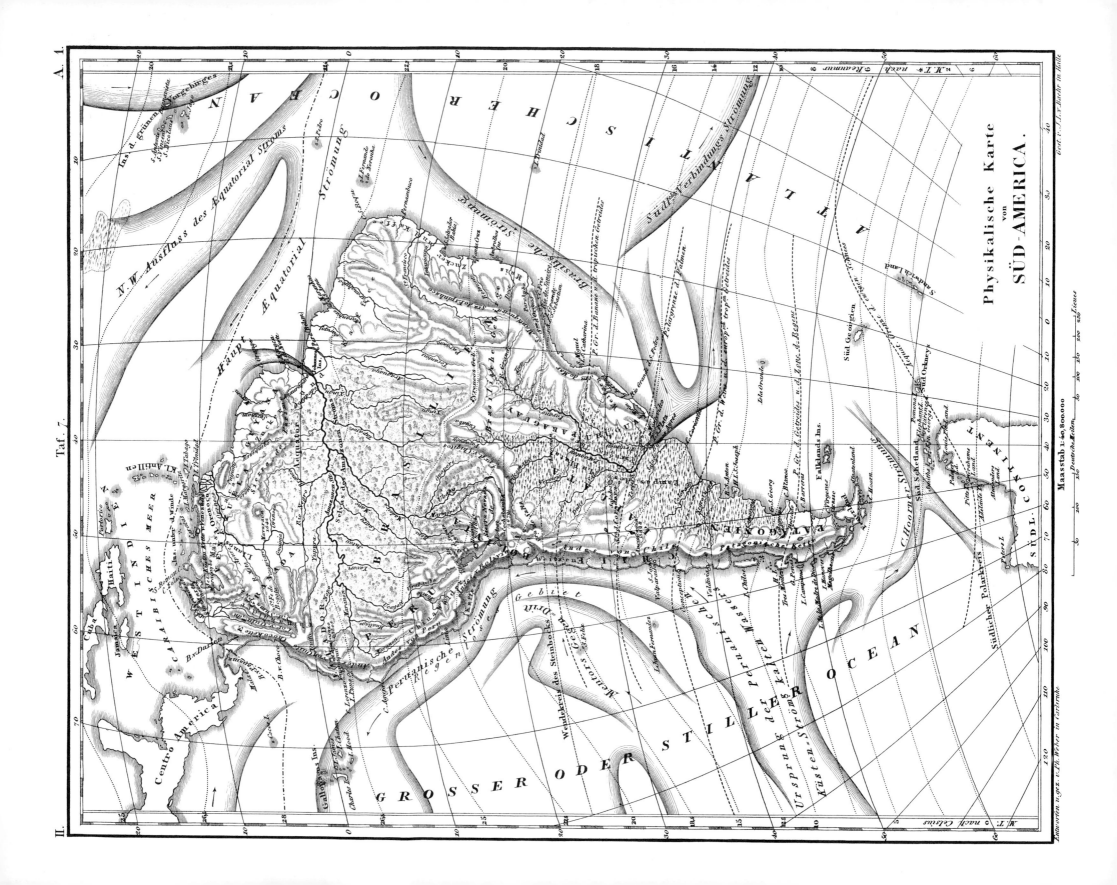

Physikalische Karte von
SÜD-AMERICA.

Maasstab 1:40,800,000

I. Herodots Erdtafel.

Nördlicher Oceanus — Scythisches Meer

Ethiopischer Oceanus

1 Pontus-Euxinus   3 Kaspisches Meer
2 Macotis See   4 Mittelländ: Meer

III. Ptolemäische Erdtafel.

AFRIKA

INDISCHER OCEANUS

II. Strabo's Erdtafel.

EUROPA

LIBYEN — ÆTHIOPIEN

Windtafel der Griechen
(Nach Aristoteles)

Windtafel der Römer
(Nach Vitruvius)

IV. Die bekannte Welt des Alterthumes.

ATLANTISCHER OCEANUS

EUROPA

MITTELLÄNDISCHES MEER

AFRIKA — LIBYEN

ÆTHIOPISCH: OCEANUS

ÆTHIOPIEN

SKYTHIEN

INDIEN

ROTHES ODER ERYTHRÆISCH: MEER

Maasstäbe.

Hebräische Stadien, wovon 750 a.d.Gr.
Olympische Stadien, wovon 600 a.d.Grad.
Ptolemäische Stadien, wovon 700 auf den Grad.
Römische Meilen, wovon 75 auf den Grad.

Maasstäbe.

Persische Parasangen, wov. 25 a.d.Gr.
Ægyptische Schöne, wovon 18⅔ a.d.Gr.
Gallische Wegestunden, wovon 50 auf den Grad.
Geographische Meilen, wovon 15 auf den Grad.

J.L.v.Baehr sculp!

REICH ALEXANDER'S
DES GROSSEN

Olympische Stadien, 600 auf den Grad.
500 1000 2000 3000 4000
Deutsche Meilen, 15 auf den Grad.
0 10 20 40 60 80 100
---- Alexander's Heerzüge.

Zerstückelung des Reiches

REICH DER SELEUCIDEN

1 Pergamus
2 Bithynien
3 Pontus
4 Cappadocien
5 Judaea

EUROPA
EUROPÄISCHES SKYTHIEN
ASIATISCHES SKYTHIEN
MARE CASPIUM ODER
PONTUS EUXINUS (SCHWARZES MEER)
MARE HYRCANUM
MARE INTERNUM (MITTELLÄNDISCHES MEER)
MACEDONIA
THRACIA
BITHYNIA
PAPHLAGONIA
PONTUS
PHRYGIA
CAPPADOCIA
ARMENIA
BACTRIANA
SOGDIANA
MARGIANA
PARTHIA
HYRCANIA
ARIA
DRANGIANA
ARACHOSIA
PAROPAMISUS
GEDROSIA
CARMANIA
PERSIS
SUSIANA
BABYLONIA
MESOPOTAMIA
ASSYRIA
MEDIA
LIBYA
AEGYPTUS
ARABIA
Wüstes Arabien
PALÄSTINA
SYRIA
CYPERN
CRETA
RHODUS
MARE ERYTHRAEUM (INDISCHES MEER)
INDIEN
Arabischer Meerbusen
Persischer Meerbusen
Wendekreis

Athen · Sparta · Pella · Byzantium · Sinope · Trapezus · Antiochia · Damascus · Tyrus · Jerusalem · Gaza · Alexandria · Memphis · Thebae · Syene · Babylon · Borsippa · Susa · Persepolis · Pasargadae · Ecbatana · Arbela · Gaugamela · Hecatompylos · Zadracarta · Bactra · Zariaspa später Bactra · Maracanda · Cyropolis · Alexandreschata · Taxila · Nicaea · Bucephala · Pattala · Alexandria

Nil · Euphrat · Tigris · Oxus · Jaxartes · Indus · Hydaspes · Hyphasis · Araxes · Tanais · Rha (Wolga) · Danubius (Donau)

G. Heck dir.t   R. Schmidt sculp.

RÖMISCHES REICH

ZUR ZEIT

CONSTANTIN'S DES GROSSEN.

Olympische Stadien, 600 auf den Grad
Römische Meilen, 75 auf den Grad
Deutsche Meilen, 15 auf den Grad

G. Heck dir.ᵗ　　　　　　　R. Schmidt sculp.

OCEANUS ATLANTICUS

OCEANUS GERMANICUS

GERMANIA

SARMATIA

GALLIA

HISPANIA

ITALIA

MARE INTERNUM

MARE ADRIATICUM

PONTUS EUXINUS

ASIA

AFRICA

MAURITANIA

NUMIDIA

AEGYPTUS

LIBYA arida

ARABIA

ARMENIA

Roma　Constantinopolis　Carthago　Alexandria　Hierosolyma　Antiochia

Corsica　Sardinia　Sicilia　Creta　Cyprus

VENEDICUS SINUS

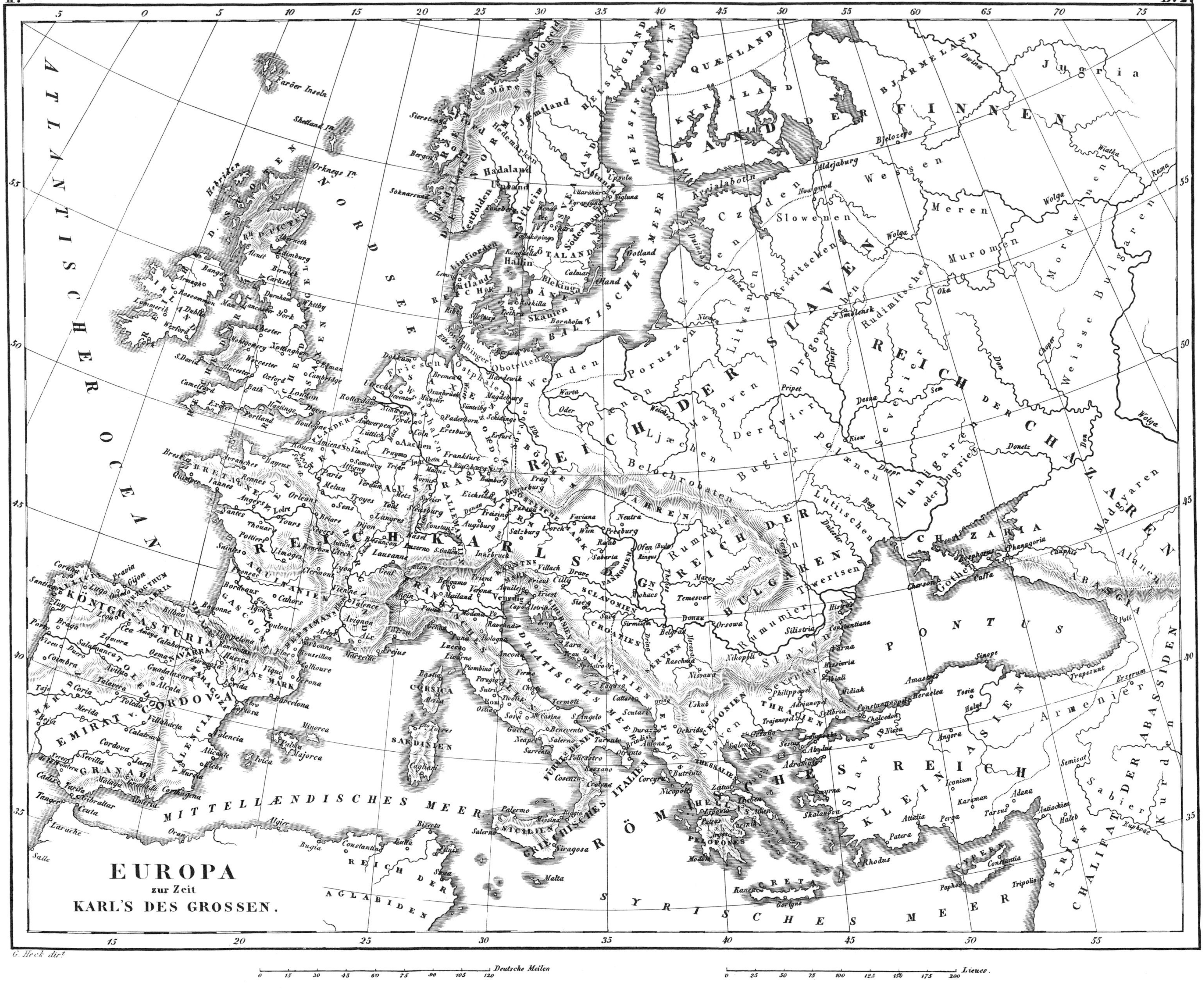

EUROPA
zur Zeit
KARL'S DES GROSSEN.

G. Heck dir!

Deutsche Meilen

Lieues

EUROPA
ZUR ZEIT DER KREUZZÜGE.

1. Zug unter Godfried von Bouillon 1097–1100. 4. Zug unter Richard I. u. Phil. August 1191–1192.

2. Zug unter Conrad III. u. Ludwig VII. 1147–1149. 5. Zug unter Kaiser Friedrich II. 1228–1229.

3. Zug unter Friedrich Barbarossa 1188–1190. 6. Zug unter Ludwig IX. v. Frankr. 1248–1250.

Deutsche Meilen. 15 auf den Grad.

Französische Lieues. 25 auf den Grad.

G. Heck dir.t   J. L. v. Baehr. sculp.

EUROPA
VOR DER FRANZÖSISCHEN REVOLUTION.
(1789)
Erklärung der Zahlen

1. Oesterreichische Landestheile . . . . . | 4. Republik Venedig . . . .
2. Preussische Landestheile . . . . . | 5. Republik Genua . . . .
3. Schwedische Landestheile . . . . . | 6. Herzogthum Parma . . . . . .
7. Herzogthum Modena . . . . .

Deutsche Meilen, 15 auf den Grad
Französische Lieues, 25 auf den Grad

ATLANTISCHER OCEAN

NORD SEE

OST SEE

MITTELLÄNDISCHES MEER

SCHWARZES MEER

ADRIATISCHES MEER

SPANIEN — PORTUGAL — FRANKREICH — DEUTSCHES KAISERREICH — SCHWEIZ — POLEN — RUSSLAND — OSMANISCHES REICH — SARDINIEN — MAROCCO — ALGIER — TUNIS

G. Heck dir.t   J. L. v. Baehr sculp.t

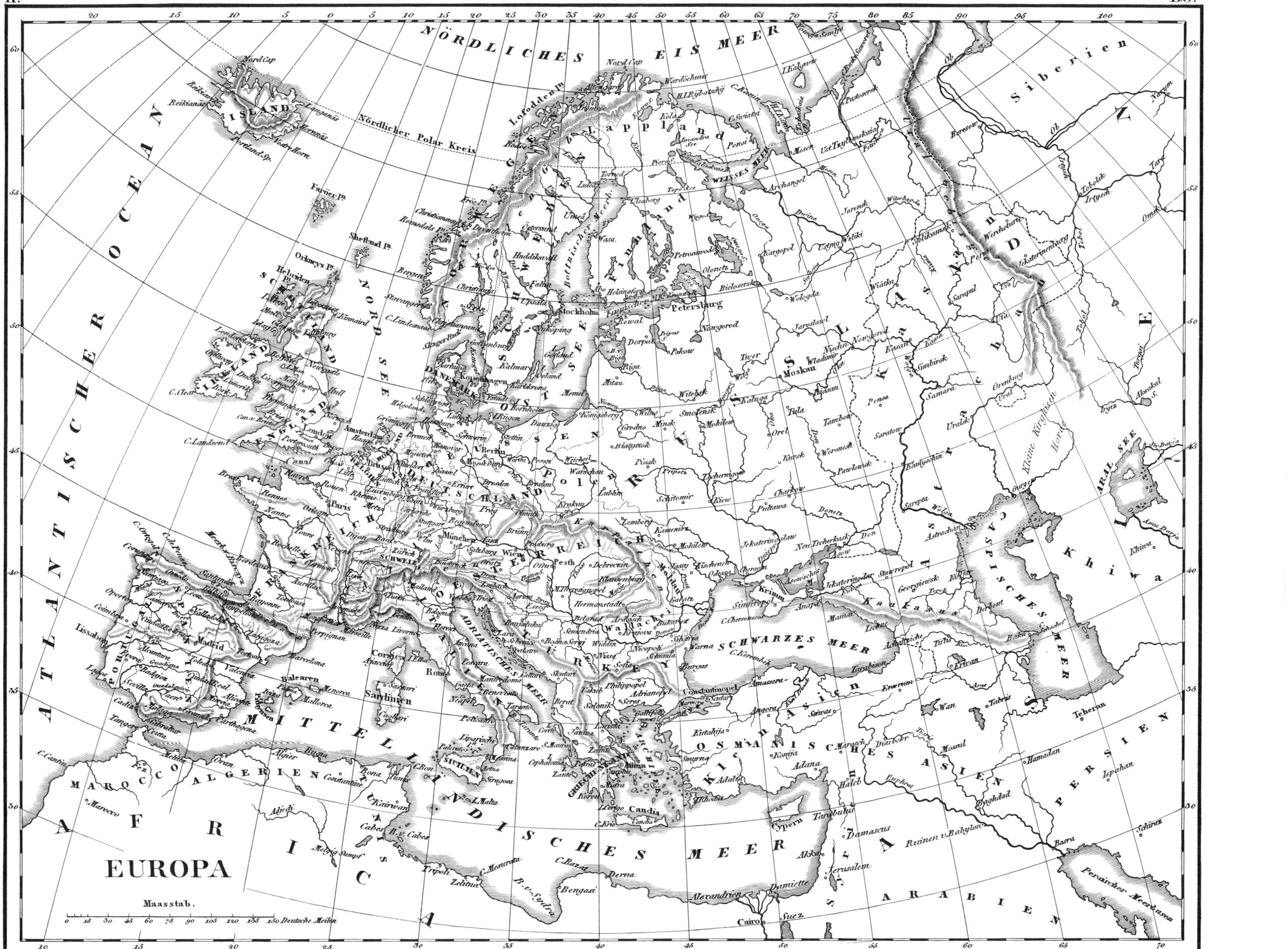

NÖRDLICHES EIS MEER

ATLANTISCHER OCEAN

NORD SEE

Siberien

EUROPA

MITTELLÄNDISCHES MEER

AFRICA

MAROCCO ALGERIEN TUNIS

SCHWARZES MEER

CASPISCHES MEER

ARAL SEE

Khiwa

PERSIEN

ARABIEN

Maasstab.

0 15 30 45 60 75 90 105 120 135 150 Deutsche Meilen

Eisenbahnkarte
von
MITTELEUROPA.

Deutsche Meilen, 15 auf den Grad.

Französische Lieues, 15 auf den Grad.

G. Heck dir.t

R. Schmidt del. et sculp.t

461 & 462.

Kaiserthum OESTERREICH.

POLEN · RUSSLAND · Podolien · GALIZIEN · Karpathisches Gebirge · BUKOWINA · MOLDAU · WALACHEI · BULGARIEN · SERBIEN · BOSNIEN · ALBANIEN · MACEDONIEN · DALMATIEN · KROATIEN · SLAVONIEN · UNGARN · SIEBENBÜRGEN · Transsylvanische Alpen · Banater Mil. Grenze · Slavonische Militair Grenze · SCHLESIEN · SACHSEN · BÖHMEN · MÄHREN · ERZHERZOGTHUM OESTERREICH · STEIERMARK · KÄRNTEN · KRAIN · TIROL · SCHWEIZ · BAIERN · WÜRTEMBERG · LOMBARDEI · VENEDIG · PARMA · MODENA · TOSCANA · KIRCHENSTAAT · NEAPEL · ITALIEN · ADRIATISCHES MEER

Frankfurt · Darmstadt · Kassel · Halle · Leipzig · Breslau · Prag · Brünn · Olmütz · Wien · München · Salzburg · Klagenfurt · Laibach · Triest · Mailand · Venedig · Rom · Florenz · Pesth · Ofen (Buda) · Klausenburg · Hermannstadt · Kronstadt · Belgrad · Bukarest · Lemberg · Krakau

G.Heck dir.t   J.L.v.Baehr sculp.t

Königreich PREUSSEN

FÜRSTENTHUM NEUENBURG

Deutsche Meilen, 15 auf den Grad.

DIE NORDSEE ODER DAS DEUTSCHE MEER

DIE OSTSEE ODER DAS BALTISCHE MEER

KATTEGAT

SCHWEDEN

RUSSLAND

DÄNEMARK

SCHLESWIG

HOLSTEIN

POMMERN

OSTPREUSSEN

WESTPREUSSEN

MECKLENBURG

HANNOVER

BRANDENBURG

POSEN

POLEN

BELGIEN

HOLLAND

OLDENBURG

WESTPHALEN

SACHSEN

SCHLESIEN

RHEINPREUSSEN

HESSEN

BAYERN

WÜRTEMBERG

BADEN

FRANKREICH

KOENIGR. BOEHMEN

OESTERREICH

Karpathen Geb.

Tatra Geb.

Gez. v. Ph. Weber in Carlsruhe.

Deutsche Meilen, 15 auf den Grad.

Französische Lieues, 25 auf den Grad.

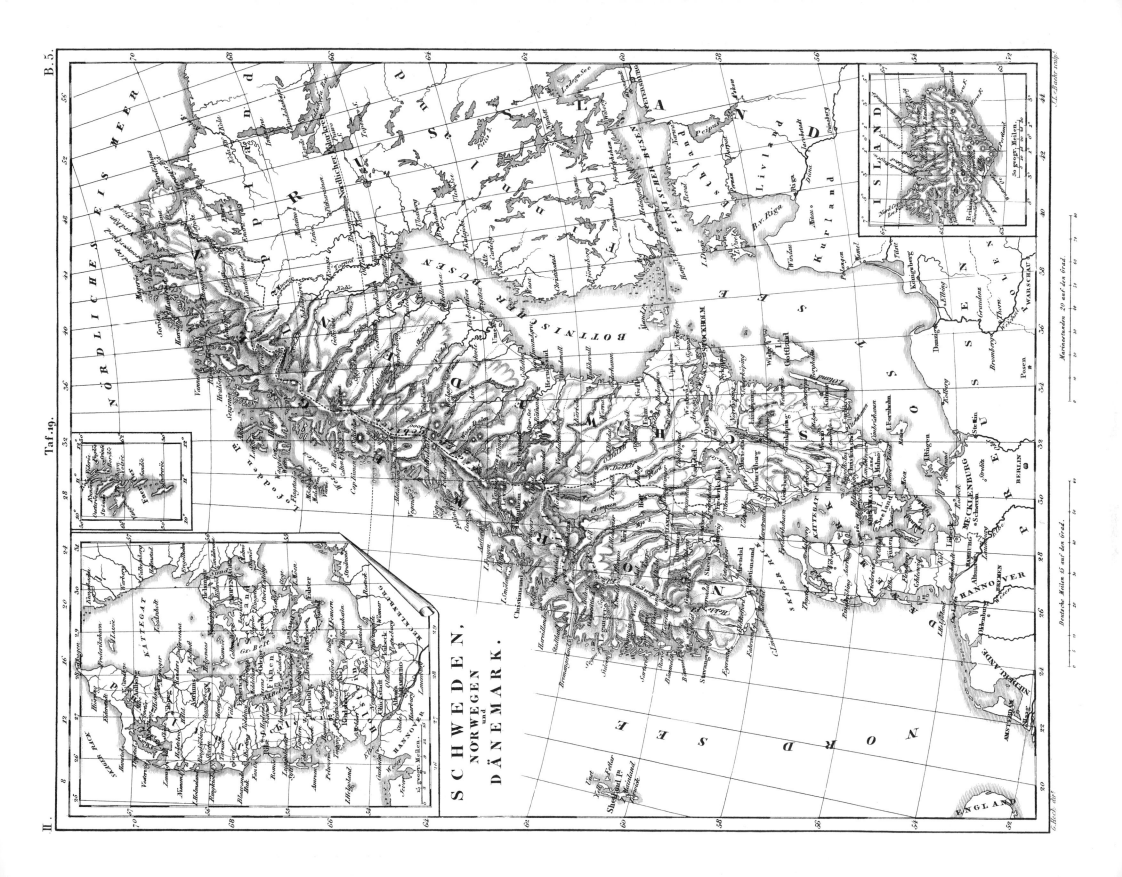

SCHWEDEN,
NORWEGEN und
DÄNEMARK.

ISLAND

Marinestunden 20 auf den Grad.

Deutsche Meilen 15 auf den Grad.

J. L. v. Baehr sculp.

GROSSBRITANNIEN und IRELAND.

Maasstäbe.

Geogr. Meilen, 15 auf den Grad.
Engl. Meilen, 69 1/10 auf den Grad.
Deutsche Meilen.

NORD SEE

ATLANTISCHER OCEAN

DER KANAL oder LA MANCHE

IRISCHE SEE

St. George's Kanal

Nord Kanal

Hebriden oder Western Inseln

Shetland Inseln

Orkney's Inseln

SCHOTTLAND

ENGLAND

IRLAND

WALES

LONDON
DUBLIN
EDINBURGH

Scilly I.

Normannische Inseln
Jersey
Guernsey

Eisenbahnen.
Kanäle.

Aberdeen — London 165 Leagues
Edinburg — London 159 Leagues
Hull — Hamburg 138 L.
Hull — London 46 L.
London — Ostende 46 L.
Bristol — London 119 Leagues
Cork — Bristol 75 Leagues

Inset maps:

GIBRALTAR
MITTELLÄNDISCHES MEER
Deutsche Meile.

HAFEN VON PLYMOUTH
Deutsche Meile.

I. GOZZO
I. MALTA
Deutsche Meilen.

HAFEN VON PORTSMOUTH
SPITHEAD
Deutsche Meile.

Ph. Weber del. Carlsruhe.

SPANIEN UND PORTUGAL.

Deutsche Meilen, 15 auf den Grad.

Französische Lieues, 25 auf den Grad.

Westliche Länge von Paris 8 · 6 · 4 · 2 · 0 · 2 · 4 · 6 · 8 Oestliche Länge von Paris

FRANKREICH.

Departemente.

1 Ain G.
2 Aisne
3 Allier
4 Alpen, Nieder - G.
5 Alpen, Ober - G.
6 Ardèche
7 Ardennen G.
8 Ariège G.
9 Aube
10 Aude S.
11 Aveyron
12 Calvados S.
13 Cantal
14 Charente
15 Charente, Nieder - S.
16 Cher
17 Corrèze
18 Corsica S.
19 Côte - d'Or
20 Creuse
21 Dordogne
22 Doubs G.
23 Drôme
24 Eure
25 Eure - Loir
26 Finistère S.
27 Gard G.
28 Garonne Ober -
29 Gers
30 Gironde
31 Heiden (Landes) S.
32 Hérault S.
33 Ille-Villaine S.
34 Indre
35 Indre - Loire
36 Isère G.
37 Jura G.
38 Kanal (Manche) S.
39 Loir - Cher
40 Loire
41 Loire, Nieder - S.
42 Loire, Ober -
43 Loiret
44 Lot
45 Lot - Garonne
46 Lozère
47 Maine - Loire
48 Marne
49 Marne, Ober
50 Mayenne
51 Meurthe
52 Maas (Meuse) G.
53 Morbihan S.
54 Mosel (Moselle) G.
55 Nièvre
56 Norden (Nord) G.u.S.
57 Nordküsten (Côtes du Nord) S.
58 Oise
59 Orne
60 Pas-de-Calais S.
61 Puy-de-Dôme
62 Pyrenäen, Nieder-G.u.S.
63 Pyrenäen, Ober-G.
64 Pyrenäen, Ost-G.u.S.
65 Rhein, Nieder-G.
66 Rhein, Ober-G.
67 Rhône
68 Rhônemündungen S.
69 Saône, Ober-
70 Saône-Loire
71 Sarthe
72 Seine, Paris
73 Seine, Nieder-S.
74 Seine-Marne
75 Seine-Oise
76 Sèvres,Beide-(Deux-Sèvres)
77 Somme S.
78 Tarn
79 Tarn-Garonne
80 Var G.u.S.
81 Vaucluse
82 Vendée S.
83 Vienne
84 Vienne, Ober
85 Vogesen (Vosges)
86 Yonne

Bemerkung

G. Grenz } Departemente.
S. See -

ENGLAND

CANAL ODER LA MANCHE

ATLANTISCHER OCEAN

SPANIEN

DEUTSCHLAND

SCHWEIZ

ITALIEN

MITTELLÆNDISCHES MEER

BELGIEN

G. Heck dir.

J.L.v.Baehr sc.

Geogr. Meilen.

Französische Lieues.

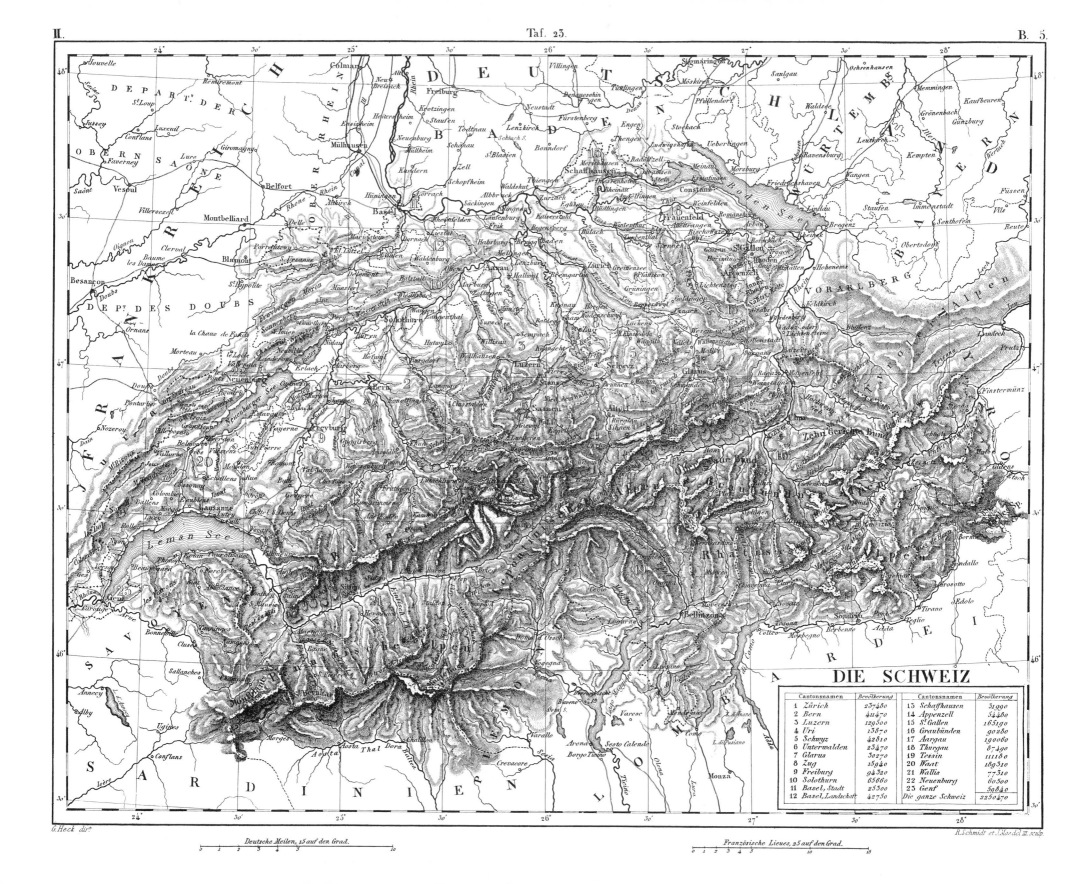

DIE SCHWEIZ

Cantonsnamen	Bevölkerung	Cantonsnamen	Bevölkerung
1 Zürich	257480	13 Schaffhausen	31990
2 Bern	411470	14 Appenzell	54480
3 Luzern	129500	15 St Gallen	165190
4 Uri	13870	16 Graubünden	90280
5 Schwyz	42810	17 Aargau	190060
6 Unterwalden	23470	18 Thurgau	87490
7 Glarus	30270	19 Tessin	111180
8 Zug	15940	20 Waat	189310
9 Freiburg	94320	21 Wallis	77310
10 Solothurn	65660	22 Neuenburg	60500
11 Basel, Stadt	25300	23 Genf	59840
12 Basel, Landschaft	42730	Die ganze Schweiz	2250470

G. Heck dir.   R. Schmidt et J. Mae del. III. sculp.

Deutsche Meilen, 15 auf den Grad.
0 1 2 3 4 5   10

Französische Lieues, 25 auf den Grad.
0 1 2 3 4 5   10   15

ITALIEN.

Maasstäbe

Französische Lieues
Deutsche Meilen

ADRIATISCHES MEER

TYRRHENISCHES MEER

MITTELLAENDISCHES MEER

LIGURISCHES MEER

Busen von Genua

Busen von Taranto

Busen v. Venedig

CORSICA

INSEL SARDINIEN

AFRICA

UNGARN

ILLYRIEN

TÜRKEI

SCHWEIZ

NEAPEL

PALERMO

TURIN

Messina

Catania

Siracusa

Cagliari

TUNIS

L. Malta

Lipärische Inseln

Stromboli

G. Heck dir.   J. L. v. Baehr sculp.

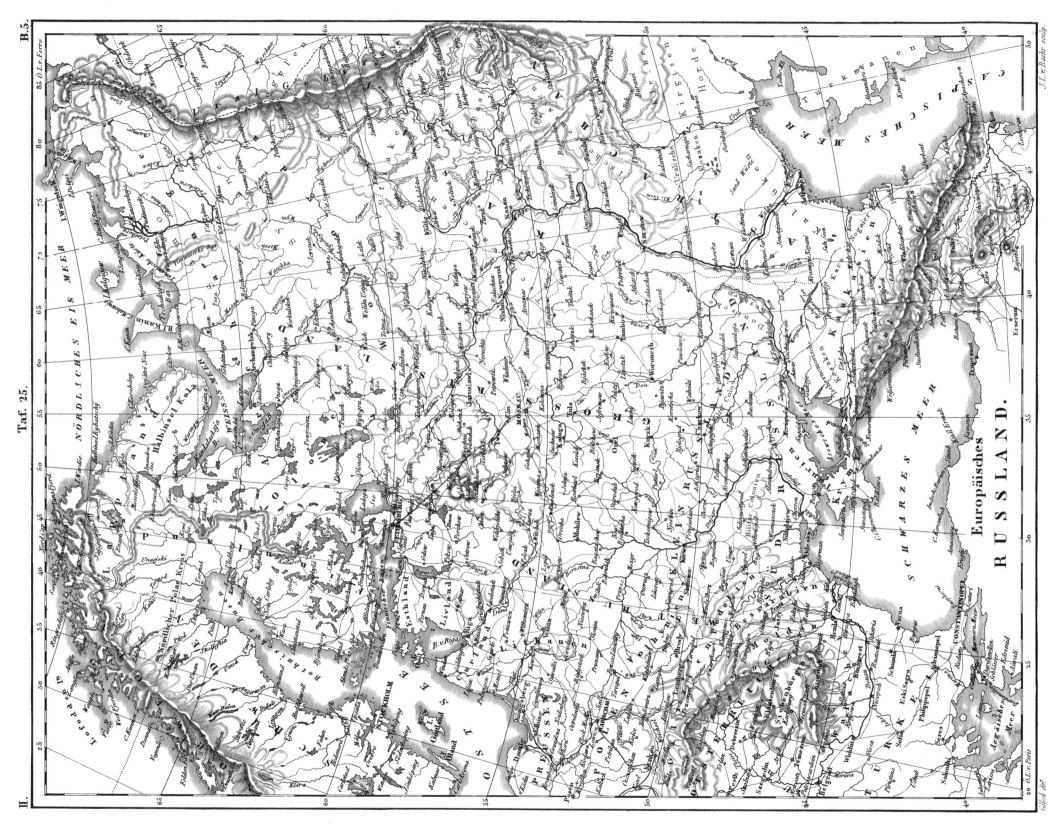

Europäisches
RUSSLAND.

OSMANISCHES REICH.

Europa	Asien	
1 Ejalet Rum-Ili	10 Ejalet Anatolien	19 Ejalet Musch
2 - Silistria	11 - Adana	20 - Baghdad
3 - Bosnien	12 - Karamanien	21 - Diarbekr
4 - Deria	13 - Marasch	22 - Urfa
5 - Kirid	14 - Siwas	23 - Mossul
6 Schutz-Staat Serbien	15 - Tarabison	24 - Haleb
7 - - Wallachei	16 - Erserum	25 - Damascus
8 - - Moldau	17 - Wan	26 - Akka
9 - - Montenegro	18 - Kars	27 - Beirut
		28 - Jerusalem

G. Heck dir.ᵗ

J. L. v. Baehr sculp.ᵗ

Deutsche Meilen   Franz. Lieus   Seemeilen   Kameelstunden

GRIECHENLAND.

38° Oestliche Länge von Ferro

EPIRUS

THESSALIEN

LIVADIEN

MOREA

ZANTE

CEPHALONIA

SANTA MAURA

JONISCHES MEER

MITTELMEER

ARCHIPELAGUS

CYCLADEN

EGRIBOS ODER NEGROPONTE

B. von Volo

Scopelo

Scyros

Chelidromia

Dio Adelphi (Die 2 Brüder)

ATHEN (Athen)

Korinth

Patras

Busen von Lepanto oder von Korinth

Arta

Prevesa

Trikkala

Lamia

Amphissa

Lebadea

Theben

Salamis

Aegina

Naplia (Napoli)

Argos

Tripolis

Sparta Mistra

Kalamata

Navarin

Thiaki

Argostoli

Thera Santorin

Naxia od. Naxos

Amorgos

Ios (Nio)

Stampalia

Zea od. Ceos

Thermia od. Cythnos

Syra

Mykone

Tine od. Tenos

Andros

Paros

Naxia

Sifanto

Serfo

Milo od. Melos

Pholegandros

Nio od. Ios

Thera Santorin

CERIGO

Maasstäbe.
Deutsche Meilen
Griechische Meilen
Marinestunden

G. Heck dir.

J. L. v. Baehr sc.

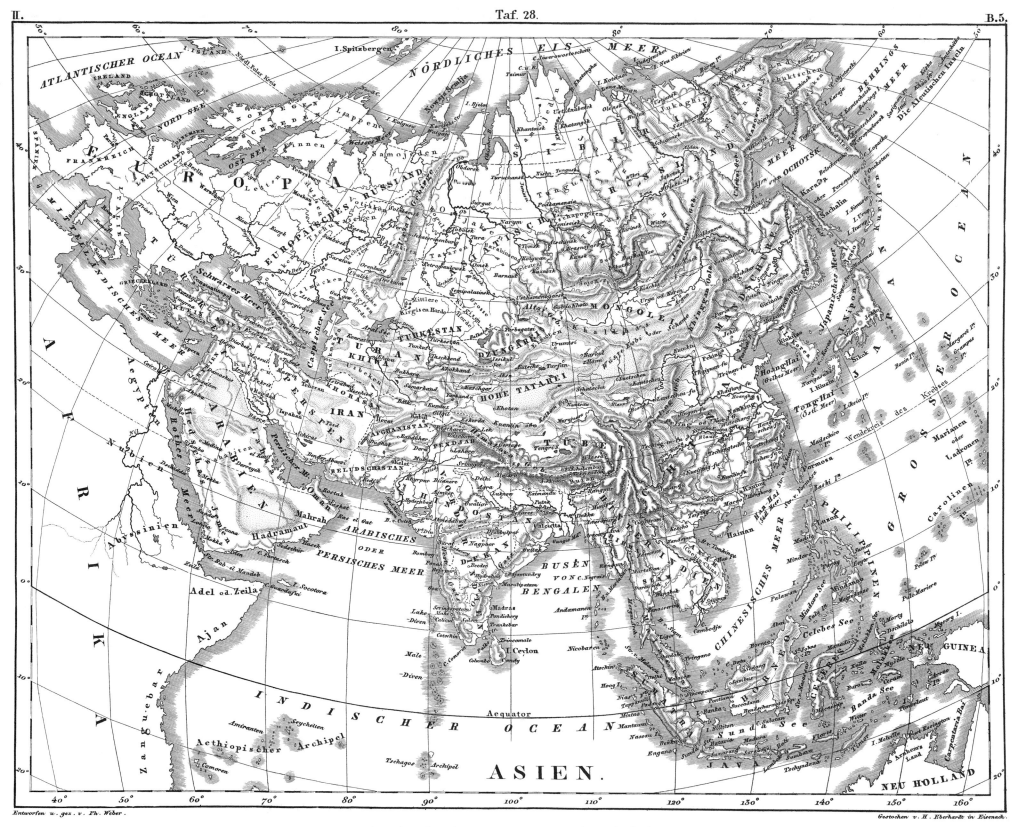

ASIEN.

50   100   150 Deutsche Meilen.   50   100   150   200   250 Lieues.

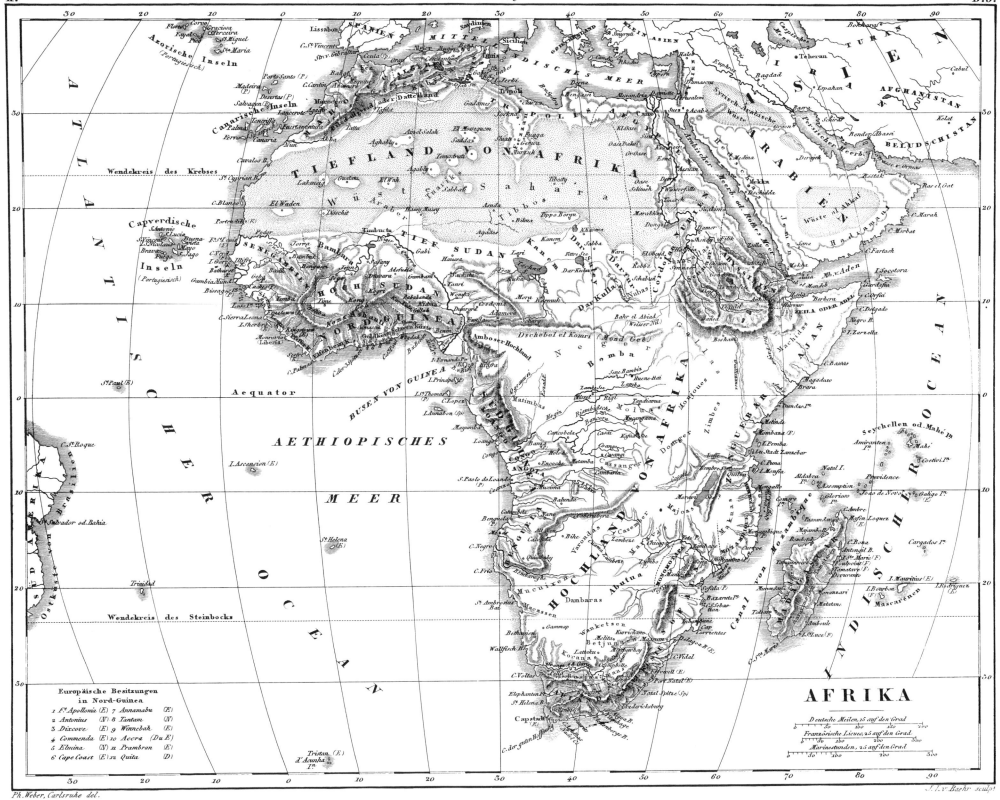

AFRIKA

Europäische Besitzungen
in Nord-Guinea

1 Ft Apollonia (E) 7 Annamabu (E)
2 Antonius (N) 8 Tantam (N)
3 Dixcove (E) 9 Winnebah (E)
4 Commenda (E) 10 Accra (Du E)
5 Elmina (N) 11 Prambran (E)
6 Cape Coast (E) 12 Quita (D)

Deutsche Meilen, 15 auf den Grad
Französische Lieues, 25 auf den Grad
Marinestunden, 25 auf den Grad

Ph. Weber, Carlsruhe del.

J. J. v. Baehr sculps.

NORDAMERICA.

Staaten der Nordamerikanischen Union

Maine	1	Louisiana	19
Neu Hampshire	2	Tennessee	20
Vermont	3	Kentucky	21
Massachusetts	4	Ohio	22
Rhode Island	5	Indiana	23
Connecticut	6	Illinois	24
New York	7	Michigan	25
Neu Jersey	8	Missouri	26
Pensylvanien	9	Arkansas	27
Delaware	10	Wisconsin	28
Maryland	11	Jowa	29
Virginien	12	Texas	50
Nord Carolina	13	**Districte**	
Süd Carolina	14	Distr. Columbia	31
Georgia	15	- - Mandan	33
Florida	16	- - Osage	34
Alabama	17	- - Ozark	35
Mississippi	18	- - Oregon	52

Staaten der Mexicschen Union

Mexico mit dem Bundesdistrict	1
Queretaro	2
Guanaxuato	3
Mechoacan	4
Xalisco	5
Zacatecas	6
Sonora und Cinaloa	7
Chihuahua mit Bolson de Mapimi	8
Durango	9
Cohahuila	10
Neu Leon	11
Tamaulipas	12
San Luis Potosi	13
Vera Cruz	14
La Puebla mit dem Distr Tlascala	15
Oaxaca	16
Chiapa	17
Tabasco	18
Unionsgebiete	
Colima	19
Californien	20
Neu Mexico	21

UMGEBUNG VON NEU YORK

Fairfield, MACKENSACK, PATERSON, Renobridge, Hanover, Lewiston, W. Farm, Manhattanville, Northfield, Durham, Belleville, Hoboken, NEW YORK, Flushing, Chegaside, Weharis, Jersey City, Bushwick, Jamai, Springfield, Union, Hoboken, Williamsburg, Westfield, Elisabeth, Camptown, BROOKLYN, LONG ISLAND, Plainfield, Lafayette, Flatbush, Brookway, Rahway, Castleton, STATEN ISLAND, Richmond, Neu Brunswick, Woodbridge, Westfield, Amboy

BEHRINGS MEER · ALEUTEN INSELN · GROSSER OCEAN · AMERICA · RUSSISCHES · EIS MEER · Nördlicher Polarkreis · HUDSONS BAY LAENDER · HUDSONS MEER · LABRADOR · Land der kleinen Eskimos · GROENLAND · BAFFINS LAND · BAFFINS BAY · OBER CANADA · NIEDER CANADA · VEREINIGTE STAATEN · ATLANTISCHER OCEAN · MEERBUSEN V. MEXICO · CUBA · HAITI · GROSSE ANTILLEN · CARAIBISCHES MEER · Wendekreis des Krebses

Entworfen u. gezeichnet v. Ph. Weber in Carlsruhe.

Gest. v. J. L. v. Baehr in Halle.

Deutsche Meilen · Lieues

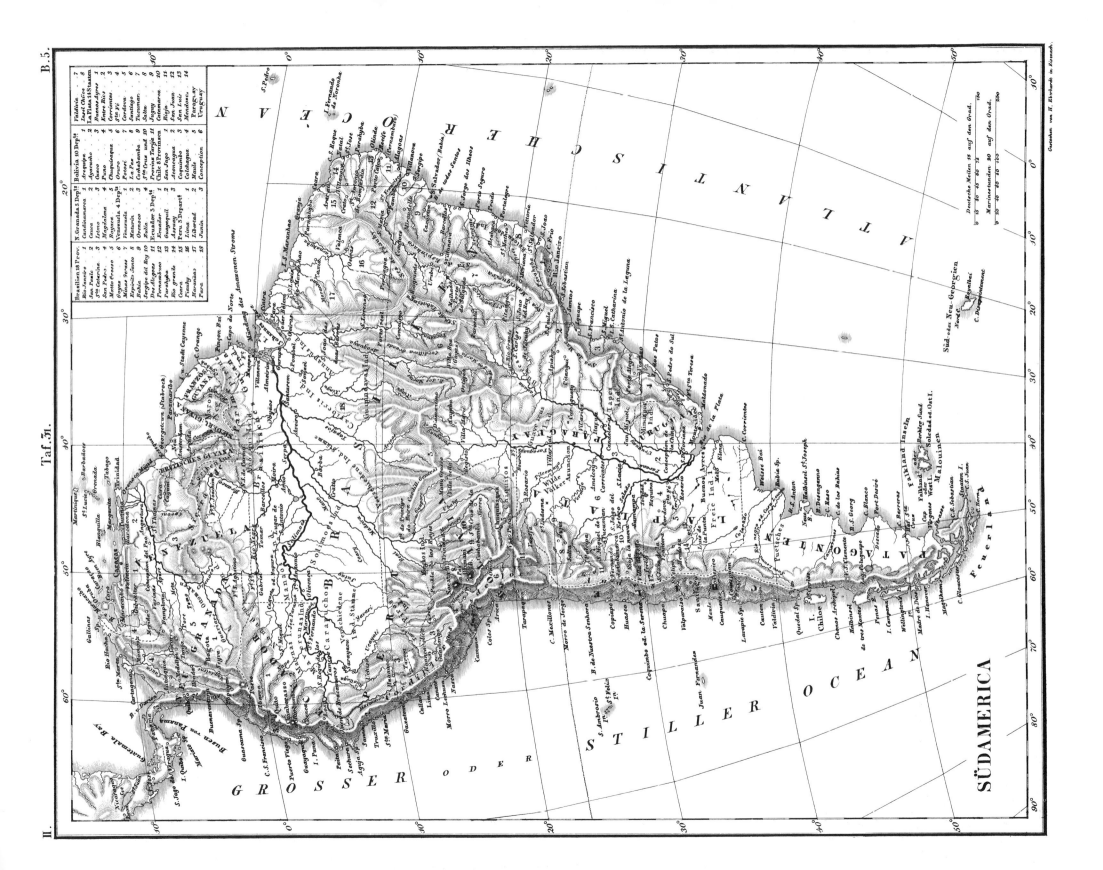

SÜDAMERICA

AUSTRALIEN

Engl. Colonien am Schwaanflusse, K. Georg's Sund und N. S. Wales.

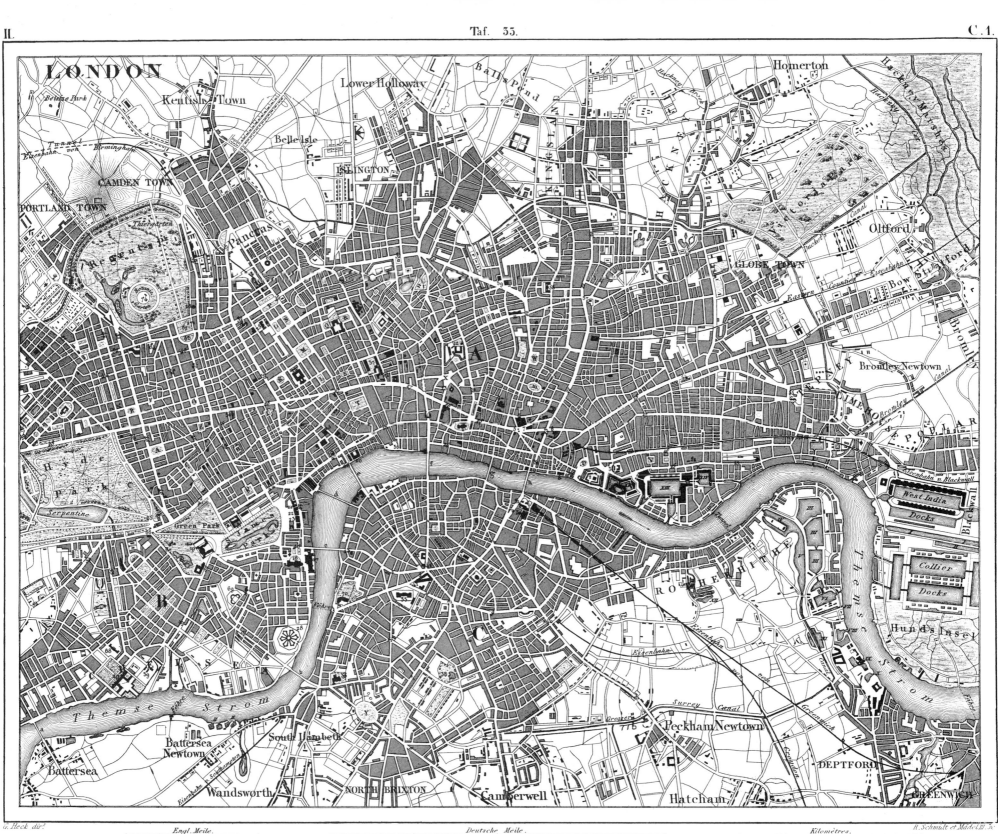

LONDON

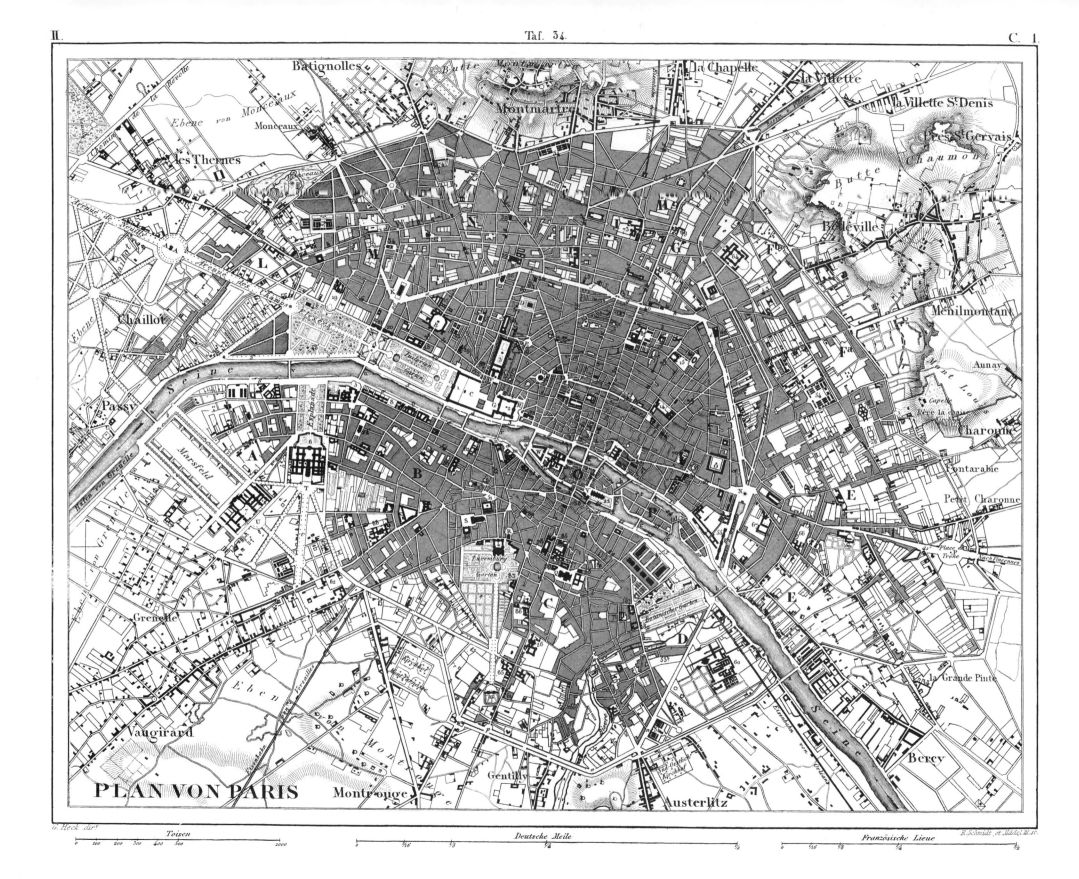

PLAN VON PARIS

Toisen

Deutsche Meile

Französische Lieue

PARIS
ALS WAFFENPLATZ.

St DENIS

Couronne de la Briche   Double Couroñe du Nord   Lunette de Stains

St DENIS

Colombes

Bezons

Petit Nanterre

Asnières

St Ouen

Courneuve

Fort de l'Est   Crèvecœur

Drancy

Gare de St Ouen

Infant. Baracken

Feldschanze

Aubervilliers

Fort d'Aubervilliers

Clichy

Glacière de St Ouen

Feldschanze

Bobigny

Courbevoie

Courcelles

Becon Château

Feldschanzen vom J. 1832

Pantin

la Folie

Bondy

Nanterre

Château de Neuilly   Villiers

NEUILLY sur Seine

les Batignolles

Chaumont

la Chapelle

la Villette

Noisy le Sec   Merlan

Fort de Romainville

Ft du Mont Valérien

Monceaux

Montmartre

Infanterie Baracken

Pré St Gervais

Romainville

Fort de Noisy

Puteaux

les Ternes

II

III

Belleville

Bagnolet

Fort de Rosny

Rosny

Surènes

I

Ménilmontant

l'Ermitage

Passy

V

VI

Charonne

Montreuil

Auteuil

X

IV

VII

VIII

Petit Charonne

VINCENNES

Fontenai sous Bois

Ft de Nogent

St CLOUD

Boulogne

Grenelle

XI

Schloss u. Ft von Vincennes

St Mandé

Nogent

Javelle   Point du Jour

XII

Bercy

Vaugirard

Petit Montrouge

Austerlitz

CHARENTON le Pont

Charenton   St Maurice

St CLOUD

Billancourt

Conflans

Issy

Vanvres

Petit Gentilly

Infanterie Caserne

St Maur

SÈVRES

Bas Meudon

Montrouge

Bicêtre

Ivry

Charentonneau

Château Gaillard

Fort d'Issy

Gentilly

Alfort

Ft de Charenton

Meudon

N. D. de Clamart

Fort de Vanvres

Ft de Montrouge

Fort de Bicêtre

Infant. Baracken

Châtillon

Arcueil

Fort à l'Anglais

Fort d'Ivry

Maisons

Clamart

Bagneux

Villejuif

GEHÖLZ VON MEUDON

Cachan

Vitry

Créteil

Fontenai aux Roses

G. Heck dir.   R. Schmidt sc.

0   500   1000   2000   3000   4000   5000 Mètres

1   2   3   4   5 Kilomètres

¼   ½   ¾   1 Lieue

¼   ½   ¾   1 Deutsche Meile

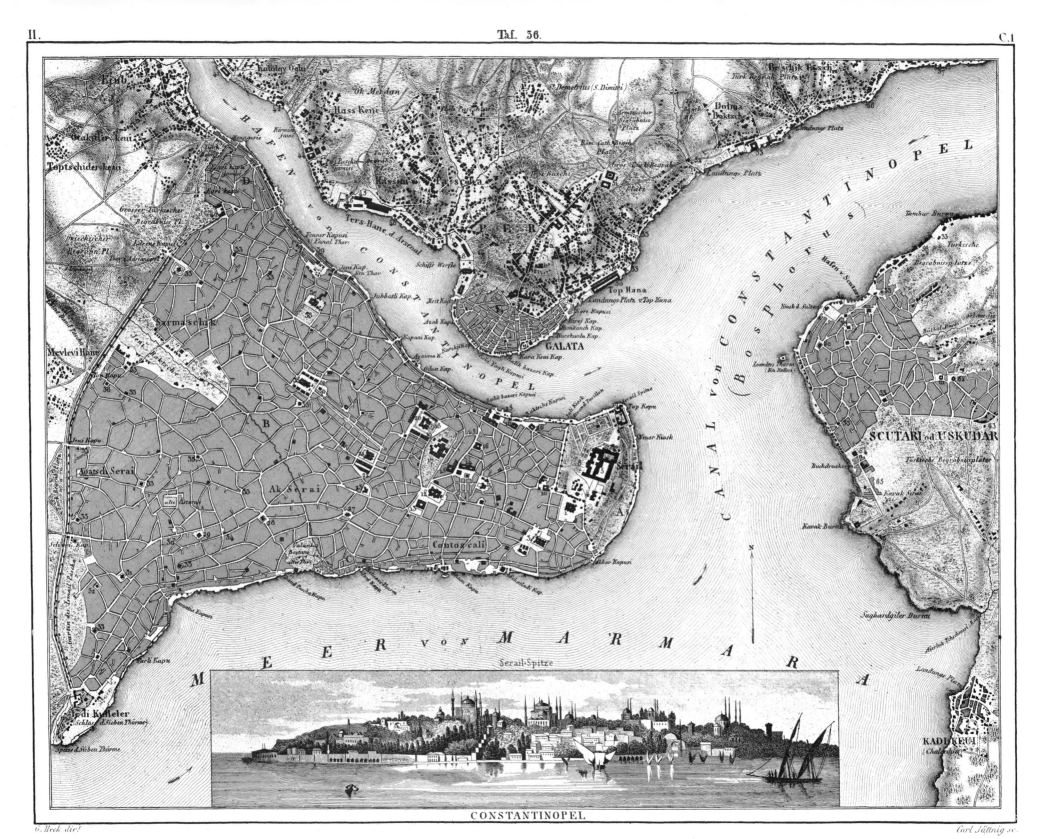

CONSTANTINOPEL

G. Heck dir!

Carl Jättnig sc.

Türkische Berri 66.67 1°   Pariser Fuss   Deutsche Meile. 15. 1°

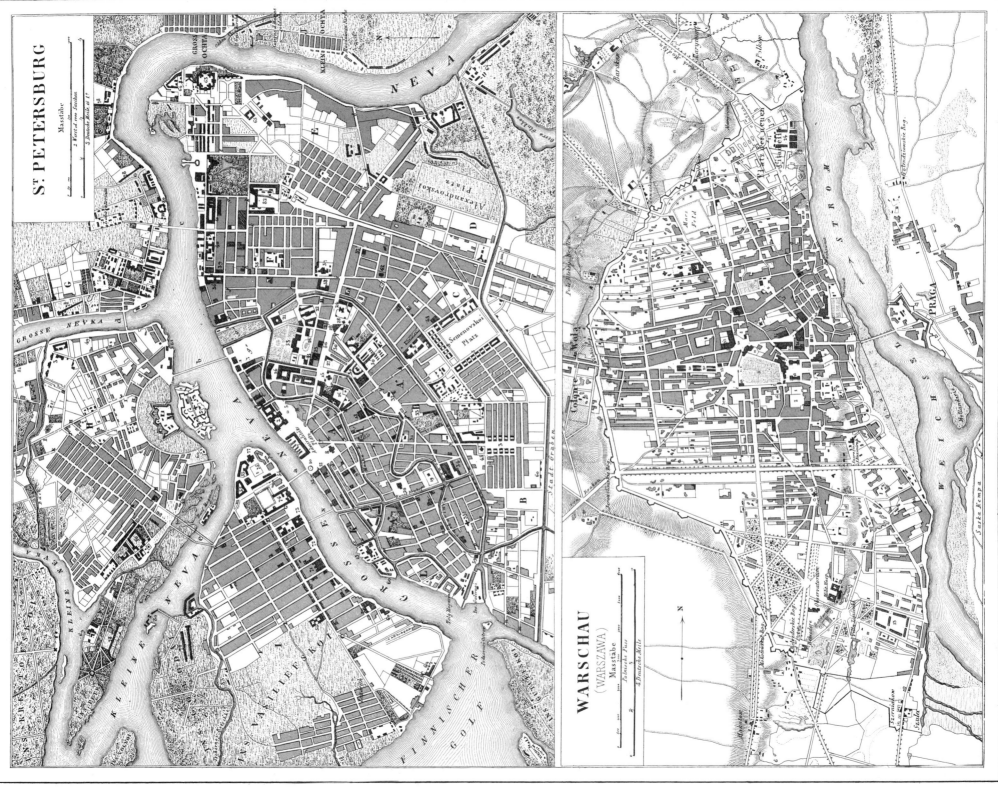

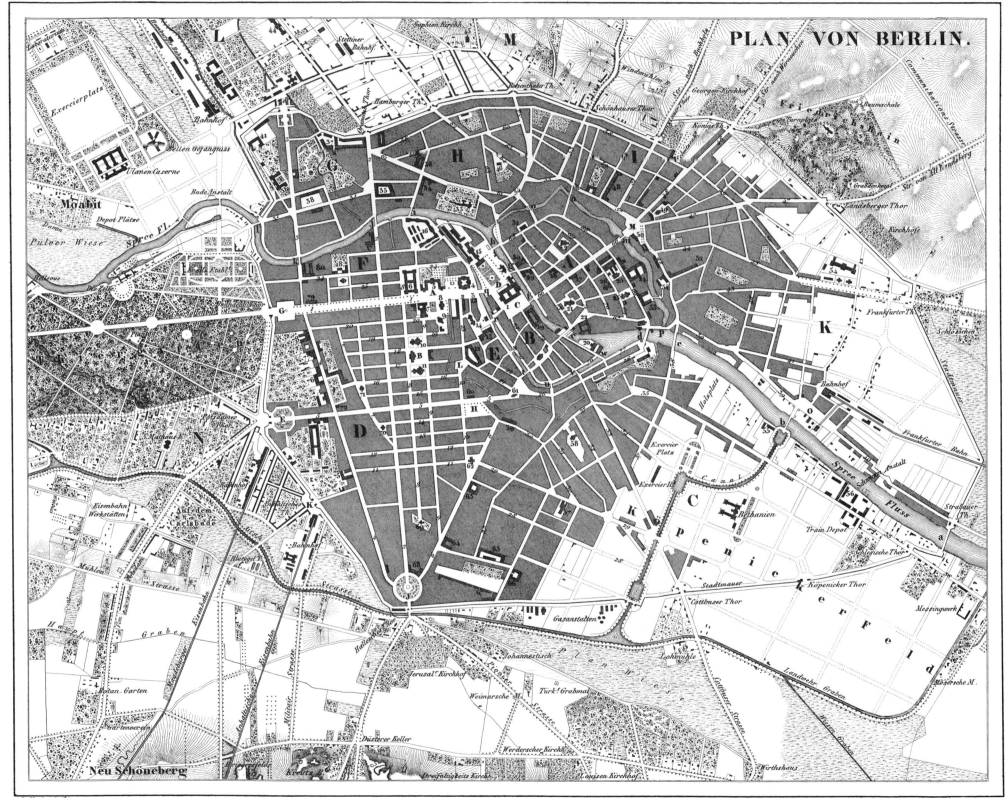

PLAN VON BERLIN.

Preussische Ruthen

G. Heck dir.t

Schlegel & Eberhardt sculp.

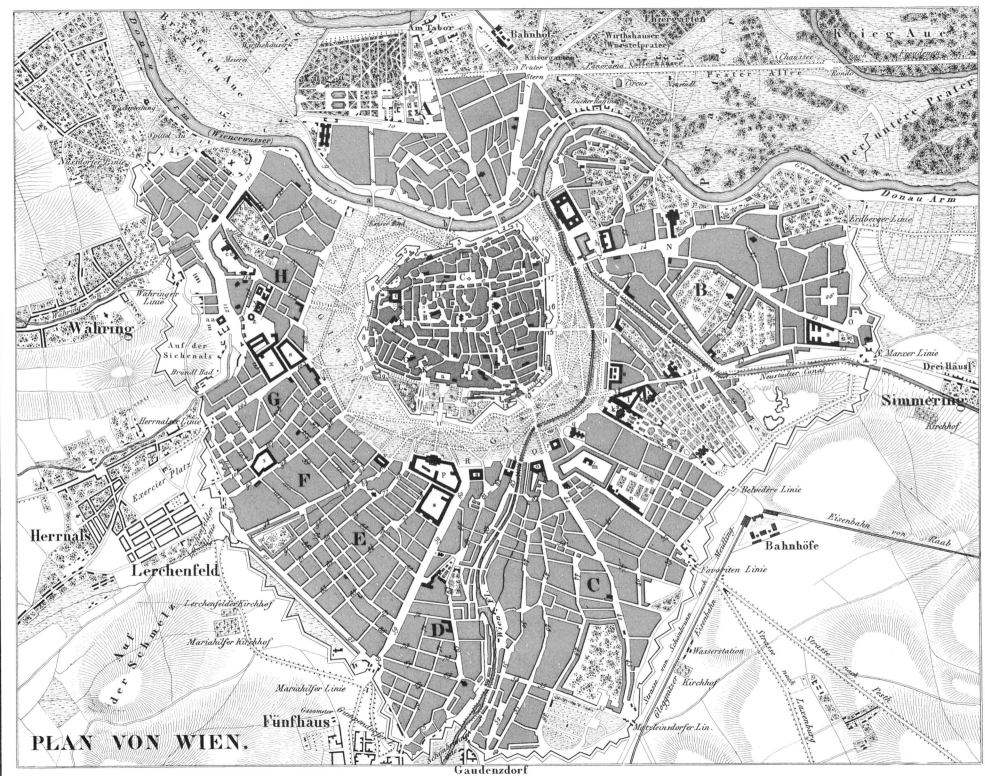

PLAN VON WIEN.

Wiener Klafter.

Deutsche Meilen.

G. Beck dir.t

Schlegel & Eberhardt sculp.

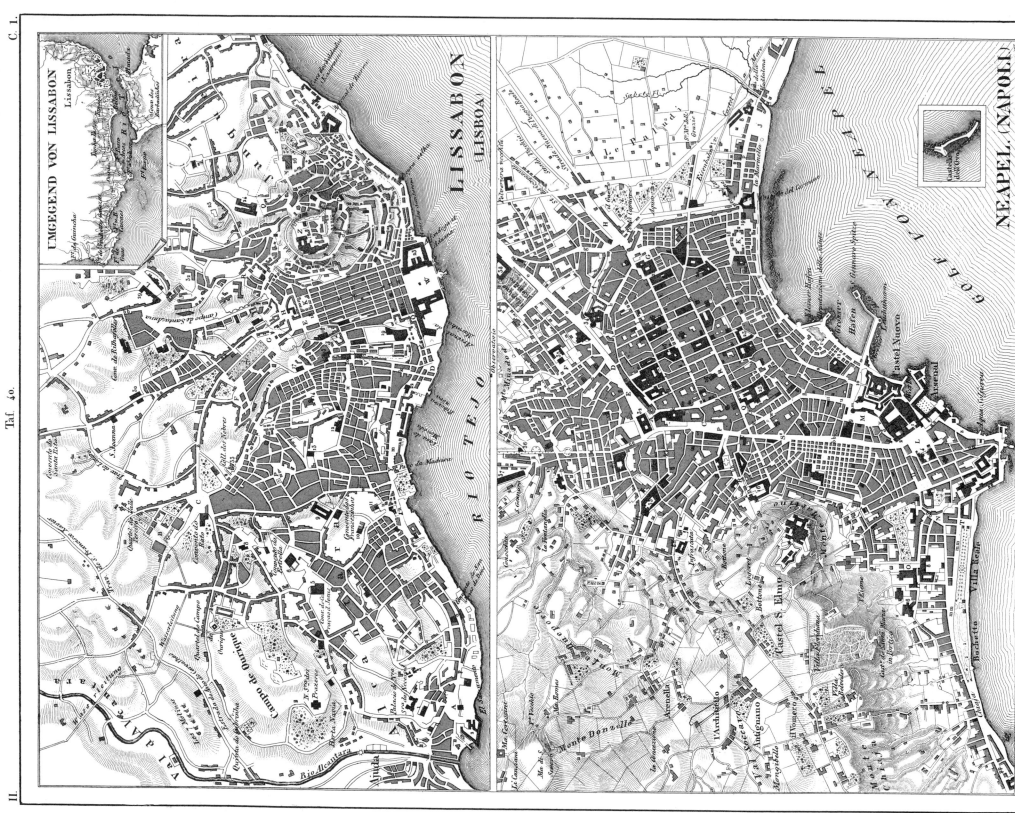

UMGEGEND VON LISSABON

LISSABON
LISBOA

RIO TEJO

NEAPEL (NAPOLI)

GOLF VON NEAPEL

Für Lissabon.

Für Neapel.

MAASSTABE

ROM
(ROMA)

Maßstäbe.

Pariser Fuss
Römische Palmen

Castello St.Angelo

S.Pietro

Mt Gianicolo

Mt Pincio

Villa Medici

Porta del Popolo

Porta Angelica

Porta Cavalleggieri

Porta Fabrica

Porta S.Pancrazio

Porta Portese

Villa Corsini

Villa Spada

Mt Esquilino

Celio

Palatino

Circo Massimo

Villa Borghese

Villa Ludovisi

o Villa Ludovisi

Porta Pia

Porta Salaria

Porta Pinciana

Porta S.Lorenzo

Porta Maggiore

Porta S.Giovanni

Via di S.Sebastiano

Via Appia

Via del Macao

Via Nomentana

Termini di S.Lorenzo

Strada Teresiana

Strada Felice

Villa Guadalupi

MAILAND
MILANO

Lazzaretto

Piazza d'armi

Arena

Strada di Circonvallazione

Circonvallazione

Strada per Novara

Str. postale per Novara

Porta Ticinese

Porta Sempione

Str. per Sempione

Str. per Segrate e Lombrate

Str. per la Reale

Str. per Venezia

Strada postale per Venezia

Str. per Trezzano

Strada per Lodi

Str. per Monzenhia

Str. per Padovarde

Il Caretto

la Parziolata

Porta Romana

Porta Tosa

Porta Nuova

Obat Nuova

Obat Vecchia

la Cacetto

Magazzeno pubblico

Pilastrello

Scuola Fabricaria

Str. per Chiaravalle

Pariser Fuss
Mailänder Fuss

G. Mayer lith.

J. Mäder lith.

II.

C. L.

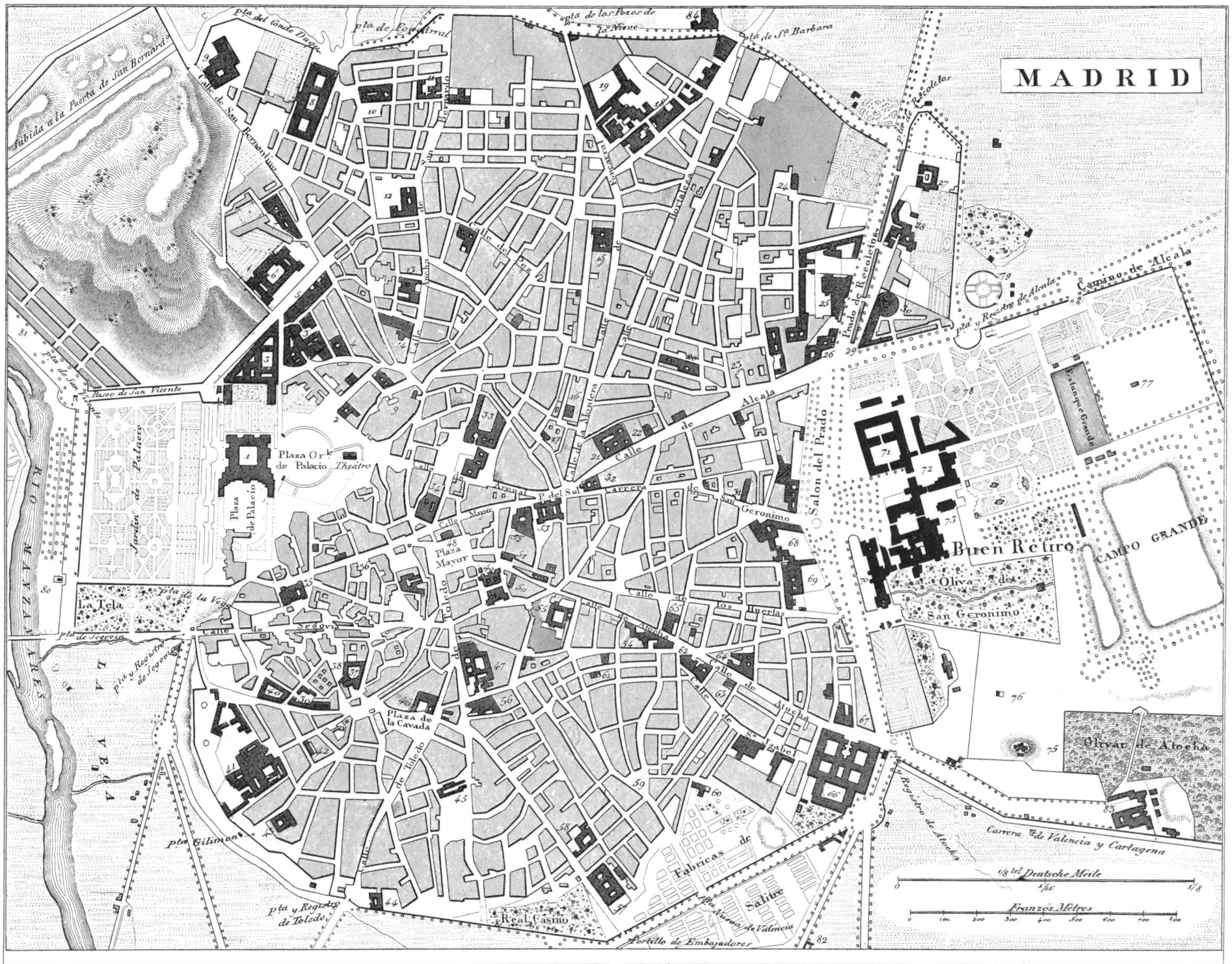

MADRID

BARCELONA

ZARAGOZA

MAR MEDITERRANEO

Fuerte Pio

Ciudadela

Barceloneta

Fuerte de Montjui

RIO EBRO

Cosso

Camino de Alfocea

Puerta de Sancho

Buen Retiro

CAMPO GRANDE

Estanque Grande

Olivar de Atocha

Salon del Prado

Plaza Mayor

Plaza de la Cavada

Plaza Or. de Palacio Theatro

Plaza de Palacio

Jardin de Palacio

RIO MANZANARES

LA VEGA

Carrera de Valencia y Cartagena

Registro de Atocha

Winkler et Lehmann sculp.

C. Hoch. delt.

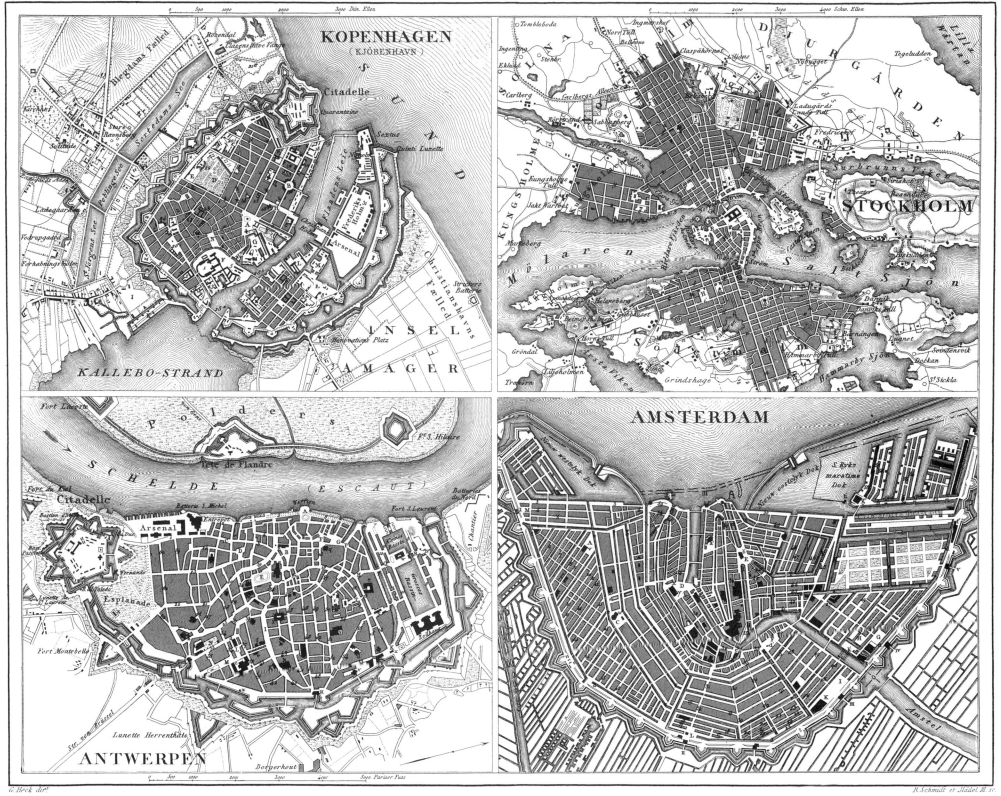

KOPENHAGEN
(KJÖBENHAVN)

STOCKHOLM

AMSTERDAM

ANTWERPEN

FLORENZ

LIVORNO

MODENA

ANCONA

ICONOGRAPHIC
ENCYCLOPÆDIA.

DIVISION III.

GEOGRAPHY AND PLANOGRAPHY.

FORTY-TWO PLATES.

[THE LIST OF THE FIGURES ON THE PLATES WILL BE FOUND IN THE TABLES OF CONTENTS OF VOL. III. OF THE TEXT.]

THE PLATES ARE NUMBERED II. 1—44.

———

NEW YORK, 1051.

PUBLISHED BY RUDOLPH GARRIGUE,

2 BARCLAY STREET (ASTOR HOUSE).

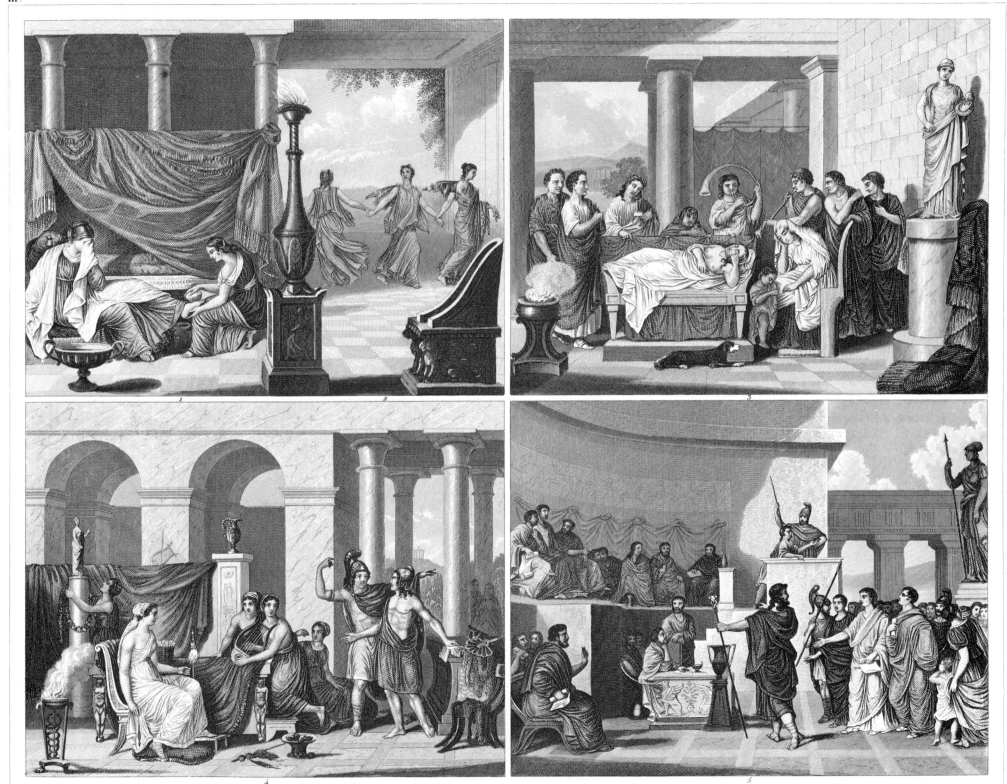

Fig. 7.

Fig. 1.

Maasstabe in Metres.

zu Figur 4   zu Figur 5. 8.   zu Figur 11.   zu Figur 9. 10.   zu Figur 13. 14.

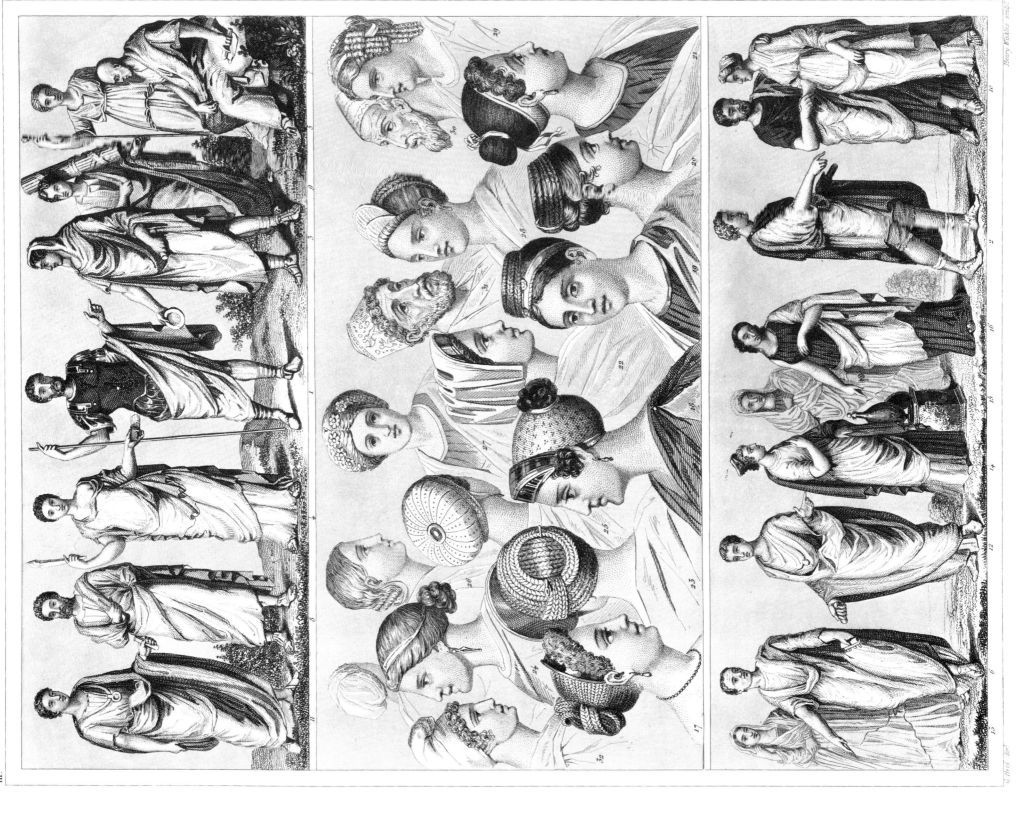

G. Heck dir.t Maschinenschrift von F. Kretschmar Leipz. Henry Winkles sculp.t

Fig. 2

Figur 1.

G. Heck del.t

H. Winkles sculp

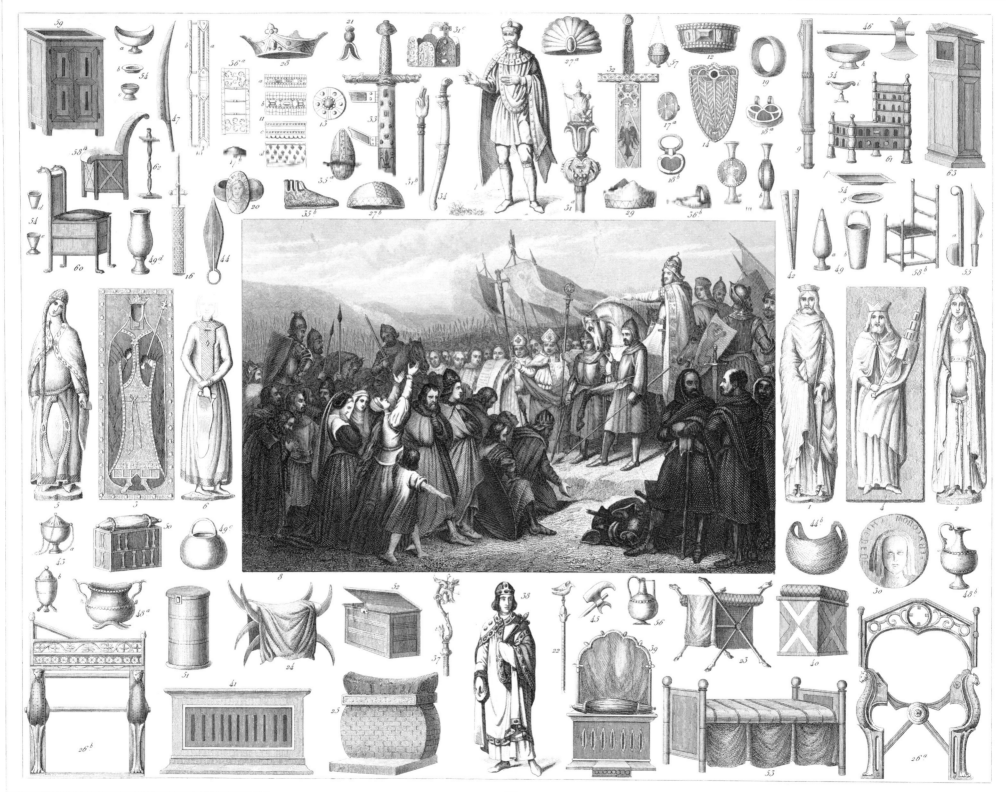

G. Heck dir.ᵗ

Henry Winkles sculp.ᵗ

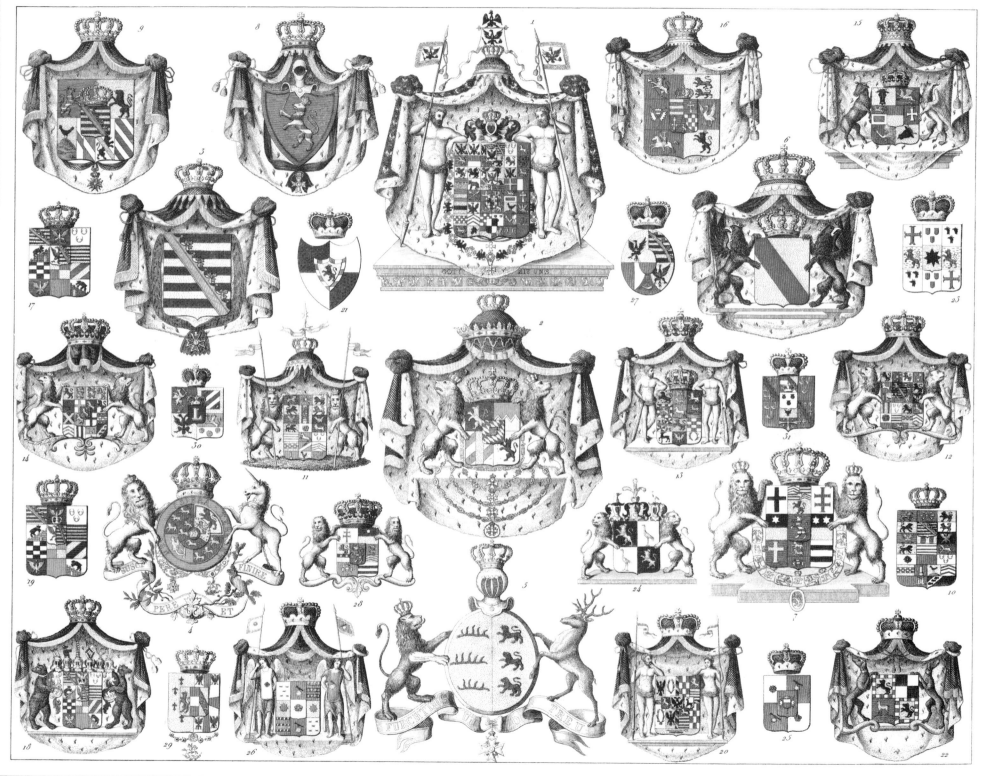

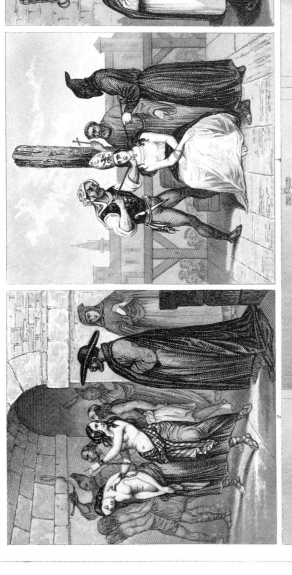

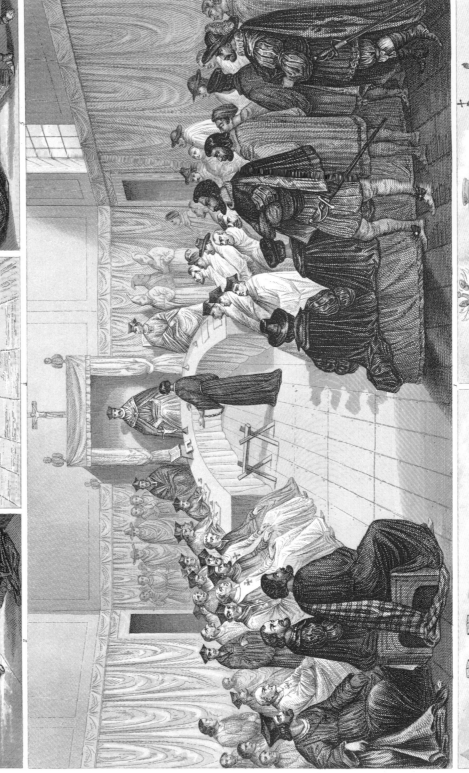

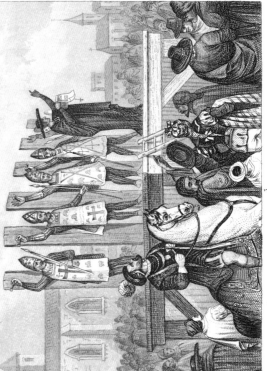

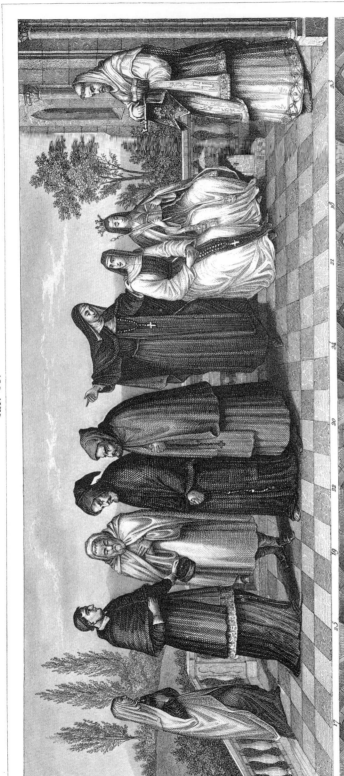

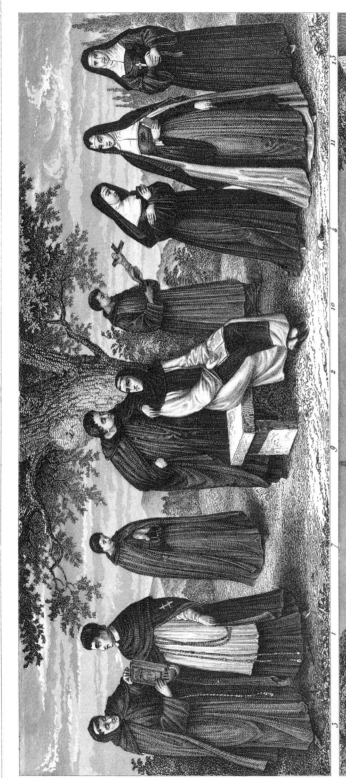

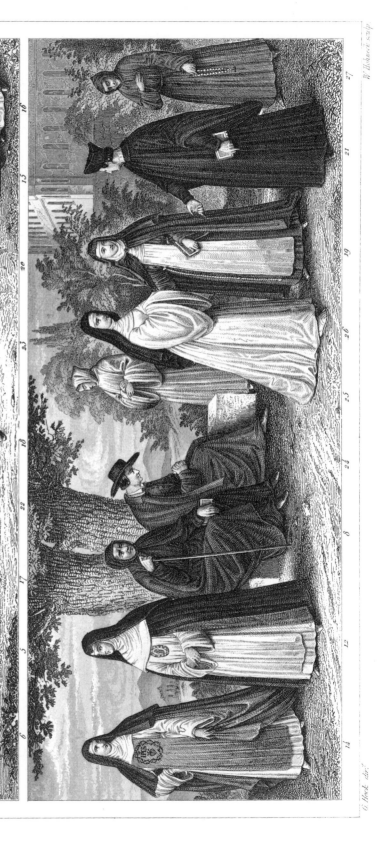

G. Heck direx.

W. Hohneck sculp.

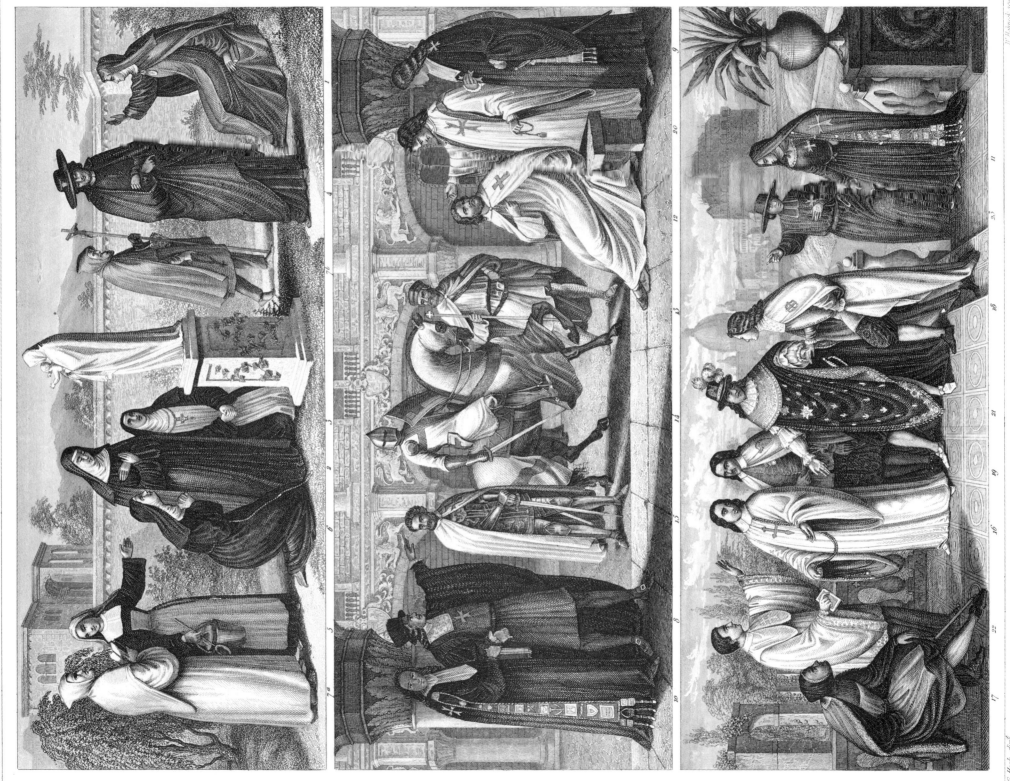

III

G. Heck del.   Henry Winkles sculpt.

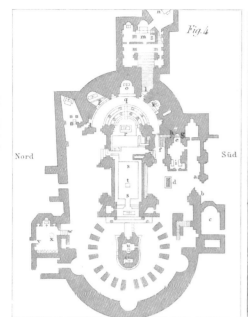

Fig. 4

Nord

Süd

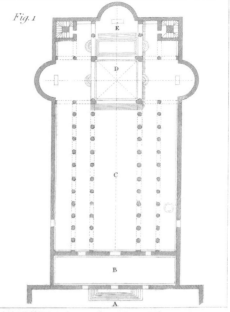

Fig. 1

5

3

6

ICONOGRAPHIC

ENCYCLOPÆDIA.

DIVISION IV.

HISTORY AND ETHNOLOGY.

EIGHTY-ONE PLATES.

[THE LIST OF THE FIGURES ON THE PLATES WILL BE FOUND IN THE TABLES OF CONTENTS OF VOL. III. OF THE TEXT.]

THE PLATES ARE NUMBERED III. 1—39, IV. 1—42.

NEW YORK: 1851.

PUBLISHED BY RUDOLPH GARRIGUE,

2 BARCLAY STREET (ASTOR HOUSE).

G. Heck direx¹

Henry Winkles sculps¹

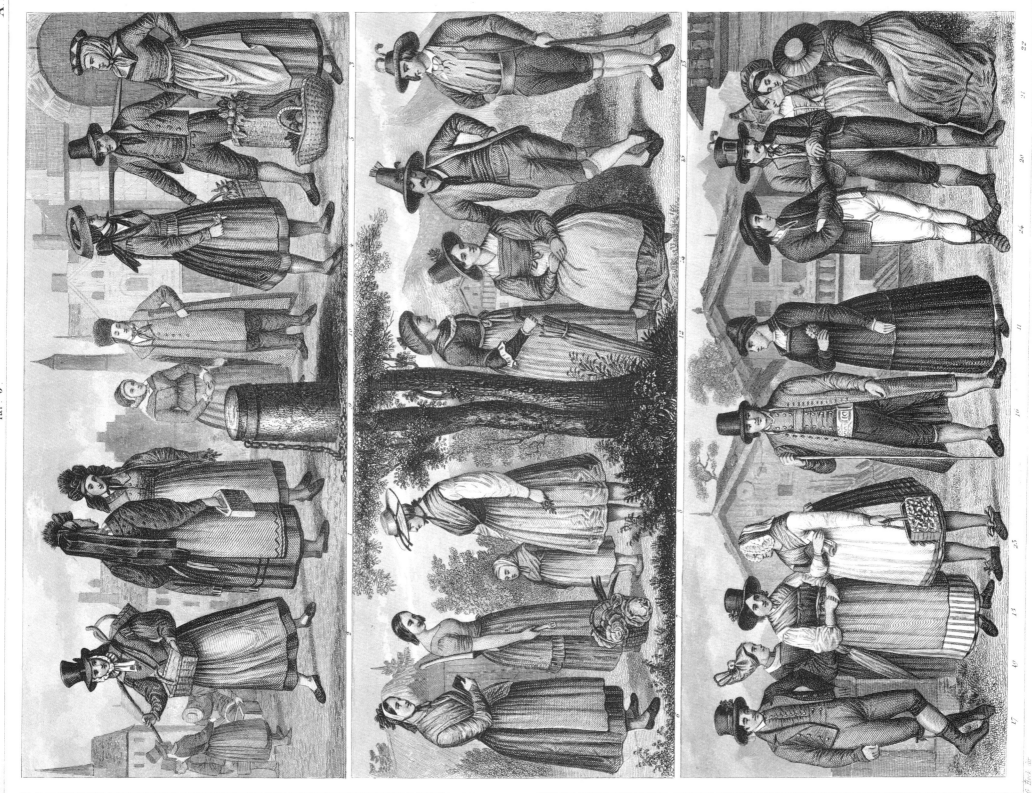

G. Heck dir! Winkles et Lehmann sculp!

G. Heck del. t

Henry Winkles sculp.t

Henry Winkles sculp.

G. Heck dir.t

Henry Winkles sculp.t

G. Heck direx.

Henry Winkles sculp.

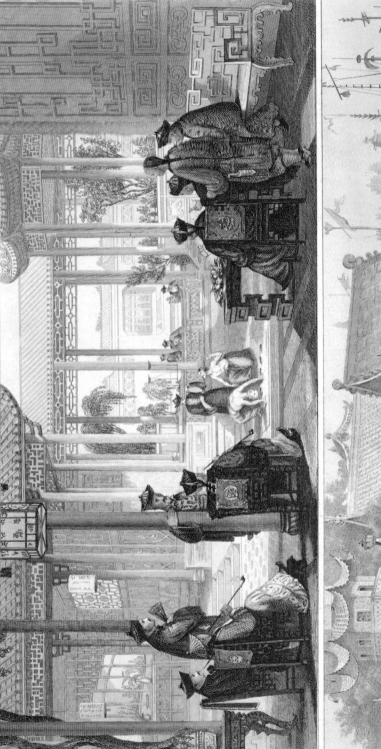

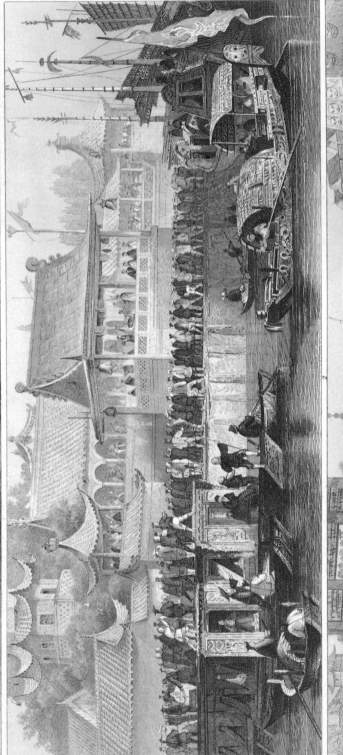

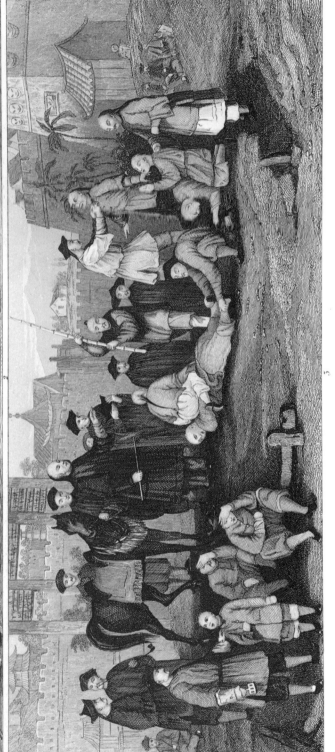

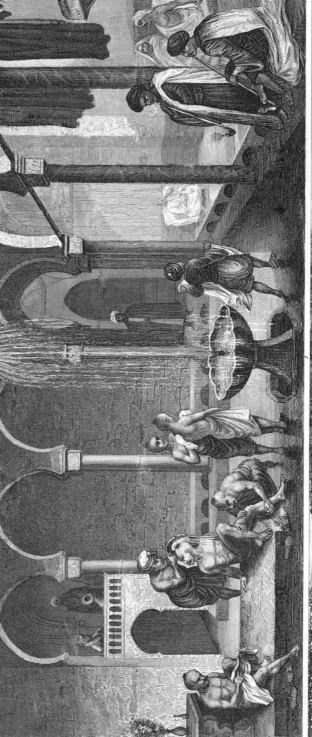

Henry Winkler sculp.

G. Heck del.t

Henry Winkles sculp.t

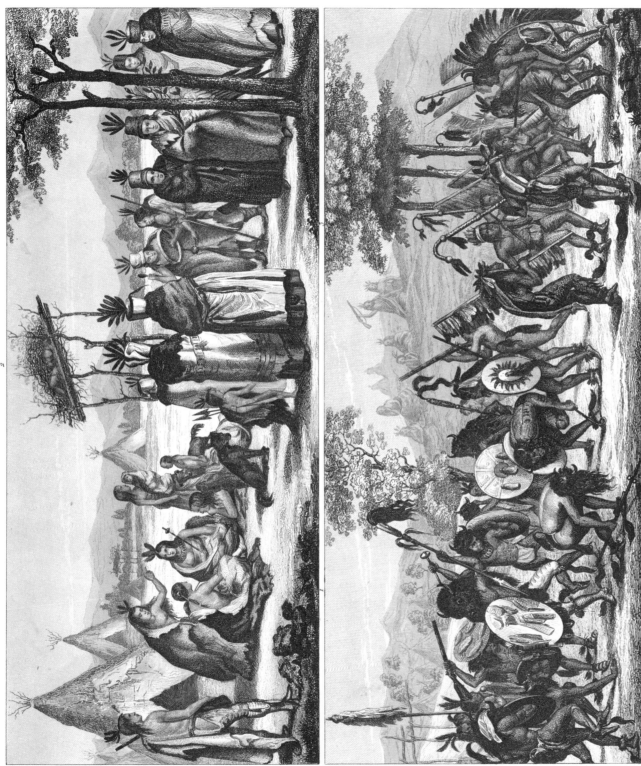

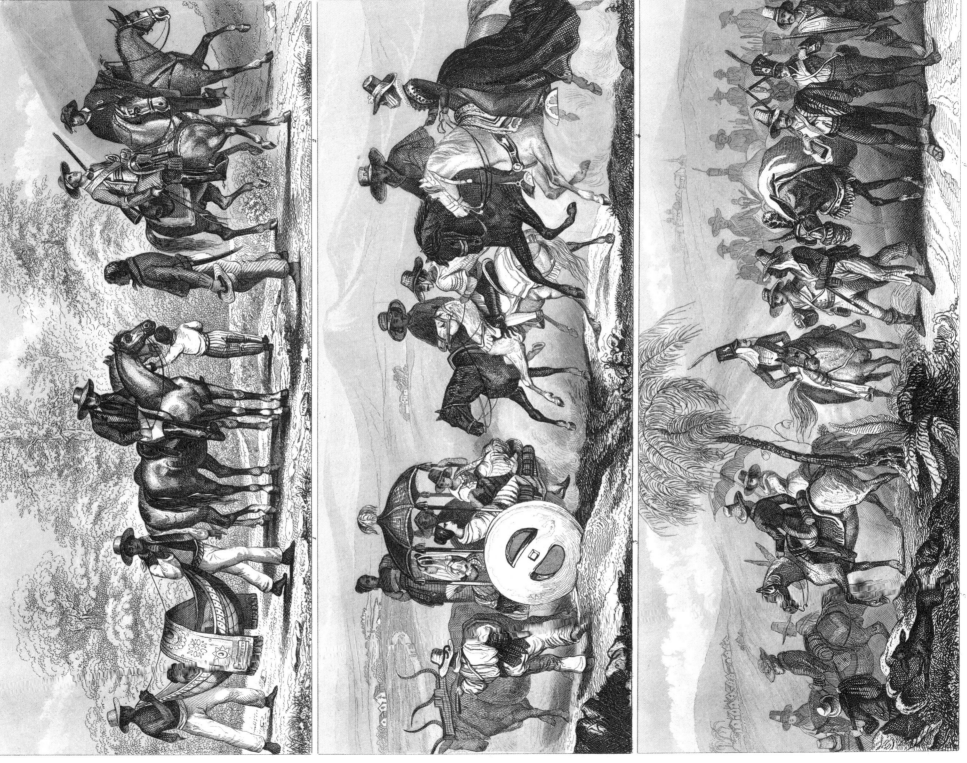

IV

G. Heck del.

Henry Winkles sculp.

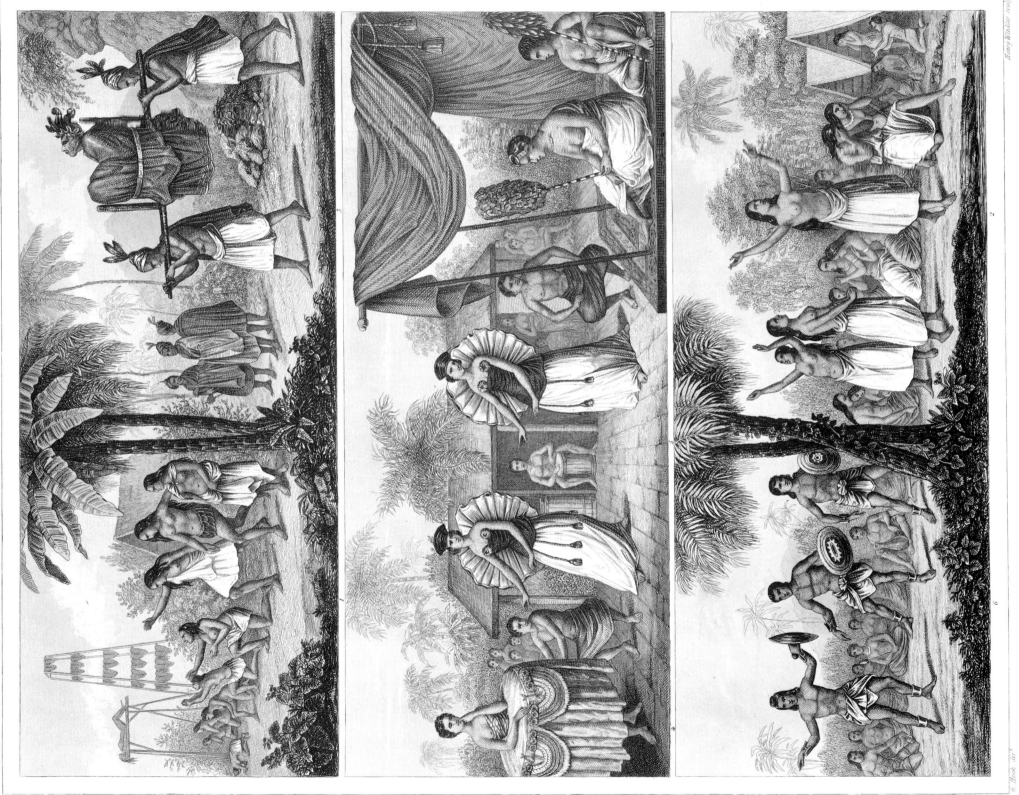

G. Beck del.

Franz Winkler sculp.

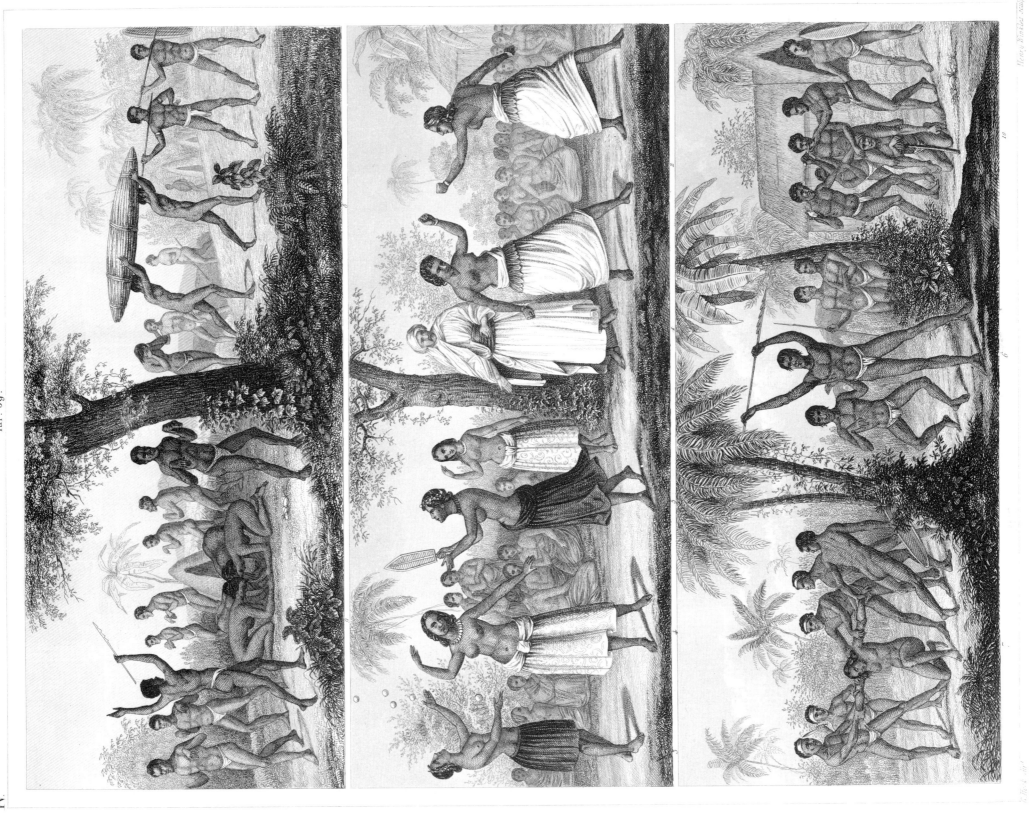

Henry Winkles sculp.